The Great Wall Street Scandal

The Great Wall Street Scandal

Raymond L. Dirks and Leonard Gross

McGraw-Hill Book Company

New York   St. Louis   San Francisco   Düsseldorf

Mexico   Toronto

123456789BABA7987654

Library of Congress Cataloging in Publication Data

Dirks, Raymond L
    The great Wall Street scandal.

    1. Equity Funding Corporation of America.
2. Fraud—United States.   3. Stock-exchange—
United States.   I. Gross, Leonard, joint author.
II. Title.
HV6698.Z9E653   364.1'63   73-21614
ISBN 0-07-017025-8

Contents

For Lee Dirks
and Roslyne Paige

Authors' Note

Equity Funding Corporation of America, a financial services institution, began operations in 1960 with ten thousand dollars. By 1973, the company purported to manage assets of one billion dollars. Its record of growth in the previous decade had exceeded that of all major diversified financial companies in the United States.

In April 1973, this growth was exposed as a fiction. The assets were real enough, for the most part, but they had been obtained by fraudulent means.

Equity Funding's stock, which had sold as high as $80 a share, was suspended from trading on the New York Stock Exchange. The corporation filed for bankruptcy. It came instantly to be known as "Wall Street's Watergate."

In November 1973, twenty-two men—twenty of them former employees of Equity Funding, the other two accountants who audited the company's books—were indicted by a federal grand jury in Los Angeles on 105 counts of fraud and conspiracy. A similar indictment was returned by a grand jury in Illinois, where Equity Funding's principal life insurance subsidiary was chartered. Still more criminal indictments were being prepared by grand juries in other states where Equity Funding did business. Myriad civil actions by stockholders and creditors are likely to continue for years. So will ruminations, and calls for reform of the public and private agencies that monitor America's business.

We have written *The Great Wall Street Scandal* as a narrative history woven through the themes it exposes. The story spans nearly twenty years. It embraces many people. For the convenience of the reader, we have listed the leading characters in the narrative, in the order of their appearance.

Documentary works are invariably reconstructed with the help of press accounts, official papers and interviews with participants. Since March 1973 we have interviewed past and present employees of Equity Funding, Securities and Exchange Commission officials, insurance commissioners, district attorneys, insurance examiners, auditors, journalists, stockholders, investment advisers, accountants, and, where permitted, the accused themselves. We have analyzed court documents, grand jury indictments, and testimony given to the Securities and Exchange Commission and the New York Stock Exchange, as well as hundreds of newspaper and magazine articles. But inasmuch as one of the authors of this book, Raymond L. Dirks, was a central participant in the events leading to disclosure of the fraud, we have been able to tell the story with an intimacy of detail and assurance as to its accuracy rarely available in a project of this kind. This book is a collaboration; because of Raymond L. Dirks' active role in the story, it is written in the first person.

Raymond L. Dirks
Leonard Gross

Characters in the Order of Their Appearance

STANLEY GOLDBLUM, President and Chairman of the Board, Equity Funding Corporation of America (EFCA).

RONALD SECRIST, an administrative officer of Equity Funding Life Insurance Corporation (EFLIC), later, vice president for administration, Bankers National Life Insurance Company, an Equity Funding subsidiary.

RAYMOND L. DIRKS, a Wall Street security analyst specializing in the stocks of insurance companies.

RAYMOND PLATT, a salesman for Equity Funding in its earliest days and a director of the company.

EUGENE CUTHBERTSON, one of the principals at the company's founding.

MICHAEL RIORDAN, the fledgling company's angel in its earliest days; later, chairman of the board.

GORDON McCORMICK, an insurance and mutual fund salesman whose ideas for combining the sale of both products formed the basis of Equity Funding.

SAMUEL LOWELL, Executive Vice President and financial officer of Equity Funding in later years.

FRED LEVIN, Executive Vice President for Marketing of Equity Funding; President of Equity Funding Life Insurance Company.

FRANK MAJERUS, EFLIC's controller.

JAMES SMITH, EFLIC's second in command.

PAT HOPPER, an administrative officer of Equity Funding, later, vice president for investments, Bankers National Life Insurance Company.

LLOYD EDENS, EFLIC's treasurer.

DONALD GOFF, a computer specialist employed by Equity Funding's Management Information Services (MIS) division.

ARTHUR LEWIS, EFLIC's actuary.

JAMES BANKS, EFLIC's corporate counsel.

PETER J. "RON" RONCHETTI, a specialist in computer systems employed by EFLIC and then Bankers National.

YURA ARKUS-DUNTOV, Executive Vice President, Investment Management Operations, Equity Funding.

LAWRENCE COLLINS, EFLIC's chief underwriter.

ROBERT OCHOA, a printer employed by Equity Funding.

RODNEY LOEB, General Counsel, Equity Funding.

GLEESON L. "TIGE" PAYNE, California Insurance Commissioner.

LAWRENCE BAKER, Deputy Commissioner, California Insurance Department.

FRED MAUCK, Illinois Insurance Director.

JAMES STEEN, Deputy Director, examinations branch, Illinois Insurance Department.

JACK DOYLE, auditor, Illinois Insurance Department.

MICHAEL BALINT, a partner of Haskins & Sells, auditors.

LARRY WILLIAMS, associate general counsel, Equity Funding.

HERBERT GLASER, Executive Vice President, Real Estate and International Operations, Equity Funding.

WILLIAM BLUNDELL, Los Angeles bureau chief, *The Wall Street Journal.*

GERALD BOLTZ, Los Angeles regional director, the Securities and Exchange Commission.

WILLIAM GOOTNICK, manager of computer operations for Equity Funding.

ROBERT SPENCER, a partner of Seidman & Seidman, auditors.

HAROLD RICHARDS, President, Fidelity Corporation of Virginia, the largest corporate stockholder of Equity Funding.

SOL BLOCK, an auditor with Seidman & Seidman.

ROBERT BOWIE, director, Institute of International Relations, Harvard University, and a director of Equity Funding.

The Great Wall Street Scandal

1.

The All-American Fraud

His office was a summit of sorts. It stood in the choicest corner of the highest floor of the handsomest building in the country's most sumptuous financial complex. From his roost on the twenty-eighth floor of 1900 Avenue of the Stars in Century City, he could—on the days when rain had washed the air or wind had blown it clean—look east to downtown Los Angeles, or north across the fairways of the Los Angeles Country Club to the mansions of Beverly Hills, his own among them, and to the winter-green, summer-brown Santa Monica Mountains. Pausing at the northern face of his financial summit, Stanley Goldblum might have taken some satisfaction from his perch above the country club. If he could not get into it, he might at least look down on it.

Turning to regard the setting in which he worked, he could nourish on the material confirmation of his rise. Twenty years before, he had shivered in the cold lockers of his father-in-law's meat packing plant, shoving sides of beef. Today he ran an empire.

He was a big man, heavily muscled, broad of chest and shoulder, six feet two inches tall. Big people like big space; his office measured twenty-five feet by thirty feet. But to Stan-

2   *The Great Wall Street Scandal*

ley Goldblum the office served an even more necessary function. It told him who he was.

He needed reassurance. He did not look the part of the chief executive officer of an important financial institution, and he knew it. His clothes were wrong—a little too bold. His manner was slightly off the mark, withdrawn, even hidden whenever possible, abrasive when flushed or cornered. A couch and two deep chairs faced each other, intended for chats, but Goldblum seldom used them. Whether meeting with visitors or his staff, he preferred to station himself behind the long, gleaming, leather-covered desk in the center of his office.

What Stanley Goldblum never understood was how greatly the setting he had contrived upset so many who came there. If the room was impressive, it was also overstated. Its style was not so much of a period as of an attitude.

Each piece, singly, was not offensive. Together, they were troubling. It was the fireplace that troubled most. A fireplace did not belong on the twenty-eighth floor of an air-conditioned building in brand-new Century City. Appropriately, it was fake.

If the fireplace was a clue, the desk was a giveaway. Save for a small clock and an elaborate inkwell, there was nothing on it, no stacks of papers, or "in" or "out" boxes, not even a telephone. The telephone was kept in a drawer. The only paper that Stanley Goldblum permitted on his desk was the one on which he was working. Everything else was hidden.

There was a paper on his desk now, this day in February 1973. It was an order Goldblum had prepared for the executive vice presidents of Equity Funding Corporation of America. It was a puzzling order. In the dozen years since its founding, Equity Funding had scarcely faltered. Under Goldblum's guidance, the corporation had risen from little more than an idea to a reputation as the nation's fastest growing insurance and financial company. Yet the order from Stanley Goldblum was for surgery on the corporate budget.

Goldblum signed the order. It was, by a later reckoning, the worst mistake of his life.

Four days later, Ronald Secrist, a slim, balding, thirty-eight-year-old vice president of an Equity Funding subsidiary in New Jersey, flew to Los Angeles for what he surmised was a routine visit to the home office. The next morning, he was fired. On March 6, 1973, Secrist made two phone calls that set in motion one of the most devastating collapses in financial history. One call was to the New York Insurance Department. The other was to me.

I am a private citizen. My profession is security analysis. I specialize in the stocks of insurance companies. I am thirty-nine, stubby and indifferent about my appearance. Although the financial world that yields me my living operates under unwritten rules as formalized as those of a private club, I try to live life as I choose. Some say I am the closest thing on Wall Street to a hippie broker. I suppose that is true. I believe in people, and distrust institutions. Ronald Secrist would later explain that he came to me because I had a reputation for skepticism and would dig into a story until I learned if it was true. The story he told me could scarcely be believed; yet, before the month was over, I had established that it was true—and Equity Funding stood exposed as the champion of frauds. The company had created 64,000 fictitious life insurance policies with a face value in excess of $2 billion, then sold them to other insurance companies for cash, a practice known as "reinsurance." Equity Funding had faked assets of more than $100 million; it had counterfeited bonds, and forged death certificates.

The exposure of this towering fraud broke a corporation, bloodied its stockholders, bludgeoned the stock market, and cast profound suspicions on Wall Street, the agencies that regulate it, and the System itself.

Equity Funding had issued nearly 8 million shares. The stock had traded in recent years in a range of $12 to $80 a share. At a representative price of $40 a share, that meant a market value of more than $300 million. In fact, Equity Funding stock was virtually worthless.

Nonetheless, as *The New York Times* noted,

> major state regulatory agencies in California and Illinois authorized and approved its operations. Established insurance companies accepted its policies at face value for reinsurance. Establishment auditors certified its accounts. Major banks extended loans. Lawyers participated in the planning and execution. Reputable Wall Street firms underwrote and repeatedly recommended its stock—and venerable institutions, the Ford Foundation, Princeton University and many others, bought it. In short, the cream of this country's business and financial community was drawn in.

This book is the story of how one of history's greatest hoaxes evolved. It is the story of the rise and fall of an American corporation—the largest fraud-induced bankruptcy proceeding in the history of finance. It is the story of immoral men—and of moral men whose concern for job security compromised their principles and kept them silent. It is the story of how the fraud was exposed and of my own role in the exposure. Although many regulatory agencies eventually took part, I am generally credited by Wall Street and the press as the man who uncovered the story. Certainly the New York Stock Exchange credits me with the disclosure; by informing my clients of the fraud in the course of exposing it, I had, the Exchange said, violated its rules. The punishment, on conviction, would be banishment from the Exchange, which, effectively, would mean an end to my career. And certainly, many holders of Equity Funding stock credit me with the disclosure; they have sued me for $100 million. As *The Commercial and Financial Chronicle* described my situation:

> In less than two months, Raymond L. Dirks has been transformed from a highly regarded, slightly unconventional insurance analyst into a beleaguered Wall Street folk hero. Mr. Dirks attained instant celebrity as a result of his virtually one-man investigation into fraud at the Equity Funding Corporation of America—a probe that led to the downfall of the large Los Angeles based mutual fund and insurance complex. Yet now he faces being barred from employment by any member firm for life. . . .

The reader may judge for himself, on the basis of the chronicle of events that led to the exposure, as to whether I did right. But these events transcend the role of one man. They raise questions whose answers are a national imperative.

There is the question of governmental regulation, so lax and haphazard that Stanley Goldblum and some of his confederates could toy with it for years. Where was the Securities and Exchange Commission, the agency of the federal government whose responsibility it was to monitor Equity Funding? Why did the SEC fail to uncover the scandal as long ago as 1968, when allegations of fraud first reached the agency? And where were the various state insurance departments, whose responsibility it was to certify the activities of Equity Funding Life Insurance Company? As lax as the scrutiny of the investment industry may be, that industry is super-regulated compared to the insurance industry. The life insurance industry—1800 companies with $1.5 *trillion* face amount in policies—has consistently fought regulation by the federal government as unnecessary and intrusive.

There is the question of life insurance, itself, and whether it is any longer an appropriate means of saving for the American investor.

There is the question of fraud by computer. Can those sleek machines disguise dishonesty in ways mortals never could?

There is the question of the system by which America's corporations are audited. Auditors are supposed to be independent scrutinizers of corporate morality, as reflected on their balance sheets. But the Equity Funding scandal indicates, as nothing else ever has, that audited statements are not always what they seem to be. What the Equity Funding scandal tells America's stockholders is that the certification of corporate figures in the annual reports they receive may very well be meaningless.

There is the question of the New York Stock Exchange, a venerated American institution which advertises the safety and security of investing in its listed companies, but which, in fact is an antique, costly and dangerous system perpetuated for the convenience of its members.

In its management and operational practices, the New York Stock Exchange operates today as it has since the invention of the telephone. The investment industry, reflected most faithfully in the activities of this major exchange, is geared to short-term profits and vulnerable to wild stories; it is not disposed to long-term stability and the cultivation of its clientele based on prolonged associations and trading in quality products. Because it is so shortsighted, the industry has never responded to modern changes in the business environment—the institution of new management techniques, computerization, a system of instant national communication, or the utilization of security analysis. Investment research is a phenomenon of recent years; it remains subordinate to the role of the salesmen, the underwriters, and the investment bankers. These are the men who bring in the quick profits.

There is the question of the pernicious philosophy of Wall Street reflected in these circumstances—a philosophy that encourages and even demands "performance" by corporations.

No concern is given to the social value of what a company does, and little attention is paid to historical trends or to long-range objectives and achievements. Rather, it is "what have you done *this* quarter"—an unworthy social and economic standard to whose pressures Stanley Goldblum yielded.

Goldblum knew that, once his corporation's earnings ceased to increase at the rate demanded by Wall Street, the price of his stock would fall. He needed a high-priced stock to raise capital and acquire other companies through an exchange of shares.

It was not the average investor who created this philosophy; it was the professional investment institutions of Wall Street that demanded spectacular growth. The number of stocks that survive this psychological wringer are few. There are perhaps fifty stocks that institutions own in quantity today. Those companies that dominate their field do well. Little or no faith is demonstrated in other companies, although they may be good ones. The long-range social and economic consequences for the country are shattering. Should the investment environment that bred the Equity Funding scandal be maintained, the inevitable results will be more and more centralization of power in fewer and fewer corporations, a virtual end to competition and ever-increasing pressures for the abandonment of moral standards in the fight for economic survival.

There is the question of the average investor, and whether he belongs in a market that gives such an extraordinary advantage to institutions and operates on such principles.

There was a time when investing was a way of life in America, a secular religion, a form of tribute to the country, an investment not so much of dollars as of faith in what this country meant. "Maybe all we could afford was a single share," Steve Shagan, the author of *Save the Tiger,* reminisced in the wake of the Equity Funding scandal. "But the whole family would gather around the kitchen table and discuss what to buy. We didn't just mention U.S. Steel or General Motors. We invoked their names with great respect. General Motors! That was America."

Today, no longer.

The stock market is a reflection of investors' value judgments on the business world. By any measure, these judgments are as harsh at this moment as they have been since the Depression. One of the best barometers of public confidence in the securities industry is the price of a seat on the New York Stock Exchange. Such seats have sold in good times for more than $500,000. In 1970, a discouraging year for the market, the price dropped below $150,000. By early 1973, the price had fallen to $100,000. Then came Equity Funding, and the price collapsed to $72,000—less than the cost of a McDonald's hamburger franchise.

In 1967 and 1968, on a scale of one to ten, confidence of investors stood near ten. They would believe any story that came along. They would not even check it out. They would just buy, because they were afraid that if they didn't someone else would and the stock would rise fifty percent before they had a chance to get in.

In January 1969 the market started down. Stocks that were bought in 1967 and 1968 began to disappoint the managers of the big mutual funds. They had bought them on the upside at almost any price, and now they sold them on the downside at any price just to get out. What the fund managers did not want was to have these bad buys on their record when they issued their quarterly reports. By getting rid of them, they could get rid of the record. But the individual investor is different. Psychologically, he can't accept his loss. He rarely sells a stock at a lower price than he paid for it. He simply hangs on to his bad investment.

By 1970, on a scale of one to ten, public confidence had sagged to four or three. It rose a bit in 1971 and 1972. Then, in 1973, it started down again, precipitously, as the country was beset by problems at home and abroad.

Had the Equity Funding scandal occurred in a time of prosperity and serene national confidence, it might have been absorbed. It did not. The scandal unfolded during a period of self-doubt unparalleled in our history. As the confidence factor sank to two or one, and stock market prices plummeted, a newspaper cartoonist pictured five vultures perched on a Wall Street corner. They represented higher gold prices, inflation, devaluation of the dollar, Watergate—and Equity Funding.

There was no smell of decay as 1973 began. The Vietnam war had ended. Richard Nixon had been returned to office with the greatest popular mandate ever accorded an American president. Wall Street had broken through its greatest psychological barrier—the 1000 figure on the Dow Jones industrial average—and was prospecting on higher ground. Then, abruptly, the air soured. The President's economic programs went awry. The world turned on the dollar. Domestic prices went crazy. In March, a Watergate defendant opened the floodgates of political scandal with a letter to a judge. Then came Equity Funding. It sent Wall Street reeling.

The scandal buckled, first, those companies that were intimately involved with Equity Funding, then the insurance stocks, and finally the stock market itself.

Consider Fidelity Corporation, with 579,000 shares the largest shareholder in Equity Funding. The shares were valued on the books of Fidelity Corporation at $23 million, or about $40 a share. After the scandal broke, investors decided that those shares were worthless. They promptly dropped Fidelity Corporation's stock from $11 a share to as low as $4. Because the company was reporting earnings of $1.50 a share, it was selling at less than three times earnings—unheard of for those who believe that stocks are conservatively priced at a multiple of ten times earnings. Investors were no longer willing to believe in that principle when it came to the largest stockholder of Equity Funding.

Then, the insurance stocks. "In the wake of the Equity Funding scandal," *Business Week* reported in its issue of April 14, 1973, "many investors decided that independent auditors, state examiners and the SEC are not reliable protection against fraud, and they indiscriminately knocked the whole group down ten to twenty-five percent." One stock, CMI Investment Corporation, dropped twelve percent in one day, even though the company had no connection whatever with Equity Funding and did not even sell life insurance.

And the market: in the week after April 2, the day *The Wall Street Journal* published its story on the scandal, the value of shares on the New York Stock Exchange dropped by $15 billion.

But the most enduring effect of the Equity Funding scandal was its impact on the mind of the average investor.

There have been frauds before. People have bought stocks before in companies that employed tricky accounting to show earnings that weren't really there. There have been instances of individual wrongdoing. But never before had there been such an instance of collective corporate maliciousness. Until Equity Funding, the public could indulge its belief that, in business, representations were essentially honest and that—most of the time, at least—you got what you paid for. But the Equity Funding scandal is cheating of a magnitude so vast, and accomplished with such ease, as to put into question the entire morality by which American conducts its business.

So Equity Funding becomes a watershed of a financial way of life. The matter of trust is critical to this country's prosperity. Institutions may dominate trading, but it is the money of the little investor that makes up the bulk of the capital by which American enterprise functions. Should the little investor remove his money from this financial pool, the effects could be everlasting.

This then is more than a story about a $2 billion insurance fraud. It is a metaphor of the moral corrosion in America's business and institutional environment.

Equity Funding is not an isolated fraud. It is a statement of our times. What is ultimately more shocking than the fraud itself is the number of decent people who knew about it and did nothing. James McCord, the man who exposed Watergate by writing to a judge, said he wouldn't have felt safe going to the Justice Department. It was the same for those who knew about the false insurance and fake assets at Equity Funding. They didn't feel safe about going to the authorities.

Equity Funding, whatever else it has done, has proved to me what I suspected to be true—that you can't place your faith in institutions. You have to look behind the statements and the figures. You have to look behind what's reported by authorities or companies. You have to get into the basic guts of an operation and into the hearts of people to find out whether what appears to be on the surface reflects what's underneath.

Two for One

They were as different as diamonds, one the Irish heir to a Jewish department store, the second a gambling lush, the third a sportsman, the fourth a brooding ex-butcher. And yet they were a likely crew—big, extravagant, single-minded men in their early thirties. What riveted their interest was a new idea in an industry that had not hatched one for a century. It was a way to make a dollar work twice.

They thought the idea was worth millions.

The first to appear was Raymond Platt, an overpowering salesman and epic drinker who was to wind up paying bar bills with shares of Equity Funding stock. Platt looked like Phil Silvers, spoke with a brogue, and ground his teeth.

Then came Eugene Cuthbertson, a husky graduate of the school of engineering at the University of Southern California, a member—along with his socialite second wife—of Huntington Harbor's boating set. Cuthbertson worked part-time as a draftsman while he tried to get a leg up in the mutual fund business, which he finally managed to do.

Next came Stanley Goldblum, the biggest of the four, his height accentuated by an awesome torso. Married at twenty-two, Goldblum had quit UCLA nine months short of his bachelor's degree because he needed money. He tried the scrap metal and war surplus business and then, two years later, entered his father-in-law's meat packing business. The muscles he had begun to develop at Vic Tanny's gym on Wilshire Boulevard in the Miracle Mile swelled under the weight of 10,000 pounds of beef hauled through the plant each day. Gold-blum worked there several years—"a bright guy making hot dogs," a onetime associate recalls—rose to plant superinten-dent and quit to try insurance.

The fourth man was Michael Riordan, whose father, a vice president of Abraham & Strauss, had taken over a bankrupt Stern's Department Store in 1932 at the behest of the banks and by 1940 owned a controlling interest.

Mike Riordan magnetized people. He was a mutual fund wholesaler whose salesmen revered him. When he walked through New York's financial district, he might be stopped ten times in a block. Legend had it that his visits to Wall Street from California in later years would lift Equity Funding's stock by several points. Big and good-looking, Riordan had been the top student and athlete at Cranwell, a Jesuit secondary school in Massachusetts, started college at Georgetown, and then transferred to Cornell, where he played second string football. He was a garrulous drinker beloved in a number of bars; bar-room pianists would announce his arrival by playing *The Im-possible Dream*. That was Mike Riordan's theme song.

Riordan eschewed intellectuals and derided Ivy Leaguers. His closest friends were the boys with whom he had grown up in New Rochelle. He might make a $20 million deal for Equity Funding during the day, then spend the evening drinking with his friends, most of them old football buddies. He read middle-brow literature omnivorously, had a salesman's memory and a love of the bizarre. He frequently quoted Sadakichi Hartmann, whom he described with a straight face as "the best understood poet in the world."

> There is no answer to the quest.
> Who knows when we'll meet again?

When Mike Riordan spotted a bum, he would have his hand in his pocket before the bum saw him. If a friend asked him for $5, he would give $15. One night years ago, his older brother, Bill, met Mike at one of his favorite hangouts, P. J. Clarke's, to ask for a large loan. Mike, who had been drinking heavily, lectured Bill for two hours. "What's the answer?" Bill said at last.

"What the hell do you mean, what's the answer? You're my brother, aren't you?" Mike replied. He gave Bill the loan.

For all his generosity, Mike Riordan never wore a hat because he hated to tip a quarter each time he left a bar.

He lived intensely, gambled, caroused. "Every night is opening night," he would proclaim. "Post time is forty-one," his brother Bill would warn him. That was the year a man settled down and made up for all his transgressions. His net worth at forty-one was more than $30 million, but he was the kind of man who could have lost it all and started over. There was a stanza from *Kismet* he truly liked:

> Princes come, princes go,
> An hour of pomp and show.

Not one of the four men had yet found his stride when a fifth man brought them together. His name was Gordon McCormick. He was the most flamboyant of them all, an imaginative, portly, expansive Californian of Barnum & Bailey dimension who ate epic lunches, liked the best cigars and hotels, and spent more for breakfast than most salesmen spend for dinner.

One by one, they signed on with McCormick. Within months after they had joined forces, the five men were fighting with all the ferocity of railroad barons for control of a tiny company.

Why men would battle for an untested idea can only be understood in terms of the time in which the struggle took place.

In the 1950s, Americans began to recognize that inflation had become a permanent way of life. It was not the infuriating variety of inflation that visited the country in 1973. It was the creeping variety, in which the purchasing power of the dollar diminished each year by an average of three percent. Few Americans were alarmed; most economists assured them that this tolerable inflation was the price they paid for an annual growth in Gross National Product of five to eight percent. *Real* growth for the average American in these circumstances was, roughly, the increase in the Gross National Product, minus the decrease in the value of the dollar to purchase goods and services. Translated into bread-and-butter language, that meant each American improved his economic lot an average of two to five percent each year.

"Controlled" inflation accompanied the country through a period of economic growth unmatched in size and scope. For the average American, it changed entirely the philosophy of investment. Investments with a small, fixed yield could do no more than keep the investor even. He needed the kind of investment that would put him ahead. He went looking for *equities*—common stocks, for the most part—that were responsive to inflation. When prices rise, companies charge more for their products, their annual earnings go up and so do the prices of their stocks.

That, at least, was the idea. It played hell with the concept of life insurance.

For the last hundred years, life insurance had been the primary form of savings for the typical American. But—the merits of protection aside—it became increasingly apparent in the 1950s that the dollars invested in a permanent life insurance plan would be worth considerably less years later, when the policy was cashed in, than the dollars that had been invested. Nonetheless, the need for protection against untimely death persisted. How could the advantages of a life insurance policy be maintained without financial loss?

The life insurance companies looked long and hard for an answer. So did many promoters.

By 1955, a new way to pay for insurance had been found.

You bought a policy with an initial cash down payment. You borrowed against the cash value of that policy (your own down payment) to pay the bulk of your subsequent premiums. You deducted the interest on your loan from your income tax.

There were two major disadvantages to this concept. The first was that the annual loan was subtracted from the face amount of the policy, so that the death benefit was constantly decreasing. The second was that, if the government disallowed the practice and prohibited the deduction of interest, the buyer would wind up with a policy he could no longer afford to carry. Because of these inherent risks, only the rich and the sophisticated participated in these policies.

Then came an innovation that put the plan within reach of the small investor. It was to increase the face value of the policy each year by the amount of the loan. The net effect was to provide level coverage. By this point, the possibility of government disapproval had diminished, as well. A new product was ready for market: the minimum deposit insurance policy. It was the hottest insurance product in years. Suddenly, the sale of insurance, which had been sluggish, began to boom. The number of salesmen multiplied. So did the number of "fence posts."

"Fence-posting" in the insurance industry is a euphemism for policies that are not totally legitimate. Eighteen years later, Equity Funding would give the term a whole new definition. But now, in 1955, fence posts were policies sold with little or no intention on the part of the buyers to keep them in force. An insurance salesman could urge a prospect to buy a policy on the promise that it would cost him nothing. He would be telling the truth.

A $10,000 life insurance policy for a man of thirty-five, for example, might cost him $180 in annual premium. But the immediate cash value of the policy would be $160. The policyholder would put up $20 in cash and borrow the cash value to pay the rest of the premium. The salesman would collect $130 in commission from the life insurance company—and refund his client $20.

So eager were some life insurance companies to capitalize on the minimum deposit fad that they offered commissions to salesmen in excess of the first-year premium "charged" the buyer of the policy. Some salesmen would collect $200 in commission for a policy with a $180 premium. "The amount of fence post business was horrendous," a veteran of those days recalls. At the end of the policy's first year, when both interest on the loan and second-year premium came due, the buyer would simply drop the policy. Obviously, this was not good business for the insurance companies. If an insurance policy was not renewed after the first year, the insurance company had lost money.

Enter Gordon McCormick.

McCormick was reputedly the leading salesman in the United States for the Keystone Fund, a Boston-based mutual fund. He also sold insurance and maintained his own brokerage firm, Gordon C. McCormick, Inc. He had been selling a great deal of minimum deposit insurance through a company called Reserve Life of Dallas. But one day Reserve Life told him it wanted no more minimum deposit. McCormick came back with an offer. If Reserve Life would guarantee a good cash value on policies of $25,000 and up, McCormick would guarantee that there would be no second-year lapses on any policy he sold. He posted a bond of $50,000 with the insurance company as evidence of his willingness to return 100 percent of his commission if there was a lapse. While lapses ran as high as ninety percent with some companies, the policies McCormick wrote remained 100 percent in force through the second year.

What Reserve Life didn't know was that much of the money used by McCormick's clients to pay their premiums came from loans on mutual funds. Selling insurance and mutual funds in tandem was rare but gaining currency throughout the industry in those days. A salesman would tell a client: "You're prepared to spend $300 a year on insurance. Instead of spending $300, spend $100—and put $200 in mutual funds." What was new was the idea of borrowing against the mutual fund investment to pay the premium on the insurance.

It was the first known use of the combination, yet McCormick offers a curious answer when asked who invented it. "Nobody did," he insists. "A lot of people think I did, and I know I didn't." Why McCormick refuses to take credit for the invention remains a mystery. It's possible that he got the idea from another mutual fund and insurance salesman, James C. Hayes. It's possible that Ray Platt may have contributed. It's also possible that the idea was McCormick's but had once cost him his job for violating company policy. In 1954, McCormick had a falling out with Investors Diversified Services, the largest mutual fund organization in the United States, for urging his clients to borrow against their assets to purchase mutual funds. Whatever the explanation, McCormick had no ambivalence about the combination. As he saw it in those days, two giants— the venerable life insurance industry and the upstart mutual fund industry—were fighting one another for the savings of the average investor.

All "fixed-dollar" money was the target of the mutual funds. Mutual fund salesmen argued with investors that they should not put their money into the 3½ percent interest, fixed-dollar situation offered by life insurance salesmen. In an inflationary economy, the most they could hope for would be to remain even.

Yet investors could not neglect the need for protection against untimely death. To solve the problem, McCormick seized on the idea of using the money twice.

The idea was the seed of Equity Funding. It was a refinement of a venerable financial practice known as "leverage." Leverage, Equity Funding would explain in later years, was "a concept used by most financial institutions and many major investors. It is using an asset which you already own to borrow money in the expectation that the earnings and growth will be greater than the interest cost." Equity Funding put the idea into lay terms in a handsome corporate booklet:

> Assume you've been spending $100 per month for groceries. At that rate, you've spent $1,200 a year—or $12,000 over the past ten years—just for food. You've spent the money, eaten the food, and now you have nothing left of either the $12,000 or what it bought. However, what if you could buy the groceries and still have your $100-a-month available for investment in a mutual fund? Here's what you could do:
> . . . First, arrange to charge your groceries and to pay the grocer only once, at the end of ten years. Naturally, you'd have to pay interest on your loan.
> . . . Second, take the $100 a month you'd have spent for food and invest it in a mutual fund.
> . . . Third, at the end of the ten years you would simply repay your loan in cash or redeem some of your mutual fund shares to pay for your groceries.
> . . . Result, if the amount earned on your investment is greater than the interest paid, you would have turned an expense into a profit. On the other hand, under adverse market and economic conditions, your investment earnings could be less than the interest cost and your expense would be increased.

A mutual fund prospectus accompanying the brochure indicated that a man who had followed the program would have earned substantially more than his cost. The booklet then explained how to apply the leverage concept to insurance.

> INVEST . . . First, you invest in shares of a mutual fund;
> INSURE . . . Second, you select a life insurance program;
> BORROW . . . Third, you borrow against your mutual fund shares to pay each annual insurance premium;
> REPAY LOAN . . . Fourth, at the end of ten years you pay the principal and interest on the premium loan, either in

cash, in part from any insurance cash values or by redeem-
ing shares.

RESULT . . . Any appreciation from your investment in
excess of the amount owed is your profit.

What McCormick never said at the time, and what Equity
Funding never emphasized subsequently, was that the only
certain two-for-one aspect of the scheme was the two commissions of the salesman.

The buyer's money *was* used twice. It bought funds. It then
served as collateral against a loan. But no matter what happened to the shares of the mutual fund, the loan was a form of
indebtedness that eventually had to be repaid. Rather than a
two-for-one advantage, the buyer bought a potential two-for-
one disadvantage. And he paid two commissions on the same
dollars—once on the insurance and once on the mutual funds.
If the transaction was leveraged, it was in favor of the salesman.

Ray Platt, Gene Cuthbertson, Stanley Goldblum and Mike
Riordan loved it.

Platt's association with McCormick predated the Equity
Funding concept. He had quit his job with Equitable Life in
New York to move to California. He had only just arrived when
he walked in off the street one day in answer to an advertise-
ment for salesmen McCormick had placed in a newspaper.
Platt's family was waiting at a motel for him to return with
money for food. McCormick promised Platt an immediate ad-
vance on commission the moment he made a sale. Two hours
later, Platt was back with a signed contract. McCormick gave
him $100. Platt insisted on taking McCormick and his wife to
the Luau in Beverly Hills to celebrate their new relationship.
The bar was jammed. While his family waited for the food
money, Platt gave the headwaiter $5, procured a table, and
bought the drinks. Platt did so well in subsequent months that
McCormick eventually sent him to San Francisco to open a
branch office.

McCormick was forever forming new ventures. In 1960, he formed one with Gene Cuthbertson, who by now was operating his own company, Diversified Mutual Funds of Southern California, Ltd. Cuthbertson threw in Diversified in exchange for a half interest in one of McCormick's companies.

Then came Stanley Goldblum.

Goldblum had worked briefly for McCormick several years before. He, too, had responded to an ad. "He was a hungry one," McCormick recalls. "I trained him. Then he decided he could do it himself. After a few months, he quit to form his own company. When it failed, he came back and said he wanted to be an office manager. He has a brilliant mind, but he's not a salesman." Time has telescoped the sequence, but McCormick's view of Goldblum's selling ability is in proportion to other sightings.

"He was not the salesman type," a colleague from those days recalls. "In order to sell, you have to have a nice disposition and be able to ingratiate yourself. Goldblum was crisp, direct, and businesslike." He was, according to other accounts, a loner who never mixed with the boys. He communicated only when he had to. His apprenticeship in insurance sales could not have come easily. He sold a package program for Pacific Mutual that was designed for average consumers. It required a salesman to make a blind telephone call. "Are you interested in saving money?" he would ask. "If I could show you the most unusual plan for saving you've ever heard of, would you be interested?" It was not the sort of assignment Goldblum would enjoy.

He moved soon to Midland Mutual Life Insurance and a more sophisticated type of selling. Midland's salesmen were trained to tailor a program to the specific needs of each client. The meat of this business was the $5,000 and $10,000 policy, but Goldblum concentrated, instead, on wealthy prospects and policies for $50,000 and $100,000.

He was the sharpest prospect Midland had seen in years. There was nothing he couldn't understand. Whatever he did he did well. Eventually, he would have prospered. But for Goldblum the conventional method of selling insurance was too slow. He was approaching thirty; he had an urgent desire to make up for lost time.

Insurance is an inexpensive business to enter. There is no inventory to buy. A salesman sells pieces of paper. Goldblum quit his job and went into business with Ralph Robbins, a companion from Midland Mutual days. The company concentrated on "executive planning." According to Robbins, Goldblum did more planning than selling. "He kept trying to generate capital. We'd have been better off if he had generated business." The partnership soon dissolved, but Goldblum kept the agency. For the next few years, he probed the insurance and mutual fund areas for opportunities. He was, in the words of a former associate, "an underdeveloped, underpaid bright guy." Finally, in 1960, while doing some consulting work for California Investors, Goldblum once again met up with McCormick.

McCormick had always liked Goldblum because he could figure in his head. Now he invited Goldblum to bring his agency into the firm and work as an administrator; once more he proposed a new joint venture, this time a California corporation into which he, Goldblum, and Cuthbertson each put $3,333.33.

It was during 1960 that the Equity Funding idea burgeoned. Goldblum, the administrator, went into the field to convert salesmen.

One day, McCormick received a call from Mike Riordan, who was heading the Keystone sales effort in New York. Riordan and McCormick had known one another casually for years. His call this day was impulsive. "The only reason I'm not number one in sales year after year," Riordan joked, "is that there's a guy out in California who beats me." McCormick laughed. Then Riordan said frankly, "I'd like to know how you do it. If you'll come to New York to explain it, I'll have all the broker–dealers who sell for me lined up for you in one room."

McCormick saw in Riordan's offer an opportunity to expand the Equity Funding concept into a national organization. He accepted. When he got to New York, he told the broker–dealers that he would continue the meeting either until they understood what he was talking about or until they lost interest. Then he began to explain his package plan for selling mutual funds and insurance—in which customers first bought mutual funds and then used them as collateral to purchase life insurance. Each day attendance grew. By midweek, McCormick was unable to handle the meeting alone. He called the West Coast for reinforcements.

That weekend, Goldblum arrived in New York. Riordan, his wife, Jackie, and McCormick met him at the airport. He spent the weekend at Riordan's home in Westchester County, and thereafter at the New York Athletic Club as Riordan's guest.

McCormick and Goldblum were to conduct a five-day training session. It lasted three months. In September, Ray Platt came in to help. McCormick, never a detail man, hadn't much patience for training salesmen. He was too busy masterminding and worrying about his mushrooming new sales force of nearly 1000 men. Goldblum and Platt were worrying, as well, about the problems of the fledgling corporation—unpaid bills, conflicting statements, reports of corporate debts they had not known about, and of other participants in the venture of whom they had been unaware. There was also the matter of their own stock. Goldblum had yet to receive his certificates of ownership in the company he had formed with McCormick and Cuthbertson. Platt had received 2500 shares of stock in Tongor Corporation of Nevada, one of McCormick's companies, in exchange for unpaid commissions. But Tongor was a shell without assets. It had been formed to own McCormick's other companies, but the companies had yet to be put into Tongor. Platt, Goldblum, and McCormick had a showdown lunch.

"Don't worry about money," McCormick said. "I have Riordan. I can get a hundred thousand dollars any time I want it."

"I want my stock," Goldblum insisted.

"Don't fool around with Riordan," McCormick warned.

By now, Goldblum was convinced that McCormick intended to get rid of him. He decided to force the issue. He asked Platt to join him in a meeting with Riordan. Platt vacillated. McCormick had helped him during a bad period in his life—but there were those 2500 shares of stock. Finally Platt agreed.

The three men met for lunch at Michael's Pub, in Midtown Manhattan, Riordan's favorite saloon. "All is not as it looks," Goldblum said. "You're McCormick's pigeon."

At first, Riordan didn't know what to do. But he knew he would soon have to take sides. He had been underwriting everyone's expenses. And he, too, was a shareholder in Tongor Corporation, the shell without assets. He had bought 1500 shares for $15,000. His investment, by now, was approaching $40,000, but he had nothing whatever to show for it. He decided to confront McCormick with questions about the financial operations. McCormick would not answer directly. "Goldblum's trying to knock everybody off," adding what Riordan took as a slur against Jews.

Riordan didn't like that. He liked Jews. Jews worked hard; his Gentile friends were lazy. "Let's all get into one room," he said now. "I want the answers."

McCormick summoned Cuthbertson to New York to help put down the revolt. But when Cuthbertson got there Goldblum and Platt convinced him that his investment might be jeopardized. The three men then called an accountant in the Los Angeles office who was authorized to sign checks. They told her to withdraw the money from corporate accounts in three different banks.

In the midst of the conversation, Goldblum had second thoughts. "But she'll have all the money," he said.

"If we can't trust her, who can we trust?" Cuthbertson replied.

The accountant had cashier's checks made out in the company's name and took the money home for the weekend, along with the company's books.

The showdown meeting began on Sunday, in Cuthbertson's suite at the Warwick Hotel. The four rebels proposed a five-way split in the corporation. McCormick flatly refused.

"If you don't sell us an interest in the company, we're going to wreck it," Platt said.

McCormick knew they could. Not only had they seized the assets, they controlled the sales force.

At one point, Mike Riordan turned to Gordon McCormick, Jr., McCormick's nineteen-year-old son. "This is getting a little rough," he said. "Maybe you ought to leave."

They talked through the day and into the night. Finally, McCormick, exhausted, agreed to a five-way split. If they followed through with their threats, he would have no organization left.

The next morning, McCormick, Riordan, Goldblum, Platt, and Cuthbertson met again in a borrowed board room at 40 Wall Street, in the office of McCormick's brother-in-law. There are two versions of what transpired.

As McCormick recalls the meeting, it began with an announcement by Goldblum that the four men were going to take over the company and he was going to be president.

"What's going to happen to you is that you're fired right now," McCormick replied.

Once again, Riordan pleaded for the five-way split.

"No," McCormick replied, "you're going to split it four ways, because I'm never going to do business with any of you guys again. You're a bunch of bastards. Whatever else you do in life, you're not going to do it with me."

The four men each offered to sign a note to pay McCormick for a share of the business.

"No, your note is no good, and neither are you," McCormick replied.

The other version is this: McCormick, refreshed by a night's sleep, had changed his mind. He said he was agreeable to a five-way split, but that he wanted $48,000 in addition for services rendered. The four others refused, and the meeting blew up. Riordan, Cuthbertson, Platt, and Goldblum decided then that the only solution was a "buyout." Either McCormick bought them out, or they would buy him out.

There is no argument about McCormick's reasoning after this point. He felt the others would wreck the business if he didn't give in. They had Mike Riordan's capital. Alone, he could not support the overhead he had created by vastly expanding his sales force. There were other opportunities. He would start his own funding company. He agreed, at last, to be bought out. The terms were complex—transfer of stock, the retirement of indebtedness, the assumption of McCormick loans. But the total bill came to just over $56,000.

Mike Riordan paid the bill. His investment was now more than $90,000. The others returned to Los Angeles, but he remained in New York. He was unwilling to leave Keystone until the idea got going.

By the following spring, he was satisfied. One evening, he met his brother Bill at Michael's Pub. "I'm going to quit my job," he said. "I'm going out to California. I'm going to make a hundred million dollars—and I'm going to make it with Jews. The only people who ever fucked me in my life have been Gentiles. I've never been fucked by Jews."

Lunch for Stanley

In the summer of 1961, a journalist friend of mine based in New York arrived in Los Angeles on a writing assignment and had dinner with an old friend of his. The friend, an attorney, told the journalist of a small new company in which he had made an investment and offered the journalist 500 shares of a large block of private stock he had bought at $1 a share. The risk was substantial, he said, but the upside potential was enormous. The journalist agreed to the purchase. On his return to New York, he sent a check to his friend along with a covering letter.

That December, the journalist was transferred abroad. As he was cleaning out his files, he found the copy of his letter to the attorney. He had completely forgotten the investment. He called his friend in high hopes, only to learn that the investment had gone sour. The friend was chagrined. "I never should have sold you those shares, and I want to buy them back," he said.

"Don't be silly," said the journalist. "I took the risk, and I'll take the loss. How much are the shares worth?"

"Eighteen cents—if you can find a buyer," the attorney replied. "Look," he went on, "this matter is on my conscience. I can afford the loss. They were my shares. I'm sending you back your five hundred dollars, and I don't want to hear any more."

The journalist argued in vain. But he was secretly relieved.

Eight years later, the two friends were reunited in Paris. "Whatever happened to that little company?" the journalist wondered.

"Let's see," said the attorney, "how many shares did you have?"

"Five hundred," the journalist replied.

A peculiar look crossed the attorney's face. He muttered something about a two-for-one split, a three-for-two split, a three percent stock dividend, a two percent stock dividend. "You would have had 1575 shares," he calculated.

"How much is each share worth?" the journalist asked.

"Seventy dollars," the attorney replied.

The journalist's "investment" had grown to $110,000. He was sick. So was his friend.

The company, of course, was Equity Funding, and the story suggests the flavor of its swift rise to success as a financial services institution.

Politicians like to speak of "an idea whose time has come." In finance, the phenomenon is reversed: there arrive fertile times for ideas. Suddenly, for no particular reason, Wall Street goes crazy for concepts. Equity Funding came into being during just such an era.

The 1950s had been a period when America reinvested its faith in Wall Street. Stocks, undervalued since the Depression, rose now to more realistic levels. But, where memory of the Depression had tempered the mood of the fifties, greed routed caution in the sixties. Investors turned their backs on the past and all but vaulted over the present in their eagerness to position themselves in the future.

The fifties had seen a tremendous upward move in the prices of stocks of large companies. The sixties assumed aspects of a treasure hunt. Investors prospected for small companies that were highly speculative but seductive with promise. A boom began in new issues. Ideas were gold dust. Any company with "computer" in its name could sell for twenty, forty, even sixty times earnings. The multiple of earnings—the ratio between what a company earns per share and the price of each share— became so high as to be all but irrelevant. Stocks sold not on the basis of present earnings but of future earnings. Even those stocks of companies that were losing money did well on the Street, on the thin assumption that the companies would earn money some day.

In 1961, the average life insurance stock went up 100 percent. Newspaper financial pages filled with advertisements touting the virtues of insurance companies as investments. Into this heady atmosphere came Equity Funding. Its concept made it a darling of the "go-go" era. It fit right in with the crowd. Through the sixties, the crowd carried it along.

But Equity Funding's swift rise was not without its problems. In 1962, the Securities and Exchange Commission had almost put the company out of business with a ruling that the company's mutual fund–insurance package constituted a security and thus had to be registered under the Securities Act of 1933. Equity Funding was caught unawares. The company was compelled to stop selling, conform its program to securities regulations and wait for the SEC's blessing. Approval was not forthcoming for eighteen months. In the meanwhile, many salesmen drifted away. Not only were they discouraged by the legal delay; the stock market recession of 1962 had cast a pall on mutual funds.

Then there was the antagonism that arose between the upstart new company and older, entrenched insurance firms. It is an axiom of the business that there are many more owners of insurance policies than there are buyers. The prime target for the salesman, therefore, is not the prospect who has no policy, but one who has one and might change it. Equity Funding's salesmen could argue persuasively to a prospect that by letting cash value sit in an insurance policy he was losing money. They would urge the prospect to let his money work twice. Cancel the old policy. Use the cash value to buy mutual funds. Borrow against the mutual funds to pay for insurance.

Convincing a man to switch policies is known in the business as "twisting." Equity Funding's salesmen didn't like that word. They spoke instead of "restructuring" insurance programs. But among one another they acknowledged that the man with cash value in an insurance policy was their most likely prospect. Waiting for a table at the Tail of the Cock one day, Ray Platt looked out over the restaurant and said to several colleagues, "What do you guys see?" They gave up. "I see two million dollars in cash values," Platt said.

Fully half of the company's legitimate insurance would eventually be transferred from other policies. As an examiner of the California Insurance Department put it, "The whole concept was a license to twist."

Another of Equity Funding's problems was Raymond Platt himself.

When Goldblum, Cuthbertson, and Platt returned to the West Coast, they all began receiving $500 a week each. Then Platt moved to Los Angeles from San Francisco to be the sales manager. Soon his expenses alone were running $2000 to $3000 a month. In the first half of 1961, he would be gone from the office as often as he was there. He missed appointments. He was known to drink all day. There were reports of fights.

There came a point where his legendary drinking became more of a liability than his selling prowess was an asset. Amsterdam Overseas Corporation, a large stockholder, was to finance Equity Funding programs. Its officers had heard disquieting reports about Platt. There was only one thing to do. On August 1, 1961, Platt resigned under pressure as an officer of Equity Funding. He stayed on as sales manager.

Then came further problems. In November, Stanley Goldblum received a call from the manager of the North Shore Club at Lake Tahoe. Platt had lost $25,000 and couldn't cover his debt. Goldblum arranged for a Milwaukeean named Pierce Rosenberg to loan Platt $25,000. Platt put up stock as collateral. Early in 1962, after promising to reform, Platt was reinstated and reelected an officer and a director. But then came word that Platt was using his stock to settle his bar bills. In May, Platt's wife called Goldblum. Her husband was at the Hotel Tropicana in Las Vegas. He had lost $12,000. A call in June came to Mike Riordan from a vice president of Metropolitan Bank. Platt had written a check to cover some gambling losses. The bank had returned the check because of insufficient funds. Finally, on August 13, 1962, Platt was removed as an officer and an employee. He remained a director until a stockholder's meeting, on September 1, when he failed to vote his own shares.

Some months later, Mike Riordan dropped into The Phone Booth, the first topless bar on Sunset Boulevard. Platt was there with Ralph Robbins, Stanley Goldblum's former partner, downing one "gazuguda"—his favorite term for a drink—after another. Platt always loved to bait Riordan, and did so now. At last, Riordan took the bait; he made a remark that Platt didn't like. "That does it, you shanty Irishman," Platt said. He challenged Riordan to a fight, and offered him the first punch. Riordan threw it. Platt shook it off. Then he shoved Riordan up against a wall, held him with his left hand, and started throwing in rights. Bloodied, Riordan stumbled down the stairs and out into the street. Robbins followed him. Moments later, Riordan shot from the parking lot in his car and careened down Sunset Boulevard. A sheriff's car stopped him. He was taken to jail, then released.

Toward the end of 1964, Platt sued Goldblum, Riordan, and Cuthbertson for twenty-five percent of all assets and profits of Equity Funding, claiming that he had been improperly excluded from participation in a joint venture. Soon thereafter, he fell from a barstool at the Luau with a drink in his hand, dead of a heart attack at thirty-eight. (Platt's wife eventually lost the suit.)

In 1964, Equity Funding took its stock public at $6 a share. All of the salesmen who had been promised stock went to a meeting in Las Vegas. There they learned that they would have to purchase the stock at the initial offering price, just like everyone else. Five managers, whose offices accounted for a large percentage of Equity Funding's sales, quit the company. One of them was Goldblum's old partner, Robbins, who asserted he had been promised 36,000 shares at ninety cents a share.

Then Gene Cuthbertson and Goldblum began to fight. Generally, the disputes concerned Goldblum's displeasure over Cuthbertson's decisions as manager of the sales force. "I'm running it," Cuthbertson would snap. The showdown was a 1965 sales meeting. Cuthbertson outlined a new sales program.

"It won't work," Goldblum said flatly.

"How do you know, since we haven't tried it?" Cuthbertson taunted.

The dispute dragged on until, at last, Cuthbertson proposed that he would buy Goldblum out or let Goldblum buy him out. With Riordan's support, Goldblum offered to buy out Cuthbertson.

On October 22, 1965, Goldblum, Riordan, and six investors bought Cuthbertson's shares for $7 apiece. He netted $870,000.

Of the original foursome, there were now just two, Mike Riordan and Stanley Goldblum. Riordan, chairman of the board, maintained contact with Wall Street and thought up new ventures. Goldblum, the president, managed the company.

Riordan took up residence in Brentwood's Mandeville Canyon, a long and fragrant cul-de-sac winding into the Santa Monica Mountains. His white two-story home was set back on a large piece of choice property, nestled against a hillside. Goldblum had long since moved from a $20,000 home in Baldwin Hills to the select Trousdale Estates in Beverly Hills. He drove a Rolls-Royce to work.

Equity Funding kept growing. Its sales force increased; so did reported volume and earnings. From the over-the-counter market, the company's stock moved onto the American Stock Exchange. Riordan and Goldblum had each owned 300,000 shares at the outset. Subsequent purchases and stock splits had increased their holdings still further. By 1968, Riordan was well on his way to the $100 million he had predicted for himself. But, in the fall of that year, he seemed suddenly to heed his brother's admonition that "post time is forty-one."

He looked bad, and he knew it. He had been smoking and drinking heavily, racing his Mark IV down Sunset at 100 miles an hour. And he'd been carousing. He'd always enjoyed a reputation as a ladies' man. He did not need to work hard to earn it; women found him compelling. There was a theory that, consciously or unconsciously, he let his infidelities be discovered as a means of punishing himself. Abruptly, he changed. Before, he had never passed up a chance to spend a night on the town or a weekend "retreat" with the boys. Now, when the invitations came, he would say, "I'm worried about Jackie." To his brother, Bill, also his closest confidant, he said, "I want to make it up to Jackie. I haven't been good to her." He became a model husband. He seemed like a convert, out to rectify a lifetime of sins.

In January 1969, Riordan took his wife to Miami for the Super Bowl. He installed her in an expensive suite. They were like lovers.

A week later from California, Mike called Bill, who had been with him at the Super Bowl. It was early Friday evening, but Mike was already in bed. He was tired, he said, so tired that he had taken the day off. "It's been raining seventeen straight days," he told his brother. What a nice life it might be to own the Miami Dolphins. He might buy the club if Bill would help him run it.

Bill said he'd think about it.

"Tell me the line again, Bill," Mike asked then.

Bill repeated the line his brother always loved to hear.

"You're only here for a short time, so take time to smell the flowers."

That evening, as Mike Riordan lay asleep in the first floor bedroom of his Mandeville Canyon home, a mudslide crashed into the room, burying him to the waist. Firemen tried to pull him out. The pain was tremendous. "Keep pulling," Riordan told them. A second slide buried him. He was forty-one.

At his funeral, William Logan sang *The Impossible Dream.*

Eight years and three months after four men seized control of a tiny company, Stanley Goldblum was alone—the chief executive officer of a corporation with reported assets approaching $200 million.

The wake after Mike Riordan's funeral was at Goldblum's new $300,000 two-story home on Whittier Drive in Beverly Hills, north of Sunset Boulevard. The day before, at the company's offices on Wilshire Boulevard, Stanley Goldblum had been elected chairman of the board of Equity Funding Corporation of America. Goldblum had not wanted the job, but now that he had it he meant to make certain that Mike Riordan's death was not misinterpreted by Wall Street. There would be no talk about corporate indecision. The prompt action by the board of directors had been taken with that in mind.

Late that year, Equity Funding moved to the top floor at 1900 Avenue of the Stars. Early in 1970, Goldblum moved into the corner office—at the time, the largest in Century City. The only photograph he kept in the room was a framed one of Mike Riordan.

The contrast in their leaderships could hardly have been greater. Riordan made people laugh. Goldblum made them stiffen.

Physically, he was awesome. He measured six feet two inches, but such was his muscular bulk that colleagues assured you he was six four. He looked like an ex-boxer or -wrestler. His small, almond-shaped eyes gave his heavy face a faint, incongruous Mongolian caste. He made people wonder if he was comfortable doing what he did. But his manner left no doubts that, comfortable or not, he was in command. He broadcast power. He wanted, and took, control of all proceedings. He would slice into discussions. He was impatient, assertive, steely, crisp. Once he called for a subordinate and was told he was away from his desk. "This is Stanley Goldblum. Find him," he said. He communicated poorly. He was a good editor but a bad writer. His advisors frequently had to warn him against acting autocratically. Despite their counsel, his memoranda managed to sound authoritarian.

"A lot of people accused him of becoming cold and standoffish after he succeeded. Not true. He was cold and standoffish in the beginning," an associate of many years observes. He confined himself to dealings with his executive vice presidents. Only top officers called him Stanley. Others called him Mr. Goldblum. Some secretaries called him "God."

It was his quizzical manner that others found most troubling. A sharp mind and silent mouth can be a disconcerting combination. Goldblum, said one intimate, combined Jewish wit and Gary Cooper silence. Once he invited a group of senior salesmen to the home office conference room for a luncheon to discuss their grievances—mostly centering on stock options and other long-range benefits. He appeared forty-five minutes late, explained that he'd had a dentist's appointment, and asked, "What are you guys here for?"

"I'd like to know if I'm going to end up with something more than a gold watch," one sales manager said.

"How would you like a color television set?" Goldblum replied.

He seemed to have little appreciation for other people's time. He always insisted on being first on the tape with corporate news, which meant that one of his public relations representatives would have to arise at 5 A.M. on the West Coast to call the financial news services. At that luncheon meeting for salesmen, one of them said to a colleague, "This is a waste of time. The man's laughing at us. By what right does he come in forty-five minutes late? He's got a salary. We're on commission."

Goldblum became chairman of the business conduct committee of the Los Angeles branch of the National Association of Securities Dealers. He was harsh on transgressors. He would give substantially stiffer penalties than had been anticipated. He was most concerned about irregularities on the part of his own people. He would pursue each case itself rather than let it be handled by subordinates.

Yet, for all his imperious ways, Goldblum had his grace notes. He was readily available. Often, he would answer the phone himself. If you called and he was busy, he would get back to you right away.

The stories of acerbic cruelty were tempered by others of sentimentality and humor. He made contributions to political campaigns and gave generously to charity (although not so generously as was generally believed). He had something of a reputation as an easy touch. Once, during a meeting in his office, his secretary came in and said, "Your brother's here." Goldblum pulled two $100 bills from his wallet, put the bills in an envelope, and gave the envelope to his secretary. "The rent's due," he said to his visitor and went on with the meeting.

He knew what he did to people, and it troubled him. He tried seriously to shed his egocentric image. He talked critically about himself, using many of the classic psychoanalytic phrases. "I'm an imposing figure, a threatening authority figure," he would acknowledge. He apologized for his detachment. It was, he said, a function of his nature. "I'm not basically a gregarious fellow. I don't have dozens of friends. How many people do? I find that most people are lonely. I need people. I love the people that I love. I don't go out of my way to seek friendships."

His few close friends included comedian Buddy Hackett and

singer Glen Campbell. In 1972, Goldblum threw a St. Patrick's Day party for 100 persons on the top floor of the Bistro. When the orchestra left at midnight, Campbell picked up a guitar and entertained his fellow guests.

Goldblum's dress, overstated in the early 1960s, now became more muted. He wore custom-tailored suits. But he still affected big cufflinks, monogrammed shirts, and a touch too much cologne.

His fortune was estimated at $30 million. He earned $100,000 a year in salary and another $150,000 to $200,000 in stock bonuses each year. His massive weightlifter's physique seemed incongruous in his delicately decorated home with its expensive—and exquisite—Picasso and Chagall lithographs. Goldblum respected art and knew its value. One day he visited a gallery to inspect several fine paintings by prominent artists. The prices for the paintings totaled $750,000. Goldblum offered the gallery owner a check on the spot—$500,000 for the lot. "I'll have to ask my partners," the dazed owner replied. He returned and said, "We accept." Goldblum didn't buy the paintings; he had simply wanted to test the relation of price to artistic value.

If the at-home Goldblum and the office Goldblum were men apart, one certain sign was the art he kept in each. The one big painting in his office was garish, atrocious.

Goldblum's off-duty humor, another contrast, combined self-deprecation with an appreciation for the ridiculous. After his troubles began, a visitor asked him why everyone thought he was six feet four inches tall when he was only six two. "I used to be six four, but now I'm bent a little," Goldblum replied. Several years earlier, at the height of his powers, Goldblum went to Rome to conclude a deal with the Vatican. The night before the meeting, he went on the town with Samuel Lowell, Equity Funding's financial officer. They returned at 4 A.M. When Lowell awakened him for the meeting, he said, "Are they sending their number one man?"

"No," Lowell replied.

"Then we're not sending our number one man," Goldblum said, and tried to go back to sleep.

He took more readily to the toys of wealth than he did to its surroundings. A mutual friend once took a Ferrari dealer to Goldblum's house to show him the newest model. "He'll ask you just two questions," the friend said. "What colors does it come in? And when can I have it?" The friend was almost right: Goldblum asked the questions in the opposite order.

One night, after a dinner at La Chaumière, Goldblum took a stockbroker guest for a ride in the Ferrari through the quiet streets of Beverly Hills at eighty miles an hour. He loved to jump on his Honda dirt motorcycle, or sail his thirty-five-foot competitive racing yacht, or drive his other car, a Rolls-Royce.

But most of all, Goldblum loved to work out, alone, in his new $100,000 weightlifter's gym, adjoining his house. It was a dream come true. Goldblum hadn't lifted weights since he was twenty-three. In 1970, he determined to find out whether a man of forty-five could develop himself physically to resemble a twenty-year-old. He liked goals; he thought he could do it. "You can be anything you want to be," Stanley Goldblum said.

Equity Funding's stock shot up so fast in the 1960s that I missed the rise. I had first learned about the company in 1964, when it went public. My reaction was twofold—curiosity at what had made the stock perform so well and regret that I had missed it.

I have always been reluctant to go into a stock after it has gone up three or four times its initial price. Moreover, I felt that Equity Funding was something of a question mark; to try to understand its specialized product would have required a great deal of time. It didn't really seem worth it.

By 1970, however, Equity Funding's stock had dropped from a high of $80 to a low of $13 a share. Nothing publicly untoward had happened to the company; it had simply shared disproportionately in the big drop in the prices of securities.

Early in 1971, I received a phone call from Chris Godchaux
of the Argosy Group, a financial public relations firm that
handled Equity Funding. Most financial public relations people
aren't very good; the Argosy Group is an exception. Godchaux
asked me if I would like to take a look at Equity Funding. I
said I'd be delighted. When Godchaux called again to ask if
I'd like to meet with Equity's executives in New York, I offered
to give a luncheon. A few weeks later, I did. We met in a room
at the New York Chamber of Commerce. As hosts, our firm
was, in effect, presenting the company to a number of our
clients. I had never met Goldblum or any of the other officers.
When he came in, I was a trifle embarrassed. It was my job to
introduce him, but I didn't know how to pronounce his name.
When I asked him, he replied, "Any way is all right. It doesn't
make much difference." His self-effacing remark was so attrac-
tively low keyed it made me wonder why his reputation was
questioned on Wall Street.

It was, and so was his company's. "Equity Funding is generally regarded as an aggressive growth-oriented marketing
organization," a private study made by Argosy in the company's behalf noted.

> To many, it smacks of the high-flying Beverly Hills com-
> panies of the Sixties: Commonwealth United, International
> Industries, National General and Republic Corp. (or even
> Litton Industries) to name a few. Management is considered
> bright and aggressive. Accounting practices are seen by
> most as complicated and by some as suspect or "creative."
> The company is regarded as an innovator both in its funda-
> mental concepts and in day to day operations. In essence,
> Equity Funding is perceived as a "go-go" company rather
> than as a fiduciary institution, and its present appeal as an
> investment vehicle clearly is to the adventurous analyst or
> portfolio manager.
>
> The more orthodox analysts are put off either by the
> company's promotional flavor, or by the apparently complex
> inter-relationships of its various financial services. While

> analysts and other key people in the investment community
> uniformly regard Equity Funding as bright, aggressive and
> fast-moving and find these an attractive combination of
> qualities, to others there is the suspicion based on many
> precedents that those who move this fast ultimately trip and
> fall. For still others, there is the sin of pride—not of being
> bright but of advertising it: "I am the greatest." Among older
> analysts and others stung in recent years by "concept
> stocks" there is a wariness of this kind of promotion.

Then the report alluded to the unmentionable pejorative.
Banking and insurance are generally considered to be among
the last great bulwarks of anti-Semitism in the commercial
world. Goldblum and most of his executive vice presidents
were Jewish.

> There are some who link the company's aggressiveness with
> the Beverly Hills look. The so-called Beverly Hills look is
> harmful for other reasons. There are those analysts who
> want no "emotional connection" with this type of "merchan-
> dise."
>   Equity Funding is largely thought of as Stanley Gold-
> blum's company. Goldblum is given good marks by the
> financial community: "competent, shrewd, dynamic, deci-
> sive and bright" are terms that continually popped up in our
> research. A few complain that he is perhaps a little too
> shrewd and something of a "hotshot."

What the report was referring to now was Goldblum's penchant for the putdown. He never sought the opportunity; he
simply couldn't resist it. Once, at an open meeting, an analyst
asked a hypothetical question: If the analyst were a director of
Equity Funding and proposed that the corporation get rid of a
certain controversial new venture, what would Goldblum do?
    "Get a new director," Goldblum replied.
    Was his projection of arrogance what Goldblum might call
a defense mechanism? Whatever the answer, the arrogance

existed, and Wall Street felt it. Analysts not only referred to Equity Funding as "Stanley's show," they worried about the lack of depth in management that was the usual characteristic of a one-man company. They felt uneasy with the complexity of the company, as well, and uncomfortable with what they interpreted as Stanley Goldblum's impatience. In truth, he did seem intolerant of those who did not quickly understand what he told them—and he had no patience whatever for the parade of analysts who arrived at his office without having done their homework.

Goldblum savored his company's maverick image in an industry of staid traditions. Equity Funding *was* youthful; its concept *was* different. But, for all men in business, certain dues must be paid. Equity Funding needed the support of financial analysts. Goldblum made frequent trips to New York.

After cocktails and lunch at the Chamber of Commerce, I rose to introduce him. "Equity Funding," I said, "is a sales-oriented company. If you're going to succeed in the insurance and mutual fund business, the real key is being able to sell. The record shows that Equity Funding knows how."

Then Goldblum spoke. His talk seemed rational and modest. Many life insurance executives in a similar situation would have made a huge sales pitch; Goldblum didn't do that. Rather, he talked with candor. Equity Funding had many salesmen, he said, but only a small percentage produced most of the business. Nonetheless, the company constantly tried to upgrade its sales force, a task made easier because of the company's innovative products. He came across not as a sharp character, but as a fairly reasonable individual. He wasn't flashy; he answered questions in a believable way. I remember thinking once again, I don't see why this guy has the reputation he has.

I next saw Stanley Goldblum eight months later, in February 1972. We met for breakfast in a midtown hotel. He came armed with worksheets of Equity Funding's performance in 1971. The figures were impressive. The company's assets were $497 million, its net worth was $118 million, its revenues for 1971 were $131 million and net earnings were $19 million. The company's earnings per share had compounded on paper at an average annual rate of 60.79 percent since 1961—which made it the fastest growing financial services organization in the United States.

Equity Funding managed three insurance companies, Equity Funding Life, Bankers National Life, and Equity Funding Life of New York, with $4.6 billion of life insurance in force; the parent company was dickering for a fourth insurance company, Northern Life Insurance. It managed and sponsored three mutual funds, Equity Growth Fund, Equity Progress Fund, and Fund of America, with assets of more than $200 million—a hundredfold increase in just five years. Its real estate division owned and managed twenty apartment complexes in California and Arizona with a selling value of $34 million. The company owned Bishops Bank and Trust Co. of the Bahamas, Liberty Savings and Loan Association, and a brokerage operation that belonged to regional stock exchanges. It ran a petroleum exploration and development subsidiary, and it managed Ankony Angus, a large cattle breeding concern. Out of 1800 insurance companies, the Equity group ranked twenty-ninth in terms of business in force.

Goldblum spent most of that breakfast meeting discussing Bankers National Life, which Equity Funding had taken over a few months earlier. He dwelt at length on the vigor with which EFCA had fired eleven of the twelve major officers of Bankers and replaced them with its own team. But what he emphasized most was how much net worth Equity Funding Corporation of America now displayed. The earnings record was terrific but "look at the net worth," he said, "$119 million."

"Well," I said, "I guess you're in a position to raise additional capital if you need it, and also to make future acquisitions, for cash as well as stock."

"We're looking at them all the time," Goldblum said.

Not long thereafter, I received a strange phone call from Goldblum. He asked if I knew whether Alan Abelson of *Barron's,* a columnist with an accounting background and a reputation for tearing down corporate financial statements, intended to write an unfavorable column about Equity Funding.

I said I didn't have the remotest idea.

"Could you find out?" Goldblum asked.

"People at *Barron's* don't normally tell anybody when they're going to do an unfavorable piece," I answered.

"I heard you know Alan Abelson."

"No, I know Steve Anreder, who sometimes works on Abelson's column."

"Would you call him up and find out?" Goldblum asked.

"Well, Stanley," I said, "I'll call him, but I don't think I'll find out anything."

Abelson was on vacation, so I asked Anreder whether he'd ever done any work on Equity Funding. He said he hadn't. Did I know anything about it? "Not much," I said.

Then I called Goldblum and told him it didn't sound as though *Barron's* was planning anything on Equity Funding. He seemed reassured. But it struck me as peculiar that the chief executive of a major corporation would call up an analyst he had met only twice and ask him to find out about a rumored story.

There were two men with Stanley Goldblum at the luncheon I had given in 1971. Both were young. Both were fat. Both were executive vice presidents of Equity Funding. One was Fred Levin, the director of marketing as well as president of Equity Funding Life Insurance Company (EFLIC); the other was Samuel Lowell, the corporate financial officer. Levin had come to Equity Funding with its newly purchased life insurance subsidiary, Presidential Life of Illinois (which later became EFLIC). Levin and Lowell became such close friends that

Lowell bought a house close to Levin's. They traveled together, referred to one another in conversation as "my best friend." For a long time after Mike Riordan's death, Stanley Goldblum relied equally on each of them. Then he began to rely more heavily on Levin, and Lowell and Levin were no longer such good friends.

Lowell was a certified public accountant who had come to Equity Funding from Dart Industries. Prior to that, he had worked for Haskins & Sells, the auditors of EFLIC. His obsessive ways with food and his sometimes lavish displays turned many people from him, but he was a brilliant, verbal man with a strong native intelligence far beyond his years. Now however he began to drift. He became careless about his hours. His thoughts seemed more and more focused on the bridge clubs and tournaments that dominated his social hours. He would show up at the executive offices in time for lunch in the executive dining room and leave shortly after he had eaten.

Levin never let up. He was a compulsive worker. He had joined Presidential Life as counsel in 1964, after graduation from DePaul University School of Law in Chicago and a stint at the Illinois Insurance Department. By the age of thirty, he was president of the life insurance company, and had taken charge of the parent company's expanding insurance operations. By 1972, that included Bankers National Life of New Jersey and Northern Life of Seattle. By 1973, his salary was $80,000 a year, plus a $12,000 expense allowance. He also received a bonus of 4000 shares of Equity Funding stock—equivalent to twice his salary if the stock was $40 a share. Lowell received the same.

As Levin's power and wealth accumulated, his personality changed. His charm was mechanical, his smile quick but unconvincing. Cruelty became his weapon. He once announced to a department head that he was bringing a new man into the department. "In whose capacity?" the department head wondered. "Yours," Levin replied.

One day a sales manager looking to improve his financial

situation dropped into Levin's office. The executive vice president was having his shoes shined. "Tell me you love me, Freddie," the sales manager said. Levin bought him a shoeshine.

It was to Levin the salesmen went with most of their complaints. They complained when the regular sales bulletins comparing regional and branch office results were stopped. "Don't worry about the numbers. They're not important anyway," Levin replied.

Levin liked to put selling on another level. He borrowed from medicine to talk about Equity Funding's "multiphasic" approach to a client—an approach from many angles, using a variety of tests, evaluation criteria, and professional personnel to arrive at a many-faceted picture of the client's "health." While the individual salesman still remained the central pivot of the marketing effort, he was "flanked by a cadre of product specialists who maintained separate line relationships with central management but who also worked horizontally with the branch managers and the individual salesmen to provide the essential quality of competence in areas where it was wasteful to train every salesman to perform competently."

It was high-blown talk that went right past the ears of the salesmen. A few branch managers were earning $100,000 a year, but smaller branch managers were struggling. What kept them struggling, whatever their complaints, was a tempting production option to buy stock at attractive prices—a prize few large insurance companies could offer, since most of them are not stock companies but mutual companies that do not issue stock. The Equity Funding salesmen could reflect on an interoffice communication entitled "Hypothetical Production Stock Option Results."

"If the present Production Stock Option plan had been in effect since 1965," the chart said, "this is what an agent earning $10,000 per year would have received." As of June 1, 1968, the salesman would have acquired, for $29,563, shares worth $88,206.

But by late 1969, as the stock market took a dive, a good many shares of Equity Funding were suddenly worth less than they cost. Not only could the company make no acquisitions, it could offer no tempting prize to its salesmen. Without a prize, salesmen disappear. Without salesmen, so does a company.

The Trouble with EFLIC

It just didn't sound right. It might not be illegal, but it surely wasn't ethical, Frank Majerus decided. He was mulling over an official announcement from his new employers, the life insurance subsidiary of Equity Funding. All employees who requested it would be issued free insurance for one year—"special-class" insurance. The policies, which the employees could retain after the year of grace by paying annual premiums, were in significant amounts, many of them for $50,000. To a cautious man like Frank Majerus, giving that much insurance free even for a year did not set well at all. He began to wonder if he'd made a mistake.

He'd had a good job in Minneapolis: assistant vice president and assistant treasurer at a small company called Minnesota National Life. One day toward the end of 1968, Jim Smith, a former colleague who had moved to Los Angeles to work for Equity Funding, had called to see whether Frank might be interested in changing jobs. Frank had said no. But Jim had called again after the first of the year. Come on out and look things over, he said. What the heck, Frank thought. It was cold in Minnesota. At worst, he'd get some sunshine.

But there was something more seductive than the climate awaiting the low-keyed, small-town Midwesterner, an offer to be controller of Equity Funding's life insurance subsidiary, Presidential Life Insurance Company of America, which was about to be renamed Equity Funding Life Insurance Company of America—EFLIC for short. It meant a good raise, more responsibility and prestige. And the company certainly seemed promising. So, in March 1969, Frank had started his new job. But now, several months later, with that special-class insurance, he wondered if the new company wasn't just a little too aggressive. He listened to the talk around the office. It was talk he didn't like. The talk was that the company had "reinsured" the free insurance. That really grated on his Lutheran conscience.

Majerus knew that all life insurance companies reinsured part of their risks with other companies. That way no one claim would have a material effect on an insurer's financial statement. But Equity Funding was engaging in a rarer type of reinsurance. It was called coinsurance. Under this, EFLIC would not only transfer a portion of the insurance risk, it would partially sell the future profits of the policy in return for a cash payment up front. This was legal, though it generally connoted a lack of capital on the part of the company that coinsures.

There were two things wrong with the practice in this instance, Majerus reasoned: First, most of the employees who accepted the free insurance the first year wouldn't renew the second. That meant the reinsuring company would be stuck with large losses. Second, the scheme was obviously a quick way to produce profits for Equity Funding. Not only did Equity Funding receive money from the reinsuring company, it had no salesmen to pay. Those proceeds looked good on the annual statement. In effect, Majerus reasoned, Equity Funding was giving away something to create an asset of no lasting value. What was unethical was the coinsuring of it to create both cash and a misleading financial statement.

Ethical considerations aside, the scheme might work in the short run, but Frank Majerus began to doubt whether his new company was for real over the long haul. He was not a man to show emotion readily; he kept his counsels to himself.

At thirty-four, slender Ronald Secrist was the old man of the staff. His boss, Fred Levin, was thirty-two. Most of the young executives were under thirty. Fred Levin liked to boast about his young staff. Secrist was not one of the boys.

Ron Secrist didn't like certain things about Levin. He found him a coarse, abusive man, given to dirty words in the office. That was Fred's inferiority complex coming out in his vocabulary, Ron decided. The role of the tough executive was to cover his baby-fat image. And Ron, who had majored in insurance at the University of Washington, wasn't too happy about the management conditions he'd encountered at the insurance subsidiary, either. He'd moved to Los Angeles from San Francisco to get out of underwriting management and into general administrative work; but he'd found conditions in turmoil and had been unable to get his administrative system set up. But what really upset him was the crazy talk he had started hearing around the office in December, barely four months after he'd started work. At first he thought they were kidding, those young corporate officers. They were talking about how it would be easier to make up "Y business" than to go out and get real business. They said it half jokingly, but they seemed so carefree and immature and wild that he'd begun to wonder.

Well, whatever it was, he was stuck with it, because this was his fourth company in twelve years, which looked bad enough on a résumé. He could ill afford to show an assistant vice presidency that ended after six months.

Don Goff was one of those people who would spot a worm and want to dissect it. He wasn't three months into his new job, but already he had a lot of questions. The first was why he had so much difficulty obtaining information about that damned Department 99. The second was why management was insisting on a computer system with a capacity to function without an audit trail. The third was why, every time he asked for an answer to questions one and two, the invariable reply was, "See Art Lewis." Art Lewis was EFLIC's actuary, and Don Goff had no quarrel with Lewis's competence. It was just that Art Lewis was hard to pin down.

The whole attitude was a contradiction of the bargain they'd struck. They'd come after him, after all. He'd been working in Port Huron, Michigan, when this stranger had called. He'd said he was running an employment search in behalf of Equity Funding. Don's name had been given him by a friend. Equity Funding was looking for a team to install a management information system. Yes, Don replied, he thought he could run a team. So he'd gone to Chicago for one interview and then to Los Angeles for another, but in both places he'd established one condition. If he was to function as systems analyst manager, he wanted the authority to run his system.

The promise wasn't being kept.

There were several instances in which the team was getting design criteria as opposed to answers to questions of how the business ran. A computer, after all, was just a big dumb adding machine. It could do a lot of work for you provided you told it what to do. But how could he do that if he was being told, in effect, "We have some special marketing business. Your billing system must have codes in it allowing for a bypass of certain billings."

What all the evasions amounted to was this: There was a certain part of the business—Department 99—that was maintained by a special run performed in bulk at the end of the year. That was the business someone didn't want him to know about. That was like asking your wife to keep the family books without access to all the checks.

He hadn't really wanted the job, Pat Hopper reminded himself. He was thirty-one, a bachelor, and suddenly wealthy. The company he had formed in Pasadena with two other young men, Independent Securities Corporation, of which he had been vice president and secretary–treasurer, had just been sold to Equity Funding, in exchange for 150,000 shares of that corporation. His portion was 10,850 shares—and an unwanted job with EFCA. ISC was only a small part of the Equity Funding picture and Pat felt no challenge. Moreover, the company had a reputation for selling people insurance and mutual fund programs they really couldn't afford. But the job was part of the deal: EFCA was buying the management along with a sales force of 1700 licensed representatives. Pat had already begun to liquidate his shares. He really shouldn't complain. Only a year before, ISC had almost gone belly up.

Pat and his partners had wanted to offer shares in ISC to the public through a major investment banking house on Wall Street. The men from one Wall Street house promised several million dollars in financing, provided ISC would build up a large sales force selling life insurance and mutual funds. Their mandate was to forget profits and concentrate on getting offices opened and agents trained and licensed. "Don't worry about the money," they were told, "we'll take care of that when you need it." As agreed, Pat and his associates spent all their money in expanding the sales force. They built one of the largest mutual fund sales forces in the country. To keep the momentum going and to make their company look good for a public offering, they needed another $5 million in capital. "No problem," said the Wall Street firm. Then the trouble began. The Wall Street firm couldn't raise the money. After several fruitless weeks, one of its partners flew to Los Angeles and checked in at the Beverly Wilshire Hotel. Pat and his two associates decided to give him an ultimatum at breakfast the next morning. "Either you come up with the five million dollars, or we'll have to go into bankruptcy," they reported. The man from Wall Street excused himself, went to his room, and threw up his breakfast.

Hopper and his associates realized then that they would either have to sell their company or drastically cut it back. If they cut back, there would be no hope of getting a good price for their stock and all their work in building a sales force would be for naught. They decided to try to sell. Even if the public would no longer buy a company with a lot of salesmen but huge operating losses, perhaps a public company would. There was no hesitation about whom to go after: the company most interested in acquisitions was Equity Funding.

The day after ISC called, Stanley Goldblum and Fred Levin had come out to see the company. Levin, the president of EFLIC, did most of the talking that day; Goldblum said little; Hopper said nothing. "Are you happy?" Goldblum asked him at last. "You don't look happy."

"I'll be happy if you buy this organization," Hopper replied. That day, they shook on the deal.

For more than two months, EFCA kept Pat Hopper in Pasadena as president of a brokerage life subsidiary. Then the parent company moved him to the home office, to work for Samuel Lowell, Equity Funding's financial officer.

Within six weeks, Hopper had developed a strong antipathy to Lowell. The man would never take a stance. "How many votes for this solution?" Lowell would ask after a staff meeting. He would never vote himself. One week later, the solution hadn't worked, and he would say, "You see, I told you it wouldn't work."

Hopper's first assignment had been to examine and detail the problems in the company's funding department where book work on the insurance-mutual fund package programs was handled. It was a troubleshooter's role, never a popular one, particularly for a new man, and Sam Lowell hadn't made it any easier. He'd taken him down to the sixth floor and said laughingly, "I want you to meet my spy."

Well, Hopper thought, he asked for it. Here goes. He rolled a sheet of paper into the typewriter, and began:

REPORT TO: Sam Lowell
                   on Funding Department
PREPARED BY: Patrick W. Hopper
                   November & December 1970

The Funding Department has many problems, but I believe that the root of its troubles lies in two major areas—lack of adequate training and the "computer" problem. If these two problems are not improved, I believe they can contribute to a total breakdown in the operation of the Funding Department.

Lack of Training

Saying that there is a "lack of adequate training" is somewhat an understatement for what is occurring in the Funding Department—and, unfortunately, through the rest of the Company. There is no formal or planned training. As a result, people simply don't know how to perform their assigned tasks, and this covers almost all of the personnel. . . .

A clerk is hired, given a few minutes' explanation about his job, told to ask questions if he has any problems, and turned loose on the job. There are cases where, after that, if the new clerk does ask questions, he is either ridiculed or given a flip answer—often by his supervisor.

A man is promoted to supervisor, or subsupervisor, after presumably showing expertise in his assigned tasks. There is, however, no evidence of his being given any training in how to function in his new job. In essence, he is just the most proficient clerk in his area unless he is trained how to be an effective supervisor. This is knowledge that can't be applied unless it has been imparted. A supervisor must be able to properly interview, hire, train, motivate and relate with his people. He must be concerned about their welfare and morale, without coddling them. All of these have to be learned before being applied. This is not happening in the Funding Department.

I don't know what criteria was used in selecting Lloyd Edens as manager of the Funding Department, but I do know that ability to deal with people was not given very heavy weight. Lloyd is extremely competent in terms of the technical aspects of funding, but he is not able to deal with people effectively. Again, as far as I have been able to determine, he has been given no guidance or training in this area. Supervisors will come to him with a problem, and, before they have a chance to relate their problem, will be told to "take a walk" or "fix it." If Lloyd knows how to solve problems, he must show those under him how to do so also. I was also appalled to run into employees in the Funding Department who didn't know who Lloyd Edens is. . . .

I have also noted an emphasis on the quantity of work accomplished, but not the quality. For example, the renewal and conservation departments grind out all kinds of files because that is where the emphasis in the section lies. However, these two areas have the greatest number of errors, and a lot of these errors are being input into the system. . . .

The lack of training, and management's inability to work with their people, has caused an employee turnover rate of monumental proportions. The rate has slackened to some extent—probably because of the tighter job market. I do, however, feel that unless something is done to improve the training of these employees and their supervisors, the rate will pick up again as the job market improves. . . .

The Funding Department has not ever been examined by the SEC, but the chances of such an examination have been substantially enhanced recently by the establishment of an Investment Company Team—which would also cover Funding companies. Both the Legal Department and I feel that the Funding Department is *not* prepared in the least for such an inspection.

"Computer" Problem

The problems generated for the Funding Department by the Management Information Systems Department are great. From conversations with various personnel I gleaned the fact that the 1970 Funding System was designed by two individuals who spent very little time in the Funding Department. To me, to attempt to program the kind of system needed by the Funding Department without a thorough understanding of how the department works—with the myriad of exceptions—is totally unthinkable. Yet, this is apparently just what happened with the 1970 Funding System. I believe that there was a lack of management ability in allowing a system to be designed in such a manner, and then enforcing the time limit when such a system was to go on line without knowing for sure just how it would work.

My conversations with various management people in the company in relation to the Funding Department often led to asides about the MIS Department, with enough facts to make me believe that a very real problem exists with this department and the way it serves the various users in the company. The results that are being gotten are not good and, in light of the amount of money being spent, are just short of a total disaster.

For example, in a context relative to the Funding Department, everyone was quick to tell me that the 1970 System was a total failure. Such quotes as a "nightmare," "an abortion" have been used to describe the system by personnel in the MIS Department, and yet they are just now coming to the realization that this system doesn't work and cannot be made to work properly—ever. What has been going on since this system was supposed to start functioning in March of this year? Why did it take these computer "experts" eight months to realize a mistake had been made? Yet my conversations with them indicate that they have just come to this realization—after eight months. . . .

A few days later, Pat Hopper took the report to Sam Lowell. Lowell read it, and said "It's a good report, but you don't understand what you're supposed to come up with."

Hopper marched to Fred Levin's office. "I absolutely will not work another day with Lowell. If you've got nothing else for me, I'll leave."

"You ain't gonna get away that easy," Levin replied. "I've got plenty for you to do."

Hopper cooled down. He liked Levin. The man was sharp,

and always candid. He was completely honest in the things they discussed. He had an excellent memory, one that gave Hopper's own good memory a workout. Right or wrong, he took responsibilities for his decisions. And Hopper knew that Levin appreciated him. The insurance company president would frequently introduce Pat to others with an allusion to the ISC acquisition: "Here's what I bought for three million dollars." Only one thing about Fred disturbed Pat. He always seemed to have meetings going on, but he hated to talk at them. He would sit, biting his fingernails until he drew blood. He would crucify his fingers.

The year 1970 had ended. It was a time in a life insurance company when the actuaries, controllers, and treasurers squirreled themselves in their offices preparing the year-end financial statements. No time now for wasted minutes at the coffee machine. The rhythm seemed normal. But to Frank Majerus, EFLIC's new controller, one feature of the operation seemed utterly bewildering. His boss, Lloyd Edens, had just informed him that they were going to rerun the company's general ledgers on the corporation for the last six months. There could be only one reason for doing that: some new business was to be inserted. Frank Majerus was dumbfounded.

A week later Edens handed him the premium figure to enter in the books. It was twice what Majerus had anticipated for the year.

"Your project is all fucked up and there's no way it can be completed under these circumstances."

Don Goff, the computer specialist, was speaking in his downstate Illinois accent, and staring resolutely through his glasses at the others in the small sixth-floor conference room. Art Lewis, Jim Smith, and Lloyd Edens were there: Lewis the small curly-headed actuary who had attended New York University's School of Engineering and College of Arts and received a dual B.S. in Chemical Engineering and Mathematics and then at

twenty-three became the youngest fellow of the Society of
Actuaries in that association's history; Jim Smith from Brown,
EFLIC's vice president, like Lewis, a fellow of the Society of
Actuaries, a veteran with Metropolitan Life and Minnesota
Life before joining Equity Funding; and Edens, the only native
Californian, an accountant and secretary–treasurer of the life
insurance company. A lot of rank to go up against, but Don
Goff didn't care. At least two men in that room knew he was
right—Ron Secrist and the representative from IBM. Goff's
boss, Bill Mercado, heavy set, Peruvian born, the manager of
Equity Funding's computer department, had asked him to give
a report on the project's status. Don Goff was the kind of man
who would assume the authority necessary to finish a job;
he was trying to do that now. He waited until everyone was
paying attention. He looked at each man in turn. Then he went
on: "You've charged us with coming up with a global picture
and not given us all the material on the globe."

There was a long silence and then a nice, healthy discussion
about cooperation and authority. Finally, Ron Secrist, the
project coordinator, asked Goff whose fault he thought it was.

Don hesitated briefly. For months the suspicion had been
laying on like lacquer. A single layer wasn't much, but after
ninety-four layers it was nigh impregnable. Once more, he
looked at each of the men. "It's everybody's in the room," he
said. "Everyone's dropping the ball."

Be more specific, someone said.

"Okay, can anyone tell me what fields you would like designed so as not to leave an audit trail?"

"All fields," someone said.

"That's ridiculous," Goff said.

"That's okay," someone else said. "That's the requirement
of the system."

It did not happen all at once. It was more like the sun emerg-
ing from an eclipse. First there were no figures available on the
amount of production of new insurance for December of 1970;

then there was the casual talk around the office after hours
down at the executive end of the sixth floor—little comments
about the billing process, how it was easier to do it "this way,"
then a suggestion about the merits of selling reinsurance, and
then a sudden quiet. But finally, the sun was out from the
moon. At a meeting one day early in 1971, EFLIC president
Fred Levin read them a release on the sales figures the company had put out that morning. He laughed that special nervous laugh. And then Ron Secrist knew.

He had seen some monthly sales figures. He had extrapo-
lated them out to get a figure for 1970. It was obvious that the
amount of business reported for the year was double the
amount that had been written.

What seemed worse was that everyone in the room seemed
to accept the knowledge that the circumstance existed. Ron
Secrist still found what they were doing unbelievable. He didn't
really think it could be done. It sounded like an expediency
that would be caught within months. The insurance business
was too highly regulated. They could never get away with it.

The gift Jim Smith, EFLIC vice president, Lloyd Edens, the
treasurer, and Art Lewis, the actuary, had given their boss,
Fred Levin, to commemorate the completion of the annual
statement, was meant to be a gag. It was a photograph of the
three of them, seated in a row. Smith had his hands over his
ears. Edens had his over his eyes, and Lewis's were over his
mouth. Hear no evil, see no evil, speak no evil. Fred Levin
liked the picture so much he hung it on his wall.

First Frank Majerus, EFLIC's controller, talked it over with
his wife. Then he talked to a minister. Then he took three
days off to think about it. Finally, he made up his mind. The
next day, he went to Lloyd Edens and told him he intended to
quit.

"Why?" Edens asked.

"I just don't like what we're having to do to produce our financial statement."

"What can I say?" Edens replied. Then he called in Frank's old boss from Minnesota, Jim Smith. Smith listened, nodded, looked at Frank and said, "It's a onetime deal. It won't happen again."

Frank hadn't been prepared for that. He'd made his decision in pain. He was in no position to move; he had neither money nor prospects. They waited for him to speak.

Finally, he said, "I'll stay around for a while." Then he went back to work.

Pat Hopper, Fred Levin's $3 million acquisition, knew how to tabulate life insurance production figures. He had been the administrative officer of a life insurance sales organization, so he had looked with special interest at the figures he was getting at EFLIC. Fred Levin had promised a big year, but the figures didn't show it. By mid-November the face amount of life insurance produced had reached $375 million, compared to $370 million the year before. Then, abruptly, weekly reports had stopped. Early in 1971, Art Lewis, the actuary, had told him that EFLIC had written $826 million in life insurance.

"Wow!" Hopper had exclaimed. "You did quite well." A number of people had really turned on at year end, he'd concluded.

But now it was April 1971 and Pat Hopper was staring at Equity Funding's annual report for 1970; and part of it made no sense. Late in 1970, while gathering material for his report on the funding programs for Sam Lowell, the corporate financial officer, Hopper had asked how many active funding programs were in existence. The men in charge of those files had estimated between 18,000 and 21,000. The annual report Hopper was holding now said that the company had over 31,000 active funding files. Hopper knew that the information had to have come from the same people he had asked. He knew, further, that there was no way the company could have worked up 10,000 files in a year, let alone a month. He decided he must not have gotten his information straight.

The invitation caught EFLIC administrator Ron Secrist unawares. He was at lunch one day late in the spring with three young associates when one of them suggested that he join them some evening in the sixth-floor conference room for a little "special work."

He thought hard before agreeing. He wasn't exactly wearing his FBI badge, but he had determined to find out what was going on and this was the way to do it.

They gave him some medical examinations to "work up." As he worked, he cast his eyes about. Six executives, several of them earning $20,000 a year or more, were doing the kind of work that clerks did during the day. But, whereas the clerks read from real work-up sheets, these young executives were making up files for the auditors.

They're treating it as a joke, Secrist thought in amazement. It's just great sport. They would pull the file of a real "insured," Xerox certain pages, then vary the information ever so slightly on a "Y" file. Some people said the symbol had been assigned by Art Lewis. Art was a mathematician. When a mathematician wants to put a name on an unknown quantity, he thinks of a symbol. That was the birth of "Y."

It was all so simple. You write a quick program, print it on a tape, act as if it's brand new business coming in from outside sales, run it right back through the new-business system, assign a few numbers in the process, and it goes on the books as in-force business.

You could even run some names through three or more times. You could run a $10,000 policy through as a $50,000 policy. You could run expired policies through as "new" policies.

Ron Secrist had no instinct at all to blow the whistle. He was sure the game would be exposed at the next triennial examination made by the state insurance departments.

It was late afternoon of July 3, 1971, part of the holiday weekend, not a pleasant day to be working. Pat Hopper was overdue at a party. But he had come into the office to prepare fourteen points of additional information for the New Jersey Insurance Department. The department wanted, among other things, a letter from Beneficial National Life, a New York company that underwrote policies for Equity Funding, detailing its procedures. The work was part of the activities relating to the purchase of Bankers National Life Insurance Company, a New Jersey firm that Equity Funding was in the process of acquiring. Hopper didn't think much of the acquisition; Equity Funding was exchanging shares of its stock with a market value of $36 for shares selling at $12.

James Banks, a young attorney, the assistant secretary of EFLIC, was preparing the letter.

Hopper walked into Banks's office. "Have you got the letter done?" he asked.

Banks handed it to him. Hopper read it. "Looks good to me," he said. "I'm going to ship it back to Beneficial for the president's signature."

"That won't be necessary. I can take care of it," Banks said. According to Hopper's later testimony in an SEC investigation, Banks then took the letter from Hopper, went to a drawer and pulled out a Beneficial policy form. Then he went to a window, placed the president's specimen signature against the window, and the letter over that. Then he traced the signature onto the letter, and returned it to Hopper.

Hopper was too dumbfounded to speak.

The meetings of the Consolidated Insurance Management Information System (CIMIS) steering committee were set for

4:30 every Monday in the sixth-floor conference room. They were generally tightly run meetings.

The group was a changing cast of characters under the direction of Jim Smith, EFLIC's vice president. Half a dozen men would be there from the life insurance company. Another four men would represent the Management Information Services (MIS) group. Three representatives of Datair, a computer services company hired to work out the CIMIS system, would also attend. And there was a newcomer on the committee, Peter J. "Ron" Ronchetti, a thirty-two-year-old Englishman who had married an American girl and moved to the States. Ronchetti was a specialist in systems and procedures, hired from a job in San Francisco to establish control procedures between EFLIC and the CIMIS system.

On this particular night, the representatives of EFLIC and Datair were hollering at each other. Datair had come in to try where IBM had failed. The three Datair representatives were beginning to sense that the same thing was going to happen to them. They were particularly bitter because all three were stockholders in Datair, and the loss of the account would hurt.

"We have been supporting EFLIC in every way possible for the last several months, and everyone knows they have been progressing on other things but this project," Datair's Brian Tickler blurted. He was a six foot six inch Englishman who weighed 265 pounds, a fact which gave extra force to his anger.

"We had to devote time to EFLIC year-end statement processing," one of the life insurance representatives replied.

"But we don't want to talk about that, do we?" Tickler said acidly. He was sitting upright, his face flushed, his tone aggravated.

To Don Goff, representing MIS, it was one more layer of lacquer. But to Ron Ronchetti, the newcomer, it was the first of many puzzles.

Ron Secrist and Pat Hopper began working together in midsummer of 1971 on a new line of executive insurance. Within a few weeks, they had gotten to know one another well—well enough, at least, for Hopper to tell Secrist about the circumstances that had brought him to Equity Funding. Pat Hopper, Secrist determined, was the man to give him some perspective on that file-manufacturing session he'd attended and all the talk he had heard.

In mid-September Secrist invited Hopper to dinner at his home in the San Fernando Valley. They ate beside the pool: steak, salad, and corn on the cob. Two dogs kept running around the table. Mrs. Secrist didn't eat. She wasn't feeling well.

After dinner, Secrist said, "What if a company had invented a lot of business?"

Hopper looked sharply at Secrist. He knew this wasn't theoretical talk. They dispensed with the fiction quickly. Secrist poured it all out. The company was writing phony policies on nonexistent people, it was counterfeiting bonds and treasury bills. When he finished, Hopper grunted, "So that's it, huh?" To Secrist's surprise, Hopper didn't seem too concerned. What Secrist didn't know was that Hopper didn't believe him.

There were things Secrist had said that Hopper knew weren't true. But he couldn't dismiss the story from his mind.

A few days later, Hopper sent a friend to ask the head of one of Equity Funding's five sales regions how much business he had done.

"Sixty-five million," the sales chief told him.

The friend got a funny look on his face. Five times sixty-five million made $325 million of annual insurance sales. Equity Funding's annual report had shown $826 million in EFLIC sales.

"If you're trying to multiply that by five, forget it," the sales chief said. He added: "I don't really care so long as the earnings go up and the stock price goes up."

The first intimation to Ron Ronchetti—after that flareup by his fellow Englishman, Brian Tickler of Datair—was a reference to some missing name and address records. Apparently 11,000 had gotten lost during a period of testing and trial runs on the computers. By itself, the loss wasn't all that suspicious. When you have as many prospective clients as Equity Funding did, that mere fact alone created a long list of names. Each prospect got a computer work-up. Then there were lists of names for premium notices sent out, lists for lapsed policies, lists for changes in mode of payments, lists for payments of death benefits.

But one day, Gene Thibodeau, a colleague he had gotten to know and like, showed him a list that had been prepared for the Policy Services Department. There was a significant gap in the series of numbers—a gap of almost 12,000. The numbers broke at 7099000 and resumed at 7111000. There was nothing unusual in gaps of a real working file—a few here, a few there, maybe as many as a dozen. But not 12,000 numbers. Ronchetti wrote a memo to himself; he thought the information might be useful.

Some weeks later, while running a test on a real file, Ron Ronchetti found that among the items selected for the test block were a number of policies in the 7100000 series.

"Hel-lo," he said to himself.

As fall began, Equity Funding's stockholders approved the acquisition of Bankers National Life. When, a few days later, Frank Majerus told Jim Smith that he'd been offered another job, Smith asked him to consider a position at Bankers before he made up his mind. "We won't be messing around with that," Smith promised his old friend from Minnesota. Majerus agreed to take a look. But he didn't count on staying.

Dinner in New Jersey

Ron Secrist was ecstatic. He was sitting in the office of Fred Levin with several other young executives, and Levin was telling them that they were going to New Jersey the following week to take charge of Bankers National Life Insurance Company, Equity Funding's newest acquisition. Levin had just announced that Ron Secrist would be vice president for administration. That solved everything. It gave him a title. It would buy a year's time, a year to fatten that entry on the resume. And it would get him away from the phony business.

That evening, Ron Secrist and his wife celebrated their release from purgatory. They didn't even mind trading their swimming pool in the San Fernando Valley for a winter in New Jersey.

The acquisition of Bankers National was completed on October 15, 1971. On Monday, October 18, Ron Secrist and Pat Hopper flew East together. With them was Tom Patterson, a former aerospace industry executive who had gone to work for Equity Funding at half his old salary after a long period of unemployment; he was to be in charge of personnel. Hopper, the only man with investment experience, was going back at the request of Fred Levin to look over Bankers' investment portfolio. He was still flabbergasted by the purchase of Bankers for triple its market price.

You don't pay that outlandish an amount to run a life insurance company in the normal fashion, Hopper concluded. He thought about the things Ron Secrist had told him a month earlier. He thought there might be a connection. Exactly what kind of connection he didn't quite know; but he aimed to find out.

It didn't matter financially any more. The month before, he had sold the last of the Equity Funding shares he'd received when Equity took over his company. The average sales price for the 10,850 shares he'd owned had been $35. That was $380,000, and he was thirty-two. He had plans to invest that money. There was some property on a Caribbean island that seemed like a good investment. He'd look in on Bankers, and play it by ear.

At 11 o'clock that evening, the men from Equity Funding assembled in Jim Smith's room at the Governor Morris Inn in Morristown. Smith, EFLIC's number two man—and now the new executive vice president of Bankers National as well—announced that Pat Hopper was to be vice president for investments of Bankers.

"But I live in California," Hopper protested.

"That's your problem to solve," Smith said.

Fred Levin had a plan. On Tuesday, he was to fire fourteen employees of Bankers National. He wanted to do it in style. He would restage the lady-or-the-tiger story. He would sit in one office, and Jim Smith would sit in an adjoining office. He would do the firing and Smith would give the pep talks to those chosen to remain. The word would quickly spread through the offices of Bankers that, if you were going to Levin's office, you would confront the tiger; if you were summoned to Smith, your job was spared. What the employees of Bankers didn't know was that Levin and Smith planned to change offices from time to time via a connecting inner door.

At the last moment, Fred Levin canceled the plan. But he did fire the fourteen employees, and he later told the boys back in Los Angeles about his little trick.

That evening, while Fred Levin and Jim Smith worked together, eight Equity Funding employees who had journeyed from Los Angeles to consummate the Bankers National takeover went out to dinner at Mrs. Brown's Restaurant. The dinner was a good one, the talk lively and spirited.

After dinner, Ron Secrist, Frank Majerus, and Pat Hopper got into one car for the return drive to the hotel. Both Secrist and Hopper wondered about Majerus's role in the reorganization, which hadn't yet been announced. Was he there just to help out for a while? Not exactly, Majerus said. He was thinking about transferring back to Bankers. Did he intend to do it? they wondered. He might, Majerus said. He wasn't too happy with the way things were going back in Los Angeles.

"Are you referring to the phony business?" Hopper said.

Majerus's reply was evasive.

The three men then went up to Secrist's room. There, Majerus let it all out. His story confirmed great chunks of what Secrist had told Hopper. He was in a quandary, not only about his job, but about whether he should go to the authorities. He was willing to go, even if it meant implicating himself. But by himself he did not think he could get the authorities to act. He knew what was happening, but he didn't have the proof.

Hopper concurred. He felt the authorities wouldn't believe him.

"What do you think I should do?" Majerus asked the two men. His question was almost a plea.

Hopper gave a cautious reply. "If what you suspect is reasonably true, you shouldn't come back to Bankers. You know it will happen here. They're not going to leave Bankers alone."

That night, Majerus made his decision.

"Wow!" Fred Levin exclaimed. Pat Hopper had just reported that the assets of Bankers National included $28 million in coupon and bearer bonds. They bore no one's name; they could be redeemed by anyone. "Can we transfer them out to California?" Levin asked.

"No," Hopper replied evenly. "We can't do that."

Levin demanded to know why. Because, Hopper explained, Equity Funding had signed an agreement with the New Jersey Insurance Department—as a condition of its acquisition of Bankers—that it would not move any of Bankers' assets to California without prior consultation with the department. Furthermore, the transfer was not in keeping with the New Jersey insurance code.

The assets of Bankers were sizable: $70 million in bonds (including the $28 million in bearer bonds), $40 million in mortgages, $12 million in common stocks, plus a considerable number of policy loans, which were listed on the balance sheets as assets.

There were other invitations in succeeding weeks to what Hopper came to call "corporate incest." Stanley Goldblum telephoned one day to propose that Hopper make some investments in State of Israel bonds. Then Bishops Bank and Trust Company in the Bahamas, which Equity Funding owned, wanted him to buy some Brazilian bonds. On both occasions, Hopper said no. Hopper's mandate was to maximize the yield of Bankers' assets while protecting them against capital losses. The requests from Los Angeles seemed without regard to investment merits.

On October 26, Frank Majerus wrote his letter of resignation to Equity Funding. He departed two weeks later. He felt relieved to be away at last, but he didn't feel good; he would only feel good if he could unburden his conscience. The only way he could do that was to go to the authorities. He was still unwilling to do that.

Perhaps those requests had gotten to him. Perhaps it was his Catholic upbringing. Whatever the reason, Pat Hopper reacted in singular fashion when Jim Smith announced one day in November that he wanted to examine the bonds. I'm not going to let this guy alone for one instant, Hopper decided. He personally escorted the executive vice president for administration of Bankers to the vault at First Jersey National Bank in Jersey City and stood at Jim Smith's shoulder as he looked over the certificates.

There were numbers of dinners that month among the men who had left their homes in Los Angeles. One dinner at the Black Bull Restaurant in Mountain Lakes, New Jersey, was particularly notable. It ended in a pact. Pat Hopper, vice president for investments, Ron Secrist, vice president for administration, Rick Stevens, head of computer operations, and Tom Patterson, head of personnel, vowed that Equity Funding was not going to do anything to Bankers.

The first meeting of the new investment committee of Bankers National Life was convened early in December at company headquarters in Parsippany, New Jersey. The committee consisted of Fred Levin, Sam Lowell, and Tom Hitzelberger, the appointed representative of the New Jersey Commissioner of Insurance. Stanley Goldblum, Yura Arkus-Duntov, Equity Funding's vice president of investment management operations, Pat Hopper, and Hopper's assistant had been invited to attend. Hopper had prepared a written report on Bankers' assets, which he had distributed ten days earlier to those who would be at the meeting. When the preliminaries were over,

Stanley Goldblum asked a series of questions that had Hopper nodding in admiration. But Hopper's old nemesis, Sam Lowell, kept interjecting irrelevant comments. It was soon apparent to everyone that he hadn't read the report. Finally, Lowell began to philosophize about the quality of certain high-grade bonds.

"Shut up, Sam," Goldblum said.

That week, Ron Ronchetti's boss informed him that he was being transferred from the Los Angeles office to Bankers National in Parsippany, New Jersey. "Oh, shit," Ronchetti said, "just before Christmas."

Ronchetti was not all that unhappy. He'd just received a raise, to $14,700. He liked travel; he'd worked in Africa and Europe. And the transfer seemed like a legitimate one. He knew that a lot of good people from the home office were already in New Jersey. But the timing puzzled him.

It was his friend and fellow Englishman, Brian Tickler of Datair, who suggested an answer. "They don't want you around here at year-end," he conjectured.

"A-ha!" Ronchetti replied.

As he flew east a few days later, Ronchetti thought about another friend, Tom Patterson, who had preceded him to Bankers. One day in July, Ronchetti and Patterson had gone to lunch at Hamburger Hamlet. Ronchetti had ordered his usual lunch, a Scotch and a cheese-and-bacon burger. He felt burdened; he wanted to spread the load. "I've got something to tell you," he blurted. "I want your opinion about what I should do."

He told him then about the phony 7100000 series.

"I know what I'd do if it was me," Patterson said. "I'd tell the authorities."

Ronchetti had thought it over. But he hadn't taken the advice. He didn't have enough evidence. He couldn't prove a thing. It would be pointless to try.

His first day at Bankers, Ronchetti recalled that episode to Patterson. "How are things here?" he asked.

"We're trying to make sure that none of that shit happens," Patterson replied. He told Ronchetti then about the pact to keep the Equity Funding people out of Bankers' affairs.

A few nights later, Pat Hopper took Ronchetti to dinner at the Harbor Restaurant on U.S. 46. Hopper, a bachelor, had made a custom of dining out with the new arrivals from Los Angeles.

There was no coyness or hesitancy any longer about discussing everyone's favorite subject—and that was what they discussed.

Ronchetti knew that Hopper was a devout Catholic who would stop off at church every feastday on his way to work. He wondered aloud now how Hopper could equate his morality with what was going on.

Hopper shrugged. "I'm trying to protect the assets," he said.

Hopper had moved from the hotel in Morristown to a Howard Johnson's hotel near Parsippany. He was a man who would fall asleep as soon as he went to bed, but now he was using hours of his normal sleeping time in thought. And the more he thought the more he concluded that somehow, in some way, the men at Equity Funding were trying to trap him into complying with their requests. One blunder on his part would be enough to involve him.

The most recent request had been from Lloyd Edens, EFLIC's secretary–treasurer. He'd wanted Hopper to transfer $3 million from Bankers to the West Coast at the end of the year. "We'll keep it three hours and send it back to you," Edens had promised. The idea was that, because of the time difference between East and West coasts, the $3 million would show on the books of Bankers at the close of business on December 31, and also at the close of business on the books of Equity Funding Life. Once more Hopper had refused.

Later, Art Lewis, the actuary, had told him, "By refusing to go along with us, you cost us fourteen cents a share on our earnings report for the year."

What kind of outfit was that to work for? Pat Hopper asked himself. He decided he'd had enough.

The next morning, he wrote out his resignation and made an appointment to see Fred Levin, who was in from Los Angeles to work at Bankers for several days. He handed Levin the letter. Levin read it and looked up in pain. "I fully intended to increase your salary. Is that the only reason you're resigning?"

"No, I just don't like what's going on in the company. I don't like your creative accounting."

Levin nodded. For a moment he was silent. Then he sighed. "I was trapped into doing what I've been doing," he said. "I don't like it, but I can't stop." He looked directly at Hopper. "I wish I had met someone like you who would have resisted. No one I've dealt with before has ever resisted."

There was an office party at EFLIC on Christmas Eve, and Ron Ronchetti, who had flown back to Los Angeles for the holidays, was there, drinking and joking with his old colleagues and telling them about his first weeks in New Jersey. Jim Smith, EFLIC's vice president, came up. "Time to get back to Parsippany. Time to get back to Parsippany," he said.

Ronchetti laughed. "After New Year's. After New Year's," he said, and turned back to his group.

A few minutes later, Smith returned. "Time to get back to Parsippany. Time to get back to Parsippany," he repeated.

Once more, Ronchetti laughed. "After New Year's. After New Year's," he replied.

Awhile later, it happened again. And then again.

When someone says something once or twice, it's a joke, Ronchetti thought. But when they say it three or four times, you've got to wonder. He remembered what Brian Tickler had told him.

*   *   *

Just before the end of 1971, Fred Levin called Pat Hopper and asked him not to say that he was resigning. He also requested that Hopper stay on until January 31, 1972, to give Equity Funding time to find a replacement. If Hopper would remain, Levin promised, he would do nothing with the assets of Bankers. Hopper agreed. Late in January, Hopper accosted Levin at Bankers' offices. He had just talked to the man Levin had proposed as his replacement. "In thirty-three seconds, I knew that guy wasn't right," he complained.

Levin admitted that he hadn't honestly evaluated the man.

Hopper was upset. He could see himself lingering on and on. He told Levin he wouldn't do that.

"Why don't you run an ad in the paper?" Levin proposed.

Hopper did. A few weeks later, he offered his job to the most promising respondent.

"Watch out for transfers of assets to the West Coast," Hopper advised his successor.

One of Hopper's last duties was to attend an Equity Funding investment meeting in February at the company's New York office. He drove into the city with Jim Smith. After the meeting, Levin took Smith, Hopper, and one of the regional sales managers to dinner at an Italian restaurant on East 41st Street. Hopper said almost nothing at dinner; once more, he was too dumbfounded to talk. The others were openly joking about the phony sales production figures, and, in an oblique way, it seemed to Hopper that they were joking about him. They knew he was resigning; they knew he wouldn't be able to do anything with his knowledge because he didn't have any proof. It was, Pat Hopper concluded, the very height of arrogance. If he had had any sympathy or lingering doubts, they were gone. From this moment, he was absolutely, irrevocably convinced that Equity Funding was a fraud. He would remember this evening, and the gall of his companions, until his dying day.

On March 10, Hopper departed, feeling he had seen the last of Equity Funding. Then, curiously, he began to receive reports that indicated his resignation had not been made public. Fred Levin was telling people that Hopper was on vacation. An office had even been set aside for him. It was said that he would function as a consultant. Then the rumors changed to grumbling. Hopper was flaking off. He wasn't coming to work. Angrily, Hopper called Levin and told him he wanted those rumors ended. Levin responded with an invitation to a cocktail party. He wouldn't admit to anyone—even himself—that Pat Hopper had quit.

Ron Ronchetti had moved his wife and children into a rented home near Parsippany. But they hadn't remained there long. In March, he was returned to the Los Angeles office. His new work had nothing to do with the insurance company. By now, it seemed clear that his "transfer" to New Jersey had been exactly what Brian Tickler had suspected—a ploy to remove him from the premises while the year-end business was concluded. Three months later, on June 10, Ronchetti's boss asked him to stay after hours. When the other employees departed, Ronchetti learned that he was fired. Ronchetti was caught unawares. He'd made no preparations. The abrupt dismissal enraged him.

Between his return to Los Angeles and his dismissal, Ronchetti had learned one dazzling new fact. One day he had asked Don McLellan, a colleague in the funding department, for a list of funded insurance policies. He needed the list to resolve a problem regarding commissions. McLellan had given him the list. It was printed on standard long, continuous-form computer paper. Equity Funding's 1971 annual report had stated that there were 41,121 funding programs in force at the end of the year. The printout Ron Ronchetti held in his hand listed only 18,000 such programs.

Now, cleaning out his desk, he wondered what he could do with what he knew. He decided he could do nothing. He didn't think the word of one person would matter.

There was a problem with the records Don Goff of MIS had been working on with several of his colleagues. The problem had to do with "purification" of the files. Now the problem had been carried to Art Lewis's office, and they were all protesting to Lewis that if the operation were executed as ordered the Illinois auditors would be suspicious at the next triennial examination.

"No problem," Lewis said. "We can always take care of an auditor."

If anyone was looking around for a good psychological study on people with nothing to do, Bonnie Craig concluded grimly, this would be the place.

Here they were, ten girls between the ages of seventeen and twenty-two, sitting in a big windowless room at 341 North Maple Drive in Beverly Hills. Beverly Hills—some glamour. It might as well be the slums for all they saw of it. They would play cards, crochet, tell stories—and complain to one another about having nothing to do. Sometimes, they'd go wild. They'd laugh uproariously at a joke that really wasn't that good, and then the poor guy on the other side of the wall would pound it in frustration, which only set them off again. But he was right; it wasn't funny.

It hadn't started out that way. She'd actually felt pretty lucky. Earlier, she'd flunked the employment test at Occidental Life Insurance Company. Then she'd tried out at Equity, where her cousin was a bookkeeper. They'd told her she'd done well, but that they didn't have an opening. One day a man named Bill Symonds called to tell her they were opening a new department—something about having to straighten out a computer foulup. There would be a variety of duties, Symonds had said. It would be very exciting work, not some humdrum job. No shorthand or typing required. The pay was $2 an hour.

She'd started in March. It sure was different. To begin with, the office was tacky, nothing like the sleek quarters at Century City. Then, the room was all but empty. No typewriters, only some tables, rulers, pencils and red felt-tip pens. It was more like a schoolroom trip than an office.

There were three of them to start—Bonnie, a boy named Rick Gardenier, and one other girl. The first day, they'd sat around with nothing to do. The next day, five stuffed files and one empty one had been carted in. They'd sat there, making a list of every name and account number in those files. They'd done just that for weeks. It was really stupid. It was like a punishment to keep them occupied.

At last, a fellow named Mark Lewis, whose brother was some kind of big shot with the company, came in with another girl who was really snappy. After that, the room began to fill. They settled into an assembly line.

Each file contained several elements. There was an application sheet, a transmittal sheet, a settlement sheet, a medical sheet, and a retail credit sheet. They took the information out of computer readouts and put it on forms. They made up new forms exactly like the old forms. They would pass the forms around, get the information on them, then put them back in a cabinet. It still seemed dumb. All the information they were copying was already on microfilm. Whatever a doctor had written, for example, they would just copy onto another form. The forms were already signed. Otherwise, they were blank.

The girls couldn't figure out why they had to copy all this information that was on another form over. What they did figure out was that they didn't have to do much work.

Every once in a while 200 to 300 new files would come in, and then, for a couple of days, there was no more screaming, and no pounding from the other side of the wall.

One day, 300 files came over in a real rush job. "The auditors are coming. We've got to get these files out," one of the men told them. While they were working, Mark Lewis, Bill Symonds and a third fellow named Larry Collins took some of the files into a back room to examine them. They shut the door. Soon

Bonnie heard them giggling like a bunch of women. She thought that was really odd.

Two hundred guests gathered at the Sportsman's Lodge in Studio City on the Sunday before Labor Day for the marriage of Arthur Lewis. It was an afternoon outdoor wedding; the bride and groom stood under a *chuppa*, the traditional marriage canopy used at Jewish weddings. Lewis, who had converted to Judaism to marry, wore top hat and tails. It was misting when the ceremony started; the rains came just as it ended. The guests rushed inside for the reception and dinner.

Many of the guests were from EFLIC. Fred Levin was there, along with Jim Smith, Larry Collins, the chief underwriter, and Jim Banks, EFLIC's attorney. Ron Secrist had flown in from New Jersey, ostensibly on business, but actually to attend the wedding.

At dinner, Fred Levin sat next to Pat Hopper, who had been invited at the last moment. Levin wanted to know if Hopper would be interested in moving to Seattle, to take a position with Northern Life Insurance Company, which Equity Funding had just acquired.

No, Hopper replied.

Well, how about Jacksonville, Florida, for a job with Gulf Life Insurance Company, with which Equity Funding was then negotiating?

Once again Hopper said no.

Life looked rosy for Bob Ochoa. He was a Chicano from San Antonio, whose father had been a chef. Now, at twenty-seven, he was married, had three sons and a good job. His trade school printing course had paid off. By November, six months after coming to Equity Funding from Hughes Aircraft, he was running an Equity print shop in Santa Monica. As supervisor, he had two pressmen, a bindery girl, and a Girl Friday working for him. And now he'd just been put on notice by his boss that some head honchos were coming down from the home office to personally talk to him about an important printing job. They wanted him to run some tests after his regular hours.

Four of them came in. High level was right. Ochoa recognized Fred Levin from the company publication. The other three looked like they were in the same league.

They showed him some art work. There were fifty-five different certificates—securities of some of the leading American companies like Dow Chemical. Ochoa couldn't conceal his surprise. He knew a little about the market. He'd done some investing of his own, and run $4000 up to $8000. He was familiar with the securities. He recognized a number that sold for $50 to $60 a share.

"They're facsimiles of the originals," one of the men explained. "We're going to use them in a presentation by our investment operation. They're working up some retirement programs."

Ochoa nodded.

"Can you do it?" one of them asked.

He told them it was a lot of work. Doing it after hours, with no one to help him, would take a lot of time.

It had to be that way; it was a confidential job, someone explained.

Ochoa nodded. At Hughes Aircraft, he'd dealt in top secret work. Sometimes there were things that you did without knowing why.

"How do you treat the waste material?" one of his visitors asked.

"We have a shredder," Ochoa said. He showed them a portable machine that shredded the paper into pompoms. The machine had been used to destroy microfilm. All waste material was put into plastic bags; the bags were put into a dumpster and picked up three times a week. The arrangement seemed to satisfy the executives. They asked him to start at once.

Over the next few months, Bob Ochoa stayed late three

times a week. It was tough going; the art work wasn't much good. He would shoot a negative of what they'd brought him, let it dry for forty-five minutes to an hour, then cut a plate to see how it looked. If it didn't look good, they would take it back for further work.

Good or bad, everything they ran, they took with them. Even the plates. The plates never remained on the premises, except for the scraps, which Bob threw away. A couple of times, he put the honchos to work and let them get their hands dirty. They were willing apprentices.

By January, he was printing. He was elated with the results. "Boy," he joked one evening, "we ought to split these sonofabitches, start selling them ourselves. I know a pretty good stockbroker."

No one said a word.

There were two letters from EFLIC waiting for Ron Secrist when he returned to his new Dutch colonial home in Morristown one evening in January. One of the letters was addressed to Ronal Secret. The other was addressed to Ronald Crist.

Secrist slit the envelopes carefully. Inside were internal company audit forms requesting confirmation of funded programs with Equity Funding. Secrist owned no such programs. He had no such loans. But he knew what the confirmation slips were for. They were supposed to verify that loans were outstanding against one of Equity Funding's mutual funds. Secrist also knew why he had been sent them. The year before, he had signed and returned one. He wouldn't sign any more. He put the forms back in their envelopes and the envelopes in a drawer.

It was an unlikely meeting place for the New York Society of Security Analysts, a tacky hall at the tip of Manhattan. But it was a good crowd, both in quantity and quality. They had come to hear Stanley Goldblum.

"Equity Funding Corporation of America last appeared be-

fore the New York Society of Security Analysts in 1968," he
told his listeners on this cold January day in 1973. "Since that
time the company has grown, matured and made some important acquisitions. . . .

"As an organization, Equity Funding's great strength is
marketing. We have succeeded in identifying unfilled needs
in the financial services area, and have the technical capability
to develop new products to satisfy those needs. Finally, we
have the organization, manpower, and knowhow to effectively
market those products."

During 1971, Goldblum noted, only one stock life insurance
company had exceeded the $1.2 billion gain of insurance in
force achieved by Equity Funding. Only eight mutual life insurance companies in the United States had a greater net increase in insurance in force than Equity Funding. None
matched Equity's rate of growth.

Goldblum acknowledged to the analysts that Equity Funding
had been a "consumer of capital" during recent years, in order
to lend money to clients to pay their premiums. Cash flow had
been "negative" by about $20 million, he said, and would be
"negative" by another $12 million in 1973. But, said Goldblum,
by 1975, Equity Funding's cash flow would be $12 million to
the good. The reason: the "big swing." Clients who had taken
out Equity Funding programs in the early sixties would complete them in the early seventies. At that point, a client with a
$1000 annual insurance premium would owe Equity Funding
$10,000, plus interest of $4000—a total of $14,000. "When he
pays off the loans, we realize enough cash to fund fourteen new
programs of comparable size," Goldblum emphasized.

To many of his listeners it seemed clear that Equity Funding's golden years were just around the corner.

In a question-and-answer period, Sam Lowell, executive vice
president for finance, described the financial controls Equity
Funding used to avoid surprises. "Believe me," he said, "our
management likes surprises even less than you gentlemen do."

*   *   *

Earlier that month, Goldblum had increased his salary from $100,000 to $125,000 a year, effective January 15. Normally, the board of directors was required to approve an increase in the president's salary, and on past occasions it had. This time, however, Goldblum, who had received three increases since 1970, did not wait for that formality. He simply ordered the increase.

Four weeks later, Goldblum informed his executive vice presidents that they were to cut all expenses in their departments by twenty percent. That meant, effectively, a twenty percent reduction in manpower.

On February 8, Goldblum sent a memorandum to his executive vice presidents:

> As I discussed with each of you in the last several days, I am not satisfied with the indicated figures of the tentative budgets that have been received by me so far. As you will recall, I also advised you that it will be necessary for overall corporate expense reductions to be effected as soon as practical.
>
> Effective immediately, I would like to initiate several changes in policy and procedure as follows:
>
> 1. Until such time as studies have been completed and budgets have been finally approved by me, there will be no new hires without *previous personal approval by me.*
> 2. Effective February 15, travel policy will be amended so that all air travel will be conducted on the basis of economy fare only. (Of course, if anyone desires to travel first class, he can pay the difference.) Ground transportation allowance will be limited to normal cab fare. If some other means of ground transportation is chosen, the allowance will be based on the charge that would have been incurred if a cab had been used. This includes transportation to and from airports and intra-city travel.
>
>   Maximum hotel room allowance will be $30 per night. If anyone wishes to exceed this amount, he can pay the difference.

3. No further commitments for equipment purchases shall
be made without my previous written authorization.
In regard to the expense reviews that I discussed with each
of you personally, pay particular attention to marginal
purchases, marginal services, marginal employees and
salary reductions.
SG/vs

Ron Secrist flew to Los Angeles on February 12. It was just
another trip; he'd been going to the coast twice a month for
several months to supervise the policy service and claims
operations of the parent company. When he arrived at the
Holiday Inn on Wilshire Boulevard, he found a message to
call Jim Smith. It was 5 P.M. He did. Smith asked him to come
in first thing in the morning.

At 9:30 on the thirteenth, he was in Smith's office. Smith began with a long dissertation about a big economy move. Anything that extended beyond the immediate twelve-month
period had been deemed nonessential. Then Smith got to the
cutting of personnel. Twenty percent of each group had to be
let go, he said, not just a bottom line cut, but part of the heart,
blood, and brain of the organization. Some things were going
to hurt, he said. He paused. His voice was trembling. Jim Smith
was always supercool. He had completely lost his cool. Secrist
knew what was coming.

"You're going to have to go," he said, at last.

Secrist stared at Smith. He did not propose to make it easy
for him.

Then Smith outlined the details of Secrist's departure.
Normally, termination would be at the end of March, but in
his case they would run it until the end of May. Additionally,
Smith said, he would give Secrist a good recommendation.

Things are starting to churn at Equity Funding, Eric Farr
concluded. A thin, reserved man in his mid-thirties, Farr ran a
head-hunting service from a small office in Marina del Rey.

Equity Funding was one of his major clients. For some time there had been talk about Equity Funding among young men he sought out. A lot of it was what Farr would have to call sour grapes. But some of it had substance. Someone would tell him he wouldn't have any part of Equity Funding because of the company's practices and ethics; many people knew there were irregularities. So it was tough enough to sell a prospect on going with the company—and now this new twenty percent cut had made it even tougher.

Then, yesterday, Ron Secrist had come into the office, fuming. He'd been brought out here for a meeting, he told Farr, and when he arrived Jim Smith had fired him. The company wasn't going to pay for his relocation. Ron vowed that he was going to do something.

Now, here was this man from Haskins & Sells, EFLIC's old auditors, sitting in this bar in Marina del Rey, asking Farr if he would make a tape of everything he had ever heard about Equity Funding from his prospective clients.

Farr knew that Haskins & Sells had gathered a lot of stuff on Equity Funding. The accountant with whom he was having a drink had tipped him earlier that something strange might be going on.

"How about it?" the accountant said now.

As nicely as he could, Farr said no.

Well, the H & S man said, will you be on the lookout for information?

Okay, Farr said. It was one of those things where you said sure in order to keep the business.

There was another memorandum from Stanley Goldblum to the executive vice presidents on February 15:

> You may not be aware of the fact that, until budgets are approved by me, no additional hiring is to be effected without my *prior written approval*.
>
> This does not mean that you hire someone and then sub-

mit a personnel requisition afterward. It means that you submit the requisition to me for approval before you hire anyone. After the approval is received, employee recruiting can take place.

At present I have on my desk a number of personnel requisitions which relate to personnel already hired. You should be aware that in the next week or so when I have had a chance to review these requisitions, they may not be approved and these people will have to be terminated.

For at least a year, Ron Secrist had been preparing for the day when he would leave Equity Funding. He had kept an unwritten list in his mind of the people to whom he might take his story. It was a list that constantly changed. The great question was which group or person on that list could handle the job that needed doing. The more he talked to people in general terms, the more he thought about it, the more convinced he became that the regulatory bodies could not or would not do that job. The typical bureaucracy, he concluded, would build a file, think about it, and do nothing. Even if an insurance commission did act, there was a real possibility that it could never uncover the fraud. He had one bullet to shoot; it had to hit the heart.

The "right thing to do" was to go to the authorities. But if it wouldn't work, it was wrong.

Not even in his private counsels could Ron Secrist defend the time he had taken to act. Nor did he make any pretense of justifying his decision to wait. It had been a coldly practical decision, based on his concern about finding another job. The only conceivable justification for the delay in his own mind had been his conviction that the exposure would occur without his intervention. He would have vastly preferred that.

But some months after he had gone to Bankers, Ron Secrist realized that the fraud would not be exposed unless some one person took it upon himself to do it.

Late in fall 1972, Secrist had told Pat Hopper that he had

determined to expose the fraud when the conditions were right. To whom should he go? Hopper replied: "Ray Dirks."

We had met—Hopper and I—in the fall of 1970. He was in the East, visiting his brother; one day he wandered down to Wall Street. At that time, my office was located at 7 Dey Street, in the financial district. Passing, Hopper recognized the address and dropped in. He had been reading my insurance newsletter, apparently liked what he had read, and simply wanted to meet me. We talked for an hour. He told me that Equity Funding had recently acquired his company, and that he was now working for the parent corporation. Nine months later, when Equity Funding announced that it was acquiring Bankers National, I called Hopper to ask about the progress of Equity's application for approval of the deal by the New Jersey Insurance Department. He brought me up to date.

A few weeks passed. One evening, I went to a cocktail party in Manhattan. Fred Levin was there. Instinctively, I knew there was no room for small talk with him. I groped for something to say about Equity Funding. Finally, I told him how helpful Pat Hopper had been to me when I'd asked for information about Bankers.

A few days later, Levin asked Hopper, "Do you know Ray Dirks?"

"Yes," Hopper replied.

"Well, he was talking about his great source of inside information from Equity Funding, Pat Hopper," Levin said caustically.

Not long thereafter, Hopper passed the word to one of my colleagues that I had caused considerable trouble for him because of what I'd said to Levin at the party. Hopper and I hadn't spoken since.

One final factor had impelled Ron Secrist to delay. He had not wanted to be in the house when the roof caved in. Now he

didn't have to worry about that any longer. He called Pat
Hopper and told him the news. Hopper invited him to dinner.
They went to Hutch's Bar-B-Que on Walnut Street in Pasa-
dena.

Secrist was still fuming. He'd always intended to quit. How
could they have been so stupid as to fire a man with all his
knowledge? The two men concluded it was because Secrist
had been talking about the phony business with other employees; word must have gotten back. Well, it was a dumb
decision, Secrist repeated, because now he could tell his story.
But to whom?

One by one, they went down the list Ron Secrist had carried
in his mind: the insurance departments of California, Illinois,
New York and New Jersey; the Securities and Exchange Commission; the Internal Revenue Service; the auditors; Senator
Hart; Senator Kennedy; Jack Anderson; Ralph Nader.

Hopper had no faith in any of these approaches. He considered the idea of going to the Illinois Insurance Department
laughable; it had one of the worst reputations in the country—
Fred Levin had once worked there. None of the other states
had jurisdiction. The SEC had no jurisdiction over the insurance company, which was where the fraud was occurring.
The auditors were conceivably on the Equity Funding payroll.
All the other approaches presented a problem of credibility.
"They're not going to do anything about it. They're not going
to believe it," Hopper said. "I think the best way is to go to
someone who would really get the story out." Once more,
he offered my name.

When they returned to his home, Hopper showed Secrist a
profile of me *The Wall Street Journal* had published six months
earlier. It was a generous story detailing what the paper described as my unorthodox approach to security analysis. Hopper did not tell Secrist the real reason he kept insisting on me.
He felt that Secrist did not have 100 percent credibility. He
appeared to exaggerate things. When he made statements, he

would sometimes back them up with "facts" that were wrong. Someone checking his story out wouldn't be likely to go beyond the first or second exaggeration. Hopper wasn't sure how I would react, but he thought I had the necessary contacts and the credibility to expose the story.

Secrist leaned heavily on Hopper's recommendation. Both men were well aware of the consequences of what Secrist was about to attempt. Both were skeptical as to whether the exposure could succeed. But they agreed that Secrist was the one to do it. Everything Hopper had was hearsay, whereas Secrist was someone who could say "I did a file."

There had been a point early in the game when Secrist had worried that by exposing the fraud he might somehow implicate himself. He *had* done a file. He *had* signed a confirmation slip. But he had long since stopped worrying about that, and he made no mention of his concern now.

Nor did Secrist tell Hopper that, for all his doubts about the regulatory bodies, he was still considering an approach to the New York Insurance Department—in his view, the most incorruptible of the state insurance regulators. He still wanted one of the state insurance departments to blow the whistle. Otherwise, it would be the end of the insurance business as he knew it. There would be no more state regulation of insurance. The federal government would step in and take over. Senator Hart would see to that. It would be like the railroads disintegrating. He was no centralist; he believed in state regulation; he took an industry point of view.

The insurance department might never expose Equity Funding alone. And one man obviously couldn't do it, either. But the combination, to his mind, was perfect. While the insurance department began its examination, Ray Dirks would relay all of the information to the big institutions that owned large blocks of stock. The price of the stock would drop. The losses to investors would put so much pressure on the regulators that they would have to move fast. The confusion would be so great that Equity Funding wouldn't be able to cover up everything.

The SEC was out. He didn't know the SEC or what it could do. He was afraid that if the SEC halted trading in the stock, it would be a tipoff to the company which would then cover everything up. He didn't want to take that chance. Everything had to hit Equity Funding by surprise.

It required both an attack on the stock *and* the intervention of a state insurance department. One without the other couldn't bring it to light.

Six weeks later, Secrist would detail his strategy in secret testimony to the New York Stock Exchange:

> Point one, the stock price was probably the all-pervading concern of the top officers of Equity Funding Corporation of America. I had been told by various people in the company on many occasions that if anything started to break, that they were going to dump their stock, whatever they happened to have, and leave the country. I felt that if the stock broke first, the stock price, that would put a clamp on them, let's say, to stop one of their possible alternatives, number one.
>
> Number two, obviously, if the stock price broke badly, went down considerably, with very heavy trading, which I expected would happen, that this would bring the situation to the attention of numerous regulatory bodies.
>
> Then finally I felt that an analyst, such as Ray, would be able to continue putting pressure on the stock, through the press, through whatever media, and continue the stink long enough, that no matter what regulators got paid off, or who was conned out of what, there would be a big enough furor for a long enough period of time, that there would be so many people involved and of such magnitude, that nobody could ignore it finally, and that, if nothing else, the entire public would clamor for some results. Analogous to the Watergate situation of today.

Ron Secrist spent another day in Los Angeles, seeing what

was available in the job market. Then he returned to New Jersey via Atlanta, where he had a job interview lined up with the American Agency Financial Corporation. Pat Hopper knew the president and had put in a recommendation. Secrist had to wait until he had another job before telling the authorities. He really had grave doubts as to whether anyone would believe him. If he told his story and the company was able to cover it up, he would be through in the industry, through financially, through professionally.

On February 24, George Irwin of AAFC in Atlanta telephoned with a firm job offer. The last piece was in place. Ron Secrist spent the next week arranging for the move to Atlanta. Then he worked out a schedule: he would tell his story on Tuesday, March 6, and Wednesday, March 7, and leave on Sunday for Atlanta; he'd be on the road when the story broke. He wasn't as brave as everyone might later make him out to be, he admitted to himself.

The following Tuesday, Ron and his wife got the children off to school. Then she left for her job in a doctor's office. He sat down on the edge of his bed and wrote out some notes to make certain what he would say. Then he called New York City information and obtained the number for the New York State Department of Insurance. He dialed. A secretary answered. "Hello," he said, "my name is Ronald Secrist, and I have some very important derogatory information about Equity Funding that I thought you would be interested in."

He made an appointment for the next morning.

Then he called me.

Reconnaissance

I had never heard anything like it. Nor could I have imagined anything like it. Nonetheless, Ron Secrist's story bewitched me. After listening to him for some minutes, I said, "Where are you now? Why don't you come in and see me?" He said he was tied up that day in New Jersey. He could come in the following day. We made a date for noon on March 7. Then I bolted out of my office and into the office of my associate, Allen Gorrelick, a young, mod New Yorker. "Hey, Allen," I said, "I just got this crazy call."

I summarized the allegations. Then, suddenly, I remembered that Allen had once been an actuary for Congressional Life of New York, a company that had issued policies sold by Equity Funding agents. "Hey, you used to issue policies for Equity!" I exclaimed. "You'd better hear this story at lunch tomorrow."

Allen was accustomed to sudden bursts of enthusiasm on my part. He had to prepare for a visit we were to make the following week to some big Hartford insurance companies. He asked to be excused. I pleaded. "Okay," he said at last. "But it sounds crazy, like you say."

By the end of a four-hour lunch on March 7, it didn't sound all that crazy. There were many reasons why. The first was

Secrist himself. He was a clean-cut, flat-bellied WASP. His words were measured and straightforward. He seemed intelligent and a good, solid middle-management administrator. He was soft spoken, logical, made his presentation without any seeming rancor and with a touch of humor. While the allegation seemed preposterous on the surface, the information he provided was substantial, lengthy, and detailed, and held together well under questioning by two insurance analysts.

He proposed that there was a substantial amount of fake insurance on the books; that the company had made up fake death certificates; that it had created fake assets, such as certificates of deposit; that the officers of the company were not only involved in the plot but were its architects; that middle management carried out the fraud knowingly; that a substantial number of people inside and outside the company knew about the fraud; and that the fraud had evolved because of a need to boost the price of the stock so that the company could make acquisitions. The acquisitions of profitable companies could cover up the lack of profitability inherent in the Equity Funding operation.

He spoke, additionally, of rumors—about Mafia connections and passports and suitcases filled with cash and about an auditor in charge of the company's account who was actually listed in the company's directory.

He said that he had quit in disgust; that six of the eight top officers of Bankers National—by far Equity Funding's largest acquisition—had left within the last thirty days essentially for the same reasons that he had; and that Bankers had been badly bled by the imposition of $1 million in phony expenses by the parent company.

When he finished, I asked him what kind of proof he had. For an answer, he showed me two letters. One was addressed to a man named Crist, the other to a man named Secret. Both, he said, had been sent to his address; both were requests for confirmation that he owned an Equity Funding plan. He owned no such plan.

"That does look strange," I said. "Have you got anything else?"

"No," he said.

It wasn't much to go on. It crossed my mind that he could have sent the forms to himself.

"What are your motivations for coming to me?" I asked.

"I want this thing exposed," he replied. "I believe the life insurance industry performs a service and has a useful product and I don't like to see it corrupted by what these guys are doing."

I asked if he had gone to anyone else, specifically, any state insurance department. He answered that he hadn't.

"What do you expect me to do?" I asked.

"The whole thing rests on the price of the stock. If the price of the stock falls apart, the management will be devastated and somebody will have to do something."

"How does that fit in with me?"

"Obviously, you don't want to do anything based just on what I say. But, after you check around enough and get the feeling that it's true, what I'd expect you to do is talk to every institution you know—and from what I read, I guess you know a lot of them—and tell them it's a fraud."

"By the way," I asked, "what is your financial position in the stock?"

"I never owned any stock," he replied. "I had some options, but I never exercised them."

"Well, perhaps you're short the stock."

"I wouldn't do that," he said. He told me then that a man with a lot of money had offered to take a big short position in the stock if he, Secrist, would go to the authorities. When the price fell, the money man would cover his position and they'd split the profits. Secrist said he'd turned him down.

It was after four when we left the restaurant. He walked

us back to our office, but he didn't want to come up. We said good-bye on the street.

I turned to Allen Gorrelick. "What's the credibility percentage?" I asked him.

"Ten percent," he replied.

I thought it was fifty–fifty.

The reason I did—and a second reason for my willingness to believe Ron Secrist—was my conviction that amorality on Wall Street is more typical than exceptional.

The image that stays in my mind is that of a meeting and cocktail party to which I was invited at the loftiest reaches of corporate power, in the enormous board room of International Telephone and Telegraph (ITT) at 320 Park Avenue in New York. To that meeting late one afternoon in 1970 came some 100 men who comprised the cream of Wall Street: the senior officers of the country's biggest banks, mutual funds, and foundations, even the specialist from the New York Stock Exchange who makes the market in ITT stock. They were there to hear Harold Geneen, ITT's chairman, the highest paid executive in the world, offer details of the company's proposed merger with Hartford Fire Insurance Company. If consummated, it would be the biggest corporate merger in history. Harold Geneen's message was that the merger would do wonders for both ITT and Hartford Fire; as evidence he presented detailed internal projections of earnings and sales for the following five years. The translation to the assembled potentates of American finance was that they should purchase the stock of both companies.

Securities laws forbid the passing of significant information during the midst of an exchange offering—and a prospectus covering the proposed merger was at that very time before the Hartford Fire stockholders for approval. The law insists that everyone must have access to the same information. Yet the public was not to hear about the "benefits" of the merger until after the giants of Wall Street had decided whether or not to enhance their positions.

Such illegal acts are part of daily Wall Street life. The men who participate in them are not criminals. They simply profit from an illicit environment. It therefore did not shock me that some Equity Funding insiders might have attempted to share in such profits.

One of the characteristics of go-go companies is their penchant to run down other companies with characteristics identical to theirs. No matter that their own practices may be suspect; they denounce the unsavory practices of others. It was in this roundabout way that I had learned about the refusal of a company called Westamerica to be taken over by Equity Funding. Westamerica sold mutual funds; its salesmen had revolted at the prospect of a merger. My informant was George Scharffenberger, the president of City Investing, a company listed on the New York Stock Exchange. Scharffenberger commutes between his home in Beverly Hills and corporate headquarters in New York. He is the second highest paid executive in the world. City Investing was one of those stocks that was constructed through acquisitions; it had started with little more than a plot of real estate north of New York City. One of the acquisitions was a large insurance company, which accounted for my interest.

There was a certain pattern shared by City Investing and Equity Funding that came to mind following my talk with Secrist. Both companies desired a rise in the price of their shares to exchange them advantageously for shares in other companies.

The objective of the head of a company is to make a huge salary. The simplest way to do that is to get big through acquisitions. The best way to make acquisitions is to get the price of your stock up. The ideal situation is when the shares you trade are appraised highly by the market, and the shares you acquire are undervalued by the market. There are any number of improper ways to pump up the value of your own stock, if you're so inclined. One way is to fail to fully report the accounting transactions involved in an acquisition. The acquiring company uses earnings that really belong to the company acquired. For example, when Company A acquires Company B, it induces its investment banker to put a book value smaller than the market value on the securities owned by Company B. Then Company A sells the securities at the true market value—and shows an "increase" or "profit" of, say, fifteen percent. It wouldn't be a profit, but it would *look* like a profit. It would "increase" earnings per share of Company A, cause the market price of its stock to rise—and prepare it for the next acquisition.

Promotion is another method. Company A puts on a campaign that says, in effect, to Wall Street: "Over the next few years we are going to have terrific growth and earnings. Look at our current and past performance for an indication of what we're going to do in the future." (The current and past performance may reflect the kind of trick cited above.) The stock price of Company A may reflect more of what management is saying about its future than about the real underlying value of the company.

Company B, on the other hand, may be the kind of company that doesn't talk very much to Wall Street. It simply does a solid job of making money and shows a good balance sheet. Many insurance companies were in just this position in 1968, when the conglomerates started making tender offers for them. (A "tender offer" is when Company A offers to exchange its shares for shares of Company B.) The insurance companies had liquid assets in the form of stocks and bonds; their liabilities were only the unpaid claims that are a normal part of any insurance company's operation. They had no debt whatever. In many cases these companies could be liquidated for more than the selling price of their stock.

So Company A would "tender" for Company B's stock.

Company A would be selling for twenty-five times earnings, and Company B would be selling for ten times earnings; Company A would be selling for five times book value, and Company B would be selling for book value. There would be a tremendous difference in the true current value of the two companies. The inducement for Company B to sell would be the prospect of receiving shares with a market value considerably more than its own. The inducement for Company A would be the prospect of receiving hard assets in exchange for hot air.

The shareholders of Company B could immediately sell the shares of Company A they had received in the transaction; it wouldn't matter to them whether Company A survived or not. But for Company A, the transaction was a financial Fountain of Youth.

A third reason for my readiness to believe in Ron Secrist was what I knew about the origins of Equity Funding. The people from whom I had initially heard the Equity Funding story ten years earlier had been promoters. In the matter of business ethics, I place promoters at the lower end of the commercial scale.

Business practices, in my view, border on the unethical and frequently cross the line. On Wall Street, at least, someone is constantly looking over your shoulder, saying, You can do this but you can't do that. That isn't true in business. If you sell a shoddy stock to someone, you can go to jail; but if you sell a shoddy product there are no great penalties. The Better Business Bureau has no power of enforcement. The Federal Trade Commission has made notoriously poor use of its powers (Ralph Nader would be doing something else if the FTC had functioned effectively). Advertising is often an inducement to misrepresentation. And, in the climate of today, the more business is tied to Washington, the less ethical it becomes.

Some of the men who sought to profit during the period of transition in the insurance industry in the 1950s had committed fraudulent acts; one of them—who had engaged in leveraged insurance predating Equity Funding—had been in trouble with the government ever since. Even strictly moral men, faced with a financial crisis, may cross over the border of fraud, hoping to get through a bad period. It figured that Equity Funding could have experienced a bad period in 1969 and 1970, just like every other seller of insurance and mutual funds. The company had *reported* an increase in earnings for that year—but Secrist's story would explain why Equity Funding had "succeeded" where others had failed.

There was certainly a plausible motive. Stanley Goldblum had taken over the leadership of Equity Funding after Mike Riordan's death, and coincident with a deterioration of the economy. He might have permitted an expediency to become a way of life.

Yet another factor lent reinforcement to Secrist's story. Only a few years before, I had been involved in a dreadful situation with a life insurance company in Los Angeles. Los Angeles Life was a small company with only 32,000 shares outstanding—2000 given to the founder, and 30,000 offered to the public at $50 a share in 1965. The company had a vigorous sales program organized with the Los Angeles County Employees Association. When I first learned about it, LA Life was selling below the original offering price, and I started recommending it. LA Life was a "thin" stock; a few trades could affect the price considerably. The stock went from 40 to an alltime high of 270 in 1971. I was not only recommending the stock; I was making the market.

Then, early in 1971, LA Life tried to take over another insurance company in the state of Washington. The insurance department of California came in to make a triennial examination. Not long after the stock hit its all-time high, the commissioner of corporations for California suspended trading in the stock—and that was the end of LA Life.

I had been attracted to the company because of what appeared to be an extremely successful sales operation, but the company hadn't been able to raise the money it needed to cover its operations. A harbinger of Equity Funding.

I'm not a conservative man. I react to wild, preposterous ideas in an excitable manner. Rather than saying something is so preposterous that I don't want to bother, I would say this is something worth looking at precisely because it's so preposterous.

My first reaction as I walked into the office of my associate, Allen Gorrelick, to tell him about the phone call was one of intense excitement. I was delighted that Secrist had called and given me the story. I thought, This is really something if it's true—look at the implications. Moreover, it was challenging and different, something far afield from the humdrum of the analyst's daily routine.

I wasn't as morally indignant as Ron Secrist said he was about the violence Equity might be doing to the codes of the insurance industry. I don't consider the industry so upstanding or ethical, particularly in terms of the way it sells its product. Basically, the life insurance industry doesn't make clear what its product is to the man who buys it, a man who is generally ignorant about finance and protection.

I *was* morally indignant, however, about a company that might be bilking the public, my own clients included. If the charges were true, and I exposed the company, I would be performing a public service. I knew that Equity Funding was about to make yet another acquisition. If Secrist's story had merit, the stockholders of the company about to be acquired would be exchanging their valuable shares for worthless paper.

If I were to get involved, and the story proved to be wrong, Equity Funding would survive. Its stock would rebound. Its rage would be nothing next to the rage of my own clients, whom I would have gotten out of the stock. I was taking a chance; if I was wrong, my career would conceivably be finished. But in all honesty, I didn't give this possibility the mature consideration it deserved.

I *wanted* to believe Ron Secrist. I wanted his story to be true—as proof that all was not well in the corporate world, that some corporations try to get away with whatever they can.

One document in which I have never put much trust is the one by which corporations represent themselves to present and prospective stockholders: the annual report. Most annual reports are "puff pieces." They puff up the good side, and deflate the bad side. Problems are either unmentioned or glossed over. Even figures are used in a misleading manner. When insurance companies speak of their size, for example, they do so in terms of the face amount of insurance they've sold. The investor sees sales figures of hundreds of millions of dollars and he thinks, That's some big company. In fact, the important figure is not the face value of the policy, but the premium dollars earned from the sale of the policy. A sale of a life insurance policy with a face value of $100,000 may mean annual proceeds to the company of less than $1000. Annual reports magnify a corporation's apparent size 100 times by emphasizing in-force insurance.

A good example of corporate camouflage, in my view, was ITT's annual report for 1969. The report showed the company's pretax income up $56 million from 1968. Included in that $56 million was an increase of $18 million the company had labeled "dividends, interest and *other income*." (The emphasis is mine.) The "other income" included $11 million ITT had "earned" when a British subsidiary sold some property to raise some cash. This meant that approximately twenty percent of *ITT's* increase in earnings had come from a non-recurring capital gain of its subsidiary. The market had translated ITT's reported gain into an increase in the price of its stock. I promptly recommended sale so vigorously as to incur the active wrath of the company.

ITT's whole pitch to investors had been its long record of consecutive quarterly earnings increases. But quarter-to-quarter increases mean nothing when a company can manipulate figures in such a way as to obscure its condition.

By coincidence, this was one point that had held off my interest in Equity Funding until the allegations of fraud—a suspicion that Equity Funding "managed" its earnings. But there was another, more fundamental reason. Analysts like myself work with institutional clients, people with millions, sometimes billions to invest. These people are professional, as opposed to individual, investors. We assume a certain sophistication on their part, as well as an ability to make up their own minds as to whether or not to buy securities. We offer our analysis for their guidance. If our analysis proves helpful, we hope they will provide us with orders to buy or sell securities. It's from the commissions on those transactions that we receive our compensation.

That is the operative mechanism. The rationale is another matter. The only justification for our existence as analysts is that, by diligent work and observation, we ascribe realistic values to companies. In so doing, we perform a vital function in a capitalistic society. We create a flow of money into those enterprises that are productive. Conversely, if the value of stocks is distorted, then money can go into enterprises in a distorted way, which results in the nonproductive use of money.

Money represents not just purchasing power, but people's time and effort. If money is poorly used in the market place, then valuable resources—namely, time and effort—are wasted. The ultimate test of an analyst's worth is if he comes up with reasonable and accurate judgments about the worth of companies. There is no contribution to society in just making money for people, particularly when that means other people will lose. That reduces life to a game. Worse yet, here, suddenly, was the possibility that part of the game was rigged.

I'm always for the underdog in any kind of a game. What appealed to me so powerfully was the opportunity to expose the phonies as frauds. There is a connection between my nonrespect for authority and the instances of people who cloak themselves with authority and other power symbols when they haven't, in fact, earned them. I felt this might be a chance to dissect a company that was proclaiming itself as a growth stock, that was highly touted by the analysts and fund managers.

So there were multiple reasons why I was disposed to believe Ronald Secrist. I will always wonder what I would have done had I known that Secrist had lied to me several times that day and would be named eight months hence as an accomplice to the fraud.

When Allen Gorrelick and I returned from lunch with Secrist, I called the other two analysts on my staff, Gerald Lewinsohn and Fred Hackenburg, into my office, closed the door so my secretary wouldn't hear, and said, "We've heard a story. It sounds unbelievable. I don't want it spread around. If the company hears we're spreading rumors about this story we could be sued." I told Gerald and Fred what the story was. They agreed that it sounded incredible, and they pledged their silence.

Within hours, I found out how difficult silence could be.

That evening, Gerald and I went to Philadelphia for a meeting the following day with the Insurance Company of North America (INA). Bill Thomas, the insurance analyst at Old Colony Trust of Boston, a client of ours, joined us for dinner. He had requested that he be present at the INA interview. Somehow, the subject of Equity Funding arose.

"What do you know about it?" I asked guardedly.

"I don't know much, but I went to an analyst's meeting that
Edwards & Hanly had in Boston the other day, and the company made a presentation to a whole bunch of institutions."

"What do you think of it?" I asked again.

"They're certainly making a very hard sell," Bill replied.

"Do you own the stock?" I asked.

"No."

"Before you buy it—if you're thinking of buying it—let me
know." I hesitated. "I would just not even look at it, if I were
you," I said then. "If someone asks you to do a study on it,
tell them you've got something else to do."

The quarterly board meeting of Equity Funding Corporation
of America was scheduled for March 8 at the corporate offices
in New York City. Three of Equity Funding's directors were
from the New York City area; Stanley Goldblum had promised
them that one meeting a year would be held in New York.

The agenda included a year-end financial report by Samuel
Lowell, a discussion of the dividend, and consideration of a
change in the corporate name. Inasmuch as the major income
from Equity Funding was now insurance, several suggestions
had been made to reflect this fact. The leading contender:
Equity Funding Life Company.

Prior to leaving for New York, Goldblum had sought out
the corporate general counsel, Rodney Loeb. Loeb is a tall,
bearded, verbal Harvard graduate who had joined the firm
in 1969; he was surprised to see Goldblum, who had been to
his office only sporadically since then. Loeb had tried to overcome Goldblum's apparent antipathy to him. He had heard
that Goldblum was interested in Japanese netsuke, little fig-
urines, and had found information on them and sent it to him.
On another occasion, he had sent Goldblum some intellectual
puzzles. "Look," Goldblum blurted one day, "stop trying to
educate me. I want to remain the dumb boob that I am."

Now, in Loeb's office, Goldblum said, "I currently hold

the position of president and chairman of the board. I want to make Fred Levin president. What do I have to do?"

"What do you want to do?"

"I want Fred to be chief operating officer. I'll be the chief executive officer."

"Shall I put this item on the agenda?" Loeb asked.

Goldblum said No. Loeb suggested that he draft a resolution, which would be presented at the end of the meeting. Goldblum agreed. "Don't say anything," he said.

Now, at 9:30, on Thursday, the two men walked from the lobby of the Regency Hotel at the same moment. Goldblum's limousine was waiting for him; he offered Loeb a ride to the offices on 41st Street. They settled into the back seat. Goldblum said nothing. Loeb couldn't take the silence. "Did you see a movie on the flight?" he asked amiably.

"Yes," Goldblum said.

Christ, Loeb thought, he won't even volunteer which one. Loeb tried no further discussion.

It was a typical board meeting, at which Fred Levin said almost nothing and Sam Lowell talked a great deal.

Ever since Levin had outraced Lowell for the admiration of Goldblum, Lowell's interest had flagged. He was constantly being bypassed on important negotiations. He was not even current on the activities of the company. He took prolonged absences from the company. People who worked for him couldn't find him. He seemed more and more disinterested.

But Lowell could still rise to an occasion. Prior to the meeting, Goldblum had instructed Loeb to make sure that Lowell, his onetime protégé, was prepared; he was worried that Lowell wouldn't be. "Don't worry," Lowell had said. "I'll be prepared." He was. He was articulate, talkative, and petulant when interrupted. He spoke glowingly of the future.

Goldblum, in his turn, reiterated the earnings report, an optimistic one, and announced a dividend of ten cents per share.

The board of directors approved a change in the corporate name by a vote of five to four.

As the meeting was drawing to an end, Loeb walked behind Goldblum, leaned over, and whispered, "Here's the matter you said you might want to bring up at the end of the meeting."

Goldblum didn't bring it up.

In San Francisco that day, Christy P. Armstrong, chief insurance examiner for the state of California, received a phone call from Murray Krowitch of the New York Insurance Department. Krowitch relayed to Armstrong what Ron Secrist had told him. Armstrong immediately called his boss in Los Angeles, Gleeson L. "Tige" Payne.

Payne, the California insurance commissioner, had been president of Founders Life Insurance prior to his appointment. Founders was a competitor of Equity; its offices were located in a Century City building next to the one Equity occupied. Tige Payne never could figure out how Equity Funding did it. His company was the second fastest growing insurance firm in the country; Equity Funding's was third. But Equity Funding was making about three times as much money as Founders. His firm tried vainly to discover the key to Equity Funding's success; it simply couldn't fathom how Equity Funding managed to sell so much insurance at such small cost.

Now Payne did three things. First, he ordered department counsel Edward Germann to alert the Los Angeles office of the Securities and Exchange Commission. Second, he asked Armstrong to contact the Illinois Insurance Department and work out a surprise audit by examiners from several states that would be advertised as a regular triennial examination. Third, Payne put the case in charge of Lawrence Baker, thirty-seven, a deliberate, auburn-haired, conservatively dressed deputy insurance commissioner.

Baker was not mightily persuaded. All he knew was the essence of the story, and that an executive of Bankers National had told it. The executive's involvement was unclear. The hardness of the information was questionable. Baker knew of Equity Funding's reputation for aggressiveness. The company was viewed by its competitors as unscrupulous, an assiduous practitioner of "twisting"—convincing customers to drop existing policies in favor of EFLIC programs. At this moment, Baker neither believed nor disbelieved the story. Had it come from a low-level employee, he might have dismissed the charges. But Secrist had been an executive, and Baker was a cautious man. He assigned a supervisory examiner to the case: Maurice Rouble, a veteran of forty years, the department's supersleuth, a man suspicious of everything.

Fred Mauck shook his head. The young, newly appointed Illinois Insurance Director couldn't figure out how the scheme he'd been apprised of three hours earlier could work. At 3:30 James Steen, deputy director of the Illinois Department's examinations branch, had brought word of a call from California alleging the existence of phony insurance at Equity Funding Life Insurance Company; EFLIC was chartered in Illinois. What Mauck couldn't figure out was how EFLIC could make the system pay. In the first year, the company would receive 180 percent of each annual "premium" from the reinsurers. But each succeeding year, EFLIC would have to pay ninety percent of the "premium" to the reinsurer—and no premium would be coming in. If you diagrammed the scheme, it resembled an inverted pyramid, a structure that had to topple. Nonetheless, Mauck was taking no chances. He wanted his auditors in there, and he didn't want to give EFLIC a chance to argue.

Steen selected two of his best auditors, Jack Doyle and Jerry Fowler. He called them at home and told them to be ready to leave on Monday morning, to handle a special audit.

I had returned from Philadelphia late Thursday evening. When I got to the office on Friday morning, my thoughts were still focused on INA, the insurance company I had just visited, rather than Equity Funding.

Moments before I was to leave for lunch, I received a call from Dick Sieben, a fraternity brother I hadn't seen in years. He'd just been made a vice president at Continental Assurance, not only one of the major insurance companies in America, but one of the major reinsurers. He wanted to have lunch. I told him that I'd already invited several guests to lunch. But I wanted to see him, thinking I might try out on him the theory of fraud that Secrist had described, without mentioning Equity Funding. I suggested that he eat in the same restaurant, and I would meet with him after lunch. Dick readily agreed.

At 2 o'clock I joined him. He was bubbling with plans for a new department that would handle mass marketing; he was talking about generating five billion dollars worth of new business by reaching into markets that had never before been developed. Suddenly Dick said, "What do you know about Equity Funding–type programs?"

I could scarcely believe the coincidence. "Well, I have a whole file on Equity Funding," I said vaguely, "and I was just taking a look at it." And then, knowing that my friend was an actuary, and very bright, and that he was my friend, and having had a couple of drinks, I said to myself, What the hell, and I told him the story.

He was incredulous.

"Could such a thing *occur?*" I persisted.

"I don't know," Dick said. But he did have one suggestion— that we call the man in charge of the reinsurance department at Continental Assurance.

That day, Allen Gorrelick and I called Bankers National to determine whether Secrist worked there, and whether those individuals he said had left the company had, in fact, left. That part of his story checked out. But we didn't try to check out the allegations themselves. I wanted to think about them over the weekend.

I was uncertain about what to do. I thought about my clients.

I wanted them to hear the allegations—partly to protect themselves, partly to help me determine whether the allegations
were true. If the audit firms had found no irregularities, how
was I to find them? I needed all the help I could get.

Of one thing I was certain: I could not count on the authorities. If I were to go to them, there would be an excellent
chance that the fraud—if it existed—would never be exposed.
The authorities might unwittingly alert the company, and
the company would cover it up.

The first thing Monday morning, March 12, we called the
Bankers National men whom Secrist said had quit. Sure
enough, they were at home. But they wouldn't talk to us. Nothing we said could persuade them. They said they had no comments to make at all. Secrist had mentioned the Mafia. The
refusal of these men to talk to us made us wonder.

Then Allen Gorrelick called a former official in the Equity
Funding sales organization who had managed a large territory.

We had taken the production figures used by Stanley Goldblum, and divided them by the number of Equity Funding
salesmen. Each salesman had sold between $400,000 and
$500,000 of face value insurance, according to this calculation.
If Secrist's charges were true, one immediate indication would
be that the real figure would be considerably less than the
one we had calculated.

The former Equity Funding sales manager told Gorrelick
that the average face value insurance sold by his men had
been in the neighborhood of $150,000.

LOS ANGELES, March 12, 1973—Equity Funding Corporation
of America (NYSE/PCSE) a life insurance–based financial
services company, today reported record earnings from
operations of $2.81 per share for the year ending December
31, 1972, up from $2.45 per share in 1971.

Stanley Goldblum, president and chairman of the board,
said consolidated net income rose to $22,617,000 in 1972,
a 17 per cent increase over 1971 earnings of $19,332,000. . . .

> Life insurance sales in 1972 amounted to a record total
> of $2.5 billion, Mr. Goldblum said, compared with $2.0
> billion in 1971. The company's 1972 sales consisted of $1.6
> billion in individual policies and $872 million under group
> plans. As of December 31, 1972, Equity Funding's life in-
> surance company subsidiaries had $6.5 billion of life in-
> surance in force, compared to $4.6 billion at the end of
> the previous year. . . .

At 12:30 P.M., Equity Funding's 1972 earnings came over
the Dow Jones ticker. It gave me an excuse to call Stanley
Goldblum. It was 9:30 A.M. in Los Angeles; he wasn't in. His
secretary told me he would return the call.

Then we called Chick Wittenberg, the head of the reinsurance department at Continental Assurance, whose name had
been given to me the previous Friday by my old fraternity
brother. We didn't tell him about allegations of fraud. We
posed a hypothetical question. "Suppose an insurance company came to you and said, 'We have a block of business and
we want to coinsure.' How do you check out the existence
of these policies?"

"Well, we really don't," Wittenberg said.

"Suppose someone wanted to defraud you by selling you
policies that didn't exist?"

"There's really no way that we would know that," he answered. "The insurance industry is like a club. You trust certain people and you don't go through the auditing procedures.
We would rely on knowing the people who would provide us
with this coinsurance." He hesitated. "As a matter of fact I
ought to think about this. It never really occurred to me before. I wonder whether it could happen?" Once more, he
paused. "I'm going to check into it," he said.

We made other checks that day with other insurance companies. We asked all of them, in substance, how they handled
their reinsurance contracts, what kinds of records they kept,
how they checked the records of the primary company to as-

certain whether the policies were genuine, or whether they had lapsed. In most cases, the companies did not send anyone in to check the books of the firm that had sold them the insurance. Even the company that *had* sent someone in had confirmed only the existence of the policies on the books, not the existence of the people whose lives were presumably insured. When I asked Richard Weiss, an insurance consultant, whether fraud was possible, he said, "Oh, absolutely. There is no question that this could occur if the officers of the company were disposed to do it. You just couldn't rely on auditors to pick it up."

By that afternoon, Allen Gorrelick's credibility percentage had risen to twenty to thirty percent.

The young executives of Equity Funding Life Insurance Company poured from their offices to gawk at their visitors. It was early afternoon in Los Angeles; the two Illinois Insurance Department auditors had arrived unannounced to begin an inspection of the company's books. The executives were upset. Since when did the department schedule a regular audit without advising the company? Was this a surprise audit? they demanded. No, said the examiners, it was a regular audit.

Could it be rescheduled? they asked. They were in the process of filing an amended annual statement. They'd made an error in the original. No, said the examiners, it couldn't be rescheduled.

But they had no space, the corporate officials argued.

They weren't fussy, the examiners replied.

Would they at least wait until tomorrow?

Yes, the examiners replied, they would wait until tomorrow.

The next morning, the examiners were shown to an office on the twenty-eighth floor, recently vacated by an executive vice president who had resigned. The office was just down the hall from Stanley Goldblum's, separated only by the long executive dining room.

Late that afternoon, Stanley Goldblum returned my call. I was nervous, all but afraid. It had been almost two years since we had talked. Goldblum had a reputation among analysts for making them feel foolish. He did nothing to diminish that reputation now.

"I saw your earnings on the tape," I began. "It's been a long time since I did any work on Equity Funding. Are you sending something out?"

"Well, you know, Ray, we always do send out an annual report," Goldblum said sarcastically.

I asked then if he could tell me what the fully diluted earnings were—that is, the earnings depreciated by certain liabilities. He asked his secretary for them, gave them to me, and said, "Why don't you come out and see us?"

I said I would be delighted. He turned me over to his secretary. We made a date for March 27.

Back in December, I had received a call from an old colleague, Jerry Zukowski. He told me that he had just joined the Boston Company Institutional Investors Inc., and that he wanted to come in and see me. I told him to come ahead, and we made a date.

"I understand you know a lot about Equity Funding," he said when we had met a few days later.

"Frankly, I really don't," I replied. "I only know what is in my files and what I read in the newspaper, and I haven't talked to the company for a year."

"Gee, that's strange," Jerry said. "We talked to the company the other day and they told us that the two analysts who know the company best on the Street are Don Kramer at Oppenheimer and Ray Dirks."

"I don't know why they should say that," I said. I was certain there were other analysts who could be more helpful, I told him. I didn't want to waste his time.

Jerry indicated that his firm had a position in Equity Funding. He didn't say how big, but I got the impression that it was substantial. He said he intended to do a lot more work on the company, and I promised to get in touch with him if I learned anything.

Now I meant to keep my promise. I also hoped Boston Company could help me check the story out. "You told me to relay to you every bit of information that we know about the company," I said on the phone, "so I thought I ought to call you and just tell you about a conversation I had with somebody recently. You can stop me if you want to, if you don't want me to waste your time, because it really sounds incredible."

"Tell me whatever you've got," he said.

I wasn't five minutes into my story when he put Tom Courtney on the phone. Courtney, the best half-miler in the country in his day, had been an officer of a life insurance company before joining the Boston Company. He listened quietly to the story. When I finished, I said I intended to check out the auditors, who had certified the company's financial statement.

That was a good idea, Courtney agreed. Then he said he would be in New York the next day, and asked if he could see me. I readily agreed.

I had one more difficult call to make before the end of the day—to the auditors of Equity Funding in Los Angeles. My call could hardly have been more suspect. It was 7:30 P.M. New York time, by this point, long after normal working hours, and the auditors didn't know who I was.

The switchboard operator put me through to a man named Michael Balint. "Are you the auditors for Equity Funding?" I asked.

"I'm no longer in charge of the account," Balint replied. "My partner, Richard Hill, has the account. Maybe you should speak to him."

Hill, it developed, was on another long distance call.

"Are you currently doing an audit for the company?" I asked Balint.

"You ought to talk to Mr. Hill, or you ought to talk to the

company," Balint replied. He wouldn't say Yes or No. And he wanted to know who I was. I identified myself. Then he wanted to know why I was calling from New York at 7:30, and he demanded my phone number. I thought frantically for something I might say to reassure him. It was only when I mentioned that the earnings of Equity Funding had come out on the tape earlier that day that he decided I wasn't some crazy stockholder. "Oh, really?" he said. "What were they?" I told him. "Do they show anything about the life insurance company?"

"No," I said. "They just announced the earnings of Equity Funding Corporation."

"I'm amazed that they don't say anything about the life company," Balint said.

"Why?" I demanded.

"It's just very complicated," he replied. "I'm sort of amazed."

Then Balint admitted that Haskins & Sells were no longer the auditors for the life insurance company, and it was my turn to be amazed. "Why isn't there any record of this?" I asked. "Shouldn't that be reported to the SEC?"

"We're not the auditors for the parent company, and therefore I don't think we have to put it on record," Balint said. The new auditors, Seidman & Seidman, would take care of it, he assured me.

I wanted to talk to Richard Hill. But he was still on the phone.

Tom Courtney arrived at ten the next morning, two hours ahead of schedule. I suspected he might have wanted to catch me unprepared. I took him into the conference room, along with Allen Gorrelick. Then I laid out the notes of my conversations with Ron Secrist, and said, "All I have, Mr. Courtney, is this information from this individual. We've made a few other checkings, besides." I told him then that I had called Haskins & Sells.

He'd called the auditors also, Courtney replied. It was he who had been on the phone all that time with Richard Hill while I was talking to Balint.

I told Courtney that my conversation with Balint had increased my suspicions of Equity Funding. He countered that his talk with Hill had reinforced his feeling that the allegations were spurious.

Then I began to go through my notes. I take voluminous notes; it took me two hours to go through them. When I finished, I looked at Courtney.

"I find the whole thing absolutely impossible to believe," he said. Whoever my source was, he said, he was either a disgruntled former employee, a liar, or a fantasizer. He added: "These things go on all the time."

That day, we received the 1972 convention blank from Bankers National. A convention blank is a comprehensive financial statement every insurance company must file with the state insurance department that charters it. When we compared the 1972 statement to the 1971 statement we had the feeling that we were looking at two totally different companies.

The most significant difference was in the comparative fate of the "participating" and "nonparticipating" departments of the company. There are two types of whole life insurance policies sold by insurance companies. Nonparticipating policies offer a fixed guaranteed return; you get no percentage of any additional profits the company might earn on the investments it makes with your money and the money of others. Participating policies pay their owners according to how well the company invests their money.

From 1971 to 1972, the profits of the participating department, ninety percent of which belonged to policyholders, had dropped sharply, while the profits of the nonparticipating department, all of which belonged to the stockholders (in other words, Equity Funding) had increased sharply. Obviously there had been some change in the formulas, to the detriment of the policyholders and the betterment of the stockholders.

This comparison indicated that Bankers' policyholders were being deprived of profits that were rightfully theirs. Far more seriously, it indicated that Equity Funding wasn't doing nearly as well as the company maintained. Had it not been for the changes in accounting that had resulted in the shift of income from Bankers' policyholders to its stockholders, Equity Funding's 1972 earnings would have been much lower than those announced—low enough to have given the company a "down earnings" year.

On that basis alone, Allen Gorrelick concluded, he would be inclined to lighten up on the stock or sell it out completely. There was, in addition, his knowledge of Ron Secrist's allegations—which Allen's credibility estimate now placed at fifty percent.

The next day—Wednesday, March 14—Allen and I went to a luncheon given by Occidental Life. Chance put Allen at a table next to John Buszin, a young insurance analyst with Bankers Trust. On our way back to the office, Allen told me that Buszin had told him that Bankers Trust owned shares in Equity Funding. He thought the number might be substantial. I called Buszin the moment we returned, and told him I had information about Equity Funding. He told me to come on over.

I did the next day. I sat down and recited the story that Secrist had told, emphasizing that it was purely what a former employee had told us. I hadn't gotten fifteen minutes into the story when Buszin said, "I don't want to hear any more. I just want to get out of this stock. Even though this may be completely false, we're going to sell the stock. It's been a lousy performer."

I asked if he wanted me to talk to any of his portfolio managers or others who made decisions. Since Buszin was only an analyst, I assumed he couldn't make the decision alone.

"No," he said confidently, "you don't have to." Naturally, he said, "I can't give you guys the order." He added: "If you come around tomorrow and say you've got a buyer, I'll sue you."

We shared a small laugh. My heart wasn't in it. For the first time since I had heard Ron Secrist's story, I was the cause of consequences.

On March 16, Richards Barger, the former commissioner of insurance for California and now a practicing attorney, received a call from John Bolton, a Chicago lawyer retained by Equity Funding. Bolton had once been the insurance director of Illinois. "Fred Levin just called me," he said. "He worked for me for three years. An honest guy. He said two examiners from Illinois walked in on them the other day."

Bolton had called the present Illinois director, Fred Mauck, in his client's behalf, to ask if the audit could be held off. Equity Funding, he explained, was in negotiation with First Executive Corporation, the parent of Executive Life. Equity hoped to purchase Executive; the audit could foul things up. Could the audit be held off? Mauck had turned him down. Now Bolton wondered if Barger could find out from his sources at the California department what was going on.

Barger called Christy Armstrong, the chief insurance examiner. He could feel at once that something was wrong.

"A lot of things I told you as commissioner I can't tell you now," Armstrong said.

"Can you tell me who's the examiner?"

"Maury Rouble," Armstrong said.

"That's all I want to know," Barger said. "I get the vibes."

Barger then called Fred Levin. Levin asked if he could see him. The next day he came to Barger's office wearing an electric blue velvet suit. With him was Stanley Goldblum, wearing a sport jacket and an open shirt. Barger told them that the examination was a triennial audit and could not be postponed. "For all I know, someone's carrying the money away in a black bag," he said. "For all I know, it could be you."

The two men thanked him and left.

All that day I watched the ticker to see if any of Bankers Trust's Equity Funding shares would trade. But no big blocks traded.

That weekend, I tried to forget Equity Funding.

Ever since Ron Secrist's visit, I had been looking for Pat Hopper, with no success. Bankers National didn't have his number. A call to Los Angeles information was no help. Finally, on Monday, March 19, it occurred to me that his name might be on one of our old client lists. It was, along with a San Gabriel address. I soon had his phone number.

"Do you know Ron Secrist?" I asked after an exchange of pleasantries.

"Yes," he said.

"Is he somebody you would believe?"

"Absolutely."

"I guess you know why I'm calling," I said.

"I've heard the whole story from Ron."

"Do you believe it?"

"Yes."

I gave Pat Hopper the history of what had happened since Secrist's call. Just then, one of my associates stuck his head in my office to tell me that a block of 98,800 shares had just traded. Bankers Trust owned 100,000 shares. "There it goes, Pat. The Bankers Trust block just went off," I said.

"I saw it," Hopper said. He had been watching the market action on high frequency television.

"Well," I said, "I guess I'm going to be coming out there."
I never dreamed how soon.

At 4:30 that afternoon, I discovered in my client book that
Institutional Capital, a Chicago-based company, held shares
of Equity Funding the last time we had talked. I called Jerry
Dhall of Institutional and asked if they still owned the stock.
Yes, he said. "I don't know whether you want to hear this
story," I said, and began to recite the allegations.

Two minutes later, Dhall stopped me. "I better get Bill
Maloney on the phone."

Maloney, who once ran Sears, Roebuck's pension fund, was
now the president of Institutional Capital, which managed
pension funds. He was occupied at that moment. I called back
five minutes later and put Allen Gorrelick on an extension.
We elaborated the story.

Maloney listened silently for a few minutes. Then he said,
"This is a terrible allegation. Have you confirmed it?"

"I talked to Goldblum a week ago when the earnings came
out," I replied. "He didn't sound as if anything was going on."

"Have you talked to other people?"

"To one other institution," I said. I was so intimidated by
this point I was afraid to admit that I'd talked to two.

"Here you are going around the Street and telling this wild
story and you haven't even confirmed it."

"It's not that easy to confirm. I'm telling you because I'm
trying to check it out and I thought you ought to know about
it."

"You have a good reputation as an analyst," Maloney said.
"You could ruin your reputation for doing this. If I were you
I would go to Los Angeles and see Stanley Goldblum right
away."

I told Maloney that I had to be in Hartford the next week
for several important meetings and that I had an appointment
with Goldblum during the following week, on March 27.

"You should get on the next plane and go to Los Angeles and confront Stanley," Maloney insisted.

"Even if I confront him, I don't think he'll admit something like this—assuming it's true. I don't think that's the way to do it."

Maloney argued that I'd be able to tell by the way Goldblum reacted. His face would fall, or he would look at me queerly, or I would see it in his eyes.

"I don't know," I said dubiously.

"I think you ought to get on the next plane," Maloney persisted. "If you want, I'll pay your fare."

"If you think so, I guess I will," I said.

"Call me back and let me know," he said.

"Okay," I said.

I had one other surprise earlier that day. After my conversation with Maloney, I called Ron Secrist. It was the first time I had talked to him since our luncheon. The stock had been trading at $28 a share when he'd come in. I told him that a large block had gone off at $25, and I wanted him to know.

"That's great," he said. "I was wondering what you were doing."

"I'm heading out to Los Angeles," I said.

"You'd better hurry up," said Secrist. "Things are beginning to happen."

I knew at once that he must have gone to someone else. "What do you mean?" I asked. "Did you go to an insurance department?"

"I'm not supposed to tell you anything."

"Can you tell me if you've gone to the insurance department in the Far West or the Middle West?"

"In the Far East," he replied.

That meant either New York or New Jersey.

"I can't tell you anything about it, so don't ask me," he said then. "But things are really moving, so you better get going."

"Okay," I said. It was no comfort to learn that my informant had lied by telling me that he had not gone to the regulators.

I had worn a dated brown suit to work that day, which everyone in my office had mocked. All my other clothes were at the cleaners. The shop was closed. I had to go to Los Angeles as I was.

That evening, I kept a long-standing dinner appointment with two traders from Goldman, Sachs. The meeting had been arranged by Judy Wallach, a girl who had worked for me at another financial house. It was Goldman, Sachs that had done the block that day. We ate at Le Steak. I told them all that I was going to Los Angeles, but I didn't tell them why.

After dinner, I went to Bloomingdale's, bought some shirts, underwear, and socks, took a taxi to Kennedy Airport, and caught the 11 o'clock plane for Los Angeles. When I arrived at the Beverly Wilshire Hotel in Beverly Hills, it was 5:30 A.M. New York time.

When I got up Wednesday morning, I felt too exhausted to confront Stanley Goldblum. Instead, I called Pat Hopper and said, "Guess where I am?"

7.
Hide and Seek

Hopper arrived in forty-five minutes. We talked for three hours in the hotel's Hideaway Bar. He said there were eleven different reasons why he believed that what Secrist had told him was true. He ticked them off. But he had no proof. I had trouble getting him to be definite. He just let me ask him questions. Over and over again, he made it clear that he had no proof at all.

His analysis increased the probability in my mind that the story was true. It also sizably increased my discomfort.

"Who else can I talk to to get some corroboration?" I asked him. "I can't look at the books and figure it out for myself."

"Frank Majerus," Hopper said. He told me then about EFLIC's former controller. But he wasn't sure Majerus would talk. Majerus, he said, was afraid of going to jail.

Almost in frustration, I asked Hopper if he would talk to the Boston Company. I didn't think he would. But the thought of an investment banker who spoke their language expressing his conviction to the Boston Company that the story was true was highly compelling at this point. To my surprise, Hopper said okay.

On the way to my room, I stopped at the desk. There was a

message from Stanley Goldblum. I started. How did *he* know I was here?

I shoved the message in my pocket and said nothing. I didn't want Hopper to know Goldblum had called.

Hopper's conversation with the Boston Company didn't prove all that reassuring.

Within moments after he took the phone in my room, he was telling Jerry Zukowski of the Boston Company that Ron Secrist had been fired. Secrist had told me he'd resigned. That made lie number two from my principal informant.

Nonetheless, the story, as I heard Hopper relate it, seemed knowledgeable, comprehensive and convincing, particularly the narrative about the signature forging by an EFLIC attorney. When I finally took the phone, I said confidently to Jerry, "What do you think?"

"I think it's even less likely that it's true than before," Jerry said. "Secrist was fired. He told you he'd resigned. It sounds even more like a disgruntled employee story than before. It's very exaggerated—and Hopper couldn't confirm anything of substance. That thing about the signature is nothing."

That day, March 20, Rodney Loeb, Equity's general counsel, received a phone call from Kathleen Ross of the New York Stock Exchange. The activity in the stock of Equity Funding had triggered a stock watch on the computer, she informed him. Was he aware of any unusual circumstance that could account for the activity in the stock? The parent company had just announced the acquisition of First Executive Corporation, a Los Angeles insurance company, in exchange for $20 million in Equity stock, but Loeb knew this couldn't be the cause. No, he said, he wasn't aware of anything unusual.

In New York, an hour later, Yura Arkus-Duntov, Equity Funding's executive vice president in charge of investments, received a surprise visit from Jarvis Slade of New York Securities, the company that had taken Equity Funding public twelve years earlier. Slade was worried. He'd heard an upsetting remark at a luncheon. An analyst at Bankers Trust, an associate of John Buszin's, had said, "Hey, you guys want to hear of a good short? Equity Funding."

"Nonsense," Slade had replied.

"I've got it from a good source," the Bankers Trust man had insisted. "The company's issued phony insurance and sold it to reinsurers."

"That's impossible," Duntov said now to Slade. "The company would have to create phony reserves."

With Duntov that afternoon was Larry Williams, Equity's associate general counsel and vice president for compliance. Williams had been the assistant director in charge of enforcement for the Securities and Exchange Commission before joining Equity Funding. He was in New York to become acquainted with the New York Insurance Department. Both Duntov and Williams had been disturbed by the recent activity in Equity Funding stock. But Equity Funding had a tradition of running with the market, and the market was currently running downhill; as a consequence, they hadn't been overly concerned. Slade's visit gave them something to worry about. Now Duntov asked Williams to call Loeb. He did. Loeb listened to the story, then said, "Memorialize it." Williams dictated a memo to a secretary in Los Angeles.

It had been eighteen months since Frank Majerus had last seen Pat Hopper. Ten minutes ago, Hopper had called to say there was a man in town looking into Equity Funding. He was someone who might be able to get somewhere with this thing, Hopper had said. At first, Frank had hesitated, but then he'd proposed a dinner meeting for the following evening. Hopper had agreed. But Frank had just phoned his wife and learned that they were busy that evening. Impulsively, he picked up the phone and called Hopper back. "Why don't we do it now?" he said.

They agreed to meet in a bar at the Wilshire Hyatt House in half an hour. Majerus hung up and left his office. He wanted this matter off his conscience; he wanted it done with at last.

That morning, Jack Doyle, the Illinois examiner, had decided to return to Chicago for the weekend. On Monday, the twenty-sixth, he would physically count the bonds, worth more than $20 million, that were listed on EFLIC's books as on deposit at American National Bank and Trust in Chicago. He had informed Lloyd Edens of EFLIC that he would be returning to Chicago on Friday and asked Edens to make arrangements with the bank for access.

"Okay, fine," Edens replied. "I'll make the arrangements."

Now Doyle took a call from his boss, Jim Steen. He told Steen of his plans to return on Friday.

"Why not come on Thursday?" Steen proposed. "We can talk on Friday."

Doyle agreed.

It was midafternoon in Los Angeles when Rodney Loeb told Stanley Goldblum about Larry Williams's call, and the memorandum he had dictated.

"Destroy it," Goldblum said.

"Stan, your paranoia's setting in," Loeb joked.

"I said destroy it," Goldblum repeated.

"What do you know about the 'Y' business?" I asked Frank Majerus.

He looked at Pat Hopper and then at me. "What 'Y' business?" he said.

It had gone okay until I started taking notes. Then he'd begun to fidget. I put down my pen. I could understand his nervousness. An hour ago, he hadn't known that I existed; now his only assurance of my legitimacy was Pat Hopper.

I decided to lead him into it. I understood, I said, that initially the idea had been to create additional earnings by writing business on employees and coinsuring their policies. That wouldn't seem too serious; a lot of insurance companies wrote business on employees.

"That's true," Majerus said.

"Didn't it start in 1969?" I asked.

"That's true," he said.

"Well, if they had done this for employees in 1969, didn't they decide in 1970 that they could do it for 'outsiders'?"

"Yes," he said, "that's right."

Then, suddenly, some inner coil released, and Majerus was talking—about the "special-class" business, and the "Y" business, and "Department 99," and Jim Smith and Lloyd Edens and the crazy year-end figures, and of how Majerus had tried to stay out of it, and of how some people had boasted that they had really put it over on the auditors and how disgusted he was that he had to be a part of that.

I asked him about Wolfson, Weiner, the auditors of the parent company while he was there.

"Bad news," he said. He dropped his eyes, then raised them and said, "I think I'm going to jail."

"Why?" I asked.

"Because I was the controller of a life insurance company. I'm the guy who puts the finishing touches on the statement."

"Were you following instructions?" I asked.

"Yes," he said.

"Did you sign anything?"

"No."

"I don't think you're going to jail," I said. "Did you quit the company?"

"That's right."

"Did you talk to anyone about it?"

"I talked to my minister. He told me I had to think of my

family first. He told me to stay with the company until I found another job and then to leave. But he didn't advise me to report it to anybody." Majerus looked at me. "I couldn't stand it morally," he said.

Rodney Loeb had no intention of destroying Larry Williams's memo, even though he didn't put much stock in the rumor. There were always rumors about Equity Funding, dozens of them. Goldblum's reaction had really been paranoid, Loeb decided.

But his curiosity was piqued. On a hunch, he placed a call to Williams at his favorite New York steak house, Frankie & Johnnie's, on 48th Street east of Eighth Avenue. Sure enough, Williams was there. Loeb pressed his associate for more details. "You know," he said when Williams finished, "if someone is spreading rumors about the company, we have the responsibility to report it to the New York Stock Exchange."

Larry Williams agreed.

Pat Hopper drove me back to the Beverly Wilshire Hotel. I went up to my room and stared at that message from Goldblum.

I was too tired to call him back. I thought, I'll just sit here and think. I got out the file and went through it and tried to compile a list of questions for Goldblum. I decided I would call him at 9:30 the next morning. Then I started to worry.

How had he known I was in Los Angeles? I wondered again. The only way was by a call from Bill Maloney of Institutional Capital in Chicago and a subsequent call to my office to find out where I was staying. That meant Maloney had told Goldblum what I was up to.

I'd heard those stories about the Mafia. Before I went to bed, I put the few heavy chairs that were in the room up against the door. I figured maybe they might come to get me; if anything happened, I would at least have an idea they were coming.

The phone rang at 8 A.M. I picked it up.

"This is Stanley Goldblum."

I could scarcely speak. "Hi, Stanley," I managed at last. "I guess we ought to get together."

"I have some appointments this morning," he said.

"Maybe you could come to the hotel," I said. "It's not that far from your office, is it?" I didn't want to go to his office.

Goldblum said he'd be at the hotel in forty-five minutes. I decided not to wait for him in my room. I was afraid to do that. I would go to the Hideaway Bar.

Then I called my office in New York to get my messages, as well as a quote on Equity Funding. It was trading at 23½.

The phone range before I could leave. It was Jerry Zukowski at the Boston Company Institutional Investors. "We're going to sell the stock," he informed me. We think the chances are less than ten percent that the story is true. We think we may be getting out at the bottom, but we're going to get out of it."

I went downstairs, and back to the rear of the bar, so I could see Goldblum coming. I went through my notes and wrote down the name of everyone who was said to have known something of the fraud, from Fred Levin on down. I wound up with thirty names. I'll just show him the list, I thought, and see what he has to say.

He came in at last, with a little man trailing behind him. I didn't recognize his companion. Then I realized it was Fred Levin. He had lost about sixty pounds since I'd seen him at the party in New York the night we discussed Pat Hopper.

I got up. Goldblum loomed over me. "Stanley, how are you?" I said.

"Not too good. The stock just fell four points in one trade. A block of 368,000 shares crossed at 19½."

"My God, that must be the Institutional Investors," I blurted. I had no idea the company had held that much stock.

"Who else did you talk to?" he demanded.

"Bankers Trust and Institutional Capital."

"What have you been saying?"

"People have told me about fictitious policies."

"Who?" he demanded.

"I can't tell you," I said. Then my nerves gave way. "I talked to three people," I said. "One of them was Pat Hopper. But he wasn't the one who came to me first."

We were still standing. I felt menaced. I sat down.

They sat. I offered them breakfast. They didn't want any. I offered them coffee. They refused that, too. Stanley looked hurt; Fred Levin was blasé, glib. "Pat Hopper's a beach bum," he said.

"We wouldn't want somebody on our staff managing a $180 million portfolio who was going to go off to the Fiji Islands every once in a while," Stanley said.

"I understand he gave you some reasons for resigning besides those in his letter," I said to Levin.

"That's not true," Levin said.

"What are you so concerned about?" Stanley asked.

I held up my notes. "These notes comprise the story of three individuals, and the basic substance is that you have a substantial amount of business on the books called 'Y' business."

"How do you spell that—w-h-y?" Stanley asked.

"No. Just the alphabet, 'Y'," I answered.

"We have some people who've been stealing from the company. It sounds like them," Stanley said.

"Look, I've got fifteen pages of notes," I said, brandishing my papers. "Sitting here, I made up a list of thirty people who allegedly know about this."

"Let me see the list," Fred said.

He looked the list over. "There are a few people here that I don't recognize. I don't think they work for the company," he said then.

"I could have gotten the names wrong," I said.

"This is a joke," Fred said.

"Preposterous," Stanley said.

"It does sound unbelievable," I said.

"What do you intend to do with this information?" Stanley asked.

"I thought it would be a good idea to talk to you and see how the story might have gotten started and what assurances you could offer me that it wasn't true." I was trying to be as friendly as possible. I wanted to make them feel comfortable if I could, to make them believe I really wasn't convinced, that I had simply relayed a story to a few institutions that had decided not to take chances.

"You know, our statements are now certified, and the insurance examiners have been in for two weeks now, and they haven't found anything wrong," Stanley said.

That really shook me. I couldn't understand how they could have been there that long and not come up with anything. "You'd think that if they haven't found anything there wouldn't be any truth to this," I said.

"That's right," Goldblum said.

I kept offering them something to eat or drink, and they kept refusing. That made me even more nervous. Finally Stanley said, "Why don't you come over to the company? We'll show you anything you want."

"Great," I said. We walked outside. "Just a minute," I said, and rushed back to the restaurant. I couldn't remember whether I'd left a tip.

I was relieved to be away from them, if just for a minute. I was terribly uncomfortable, not simply because I was frightened, but because I felt sorry for them. If this story turned out to be true, and I exposed it, they were both going down the tubes. On the other hand, think of the public.

It did not occur to me that, by making this investigation, I might be hurting the public. I felt just the opposite. The main thing was to expose the fraud—if it was a fraud—as soon as possible, so that the public wouldn't be getting any more stock,

and the extent of future injury would be limited. On the day
Ron Secrist called me, the stock was trading at $28 a share.
If his story was true, the stock was worthless even then. My
job was to make the stock sell where it belonged as quickly as
I could. In the process of getting it from here to there, someone
unfortunately was going to get hurt. It was a game of musical
shares—the opposite of musical chairs; whoever wound up
with some shares was the one who would be stuck. Someone
was going to lose $28 a share times eight million shares, or $224
million. It didn't seem to make any great moral difference as
to who would be stuck, those who owned the stock on March
6 or those who would own it when trading stopped. The important thing was to get the stock suspended, so that the company
couldn't continue to make acquisitions—such as the one it was
about to make of First Executive, the Los Angeles insurance
company—and thereby increase even further the amount of
worthless paper and the number of unsuspecting stockholders.

Early that morning, Victor Kramer, Equity Funding's director of marketing services, had recommended to Rodney
Loeb that the company put out a press release to counteract
the rumors. Loeb had readily agreed. Kramer, Loeb, and Peter
Panarites, a Washington, D.C., attorney whose firm represented Equity Funding in SEC matters, met in the twenty-
eighth floor legal library to draft the release.

As they were working, Herbert Glaser, Equity Funding's
executive vice president in charge of the real-estate division,
came in looking for Loeb. "The stock's dropped four points,"
he announced. "I think it's a buy. Is there any prohibition
on my buying any?"

"You have to match your current buy against your last sale,"
Loeb said. "Have you sold any shares recently?"

Glaser had sold 1000 shares—one fourth of his last bonus—
five months earlier at a price of $34 a share.

Loeb reminded Glaser of Section 16b of the Securities Ex-

change Act of 1934, which required an officer of a company
to make up the difference to the company if the shares he buys
are priced lower than those he sold less than six months before.
If he bought 1000 shares at $20 a share, Glaser would have
to pay Equity Funding $14,000. There was no point in his buy-
ing.

"Oh, I forgot," Lloyd Edens said to Jack Doyle. "Those
securities aren't in Chicago any more. We sold them to purchase Northern." Northern Life was a Seattle life insurance
company Equity Funding had just bought for cash.

Only yesterday, Jack Doyle had been thinking how helpful
Lloyd Edens had been. Now the alarms went off inside. How
in hell can the controller of a corporation forget that his company sold $20 million in bonds?

Awhile later, Doyle stepped out of his office and started
down the hall. Fred Levin approached him. "Hey," he said, "I
hear you're going home on Thursday."

Doyle stared at Levin.

"Oh," said Levin, "I don't mean Thursday. I mean Friday."

There's only one way he can know that, Doyle thought.
He took an elevator to the basement, called Jim Steen from a
pay phone, and told him their calls were being monitored.

In his fifth-floor office, Victor Kramer removed a piece of
copy paper from his typewriter and looked it over.

> LOS ANGELES, March 21, 1973—Stanley Goldblum, president
> and chairman of Equity Funding Corporation, said today
> that there have been no adverse developments in the com-
> pany's operation which would account for the market activ-
> ity in EFCA stock during the past three days.
>   Mr. Goldblum said that the company is "in the strongest
> financial and sales condition in its history." He added that
> revenues, earnings and sales reached record highs in 1972,
> and that the upward trend has been continuing during the
> first quarter of 1973.

*   *   *

Later that morning, Rodney Loeb informed Kathleen Ross at the New York Stock Exchange that rumors were afloat. "Yes, we know," she replied. "A compliance man from New York Securities has already called."

Loeb walked this intelligence down the long corridor from his office in the southeast corner of the floor to Fred Levin's office on the north face. He turned the handle and started in, only to bump his head against the door. He was astonished. The door had never before been locked. "What the hell's going on in there?" he asked a secretary.

"Ray Dirks is in there."

"Who the hell is Ray Dirks?"

"An insurance security analyst."

"So what? Why the hell do they have the door locked?"

"I don't know," the secretary replied.

They took me in shifts. Names became people: Jim Smith, Art Lewis, Lloyd Edens. Each time Fred Levin would leave me alone with one of them, I would ask, "What about the 'Y' business?"

"What 'Y' business?" they'd reply.

I asked Jim Smith if the company hadn't given free insurance to employees in 1969. "It wasn't free," he said. "They paid twenty-five percent." I didn't believe him.

I asked why Bankers National and Equity Funding Life had paid virtually their entire profits the previous year to the parent company. They said that the parent company needed cash because it was generating the business. It was hardly an answer. It's unusual, at best, for an insurance company to pay out virtually its entire statutory profits. It was a case of Paul robbing Peter to hype the earnings—and thus the stock price—of the parent company.

I asked Art Lewis, the chief actuary, how EFLIC's profit margin could be so high. He went into a dissertation on how the coinsurance deals worked and how the company could show such exceptional profits under generally accepted accounting principles. He raced through his exposition so rapidly that I could see why Ron Secrist had characterized him as brilliant.

I asked Lloyd Edens if I could see a corporate balance sheet. He said there was one around somewhere, but he made no move to get one. Of all the men in the room, only he seemed uncomfortable and reluctant to talk.

From time to time, Stanley Goldblum would drop in and peer over my shoulder at my notes. "What do you think now?" he'd say. And I would tell him I was learning a lot.

On the way over to the company, I had asked Stanley about the twenty percent cut in the staff. "We always have programs to eliminate fat in the company," he said. "We're constantly looking for ways to improve operations and efficiency." It was an answer any corporate executive would have given regarding a program of cutbacks. But he didn't give me any numbers.

Now, I asked about all the departures at Bankers. We went through the list of officers, one by one. At last, Ron Secrist's name came up.

Smith said that Secrist had been anxious to move into an administrative job. There was a job he wanted, but he wasn't right for it. After his transfer to Bankers in the fall of 1971, he'd been appointed to a position with the parent company, as well. He'd carried the jobs simultaneously. Then the corporation had decided it didn't need a full time man in Secrist's position, and he had been terminated. Smith said there had been such antagonism about the termination on Secrist's part that he had sent a bitter memo to the corporation and turned in his stock options.

I wondered if I had dwelt on Secrist too long, if I had given away my informant.

It was after 12 o'clock. Goldblum reappeared and invited me to lunch. We walked down the corridor and into the executive dining room. Ahead of me was a wall of windows.

"It's the twenty-eighth floor," Levin said, "but don't worry, the windows are locked."

*   *   *

After nearly forty years as an investigator, Maury Rouble of the California Insurance Department had his own way of doing things. His reputation was that of a supersleuth, but his method was about as dramatic as his appearance. He was a jowly, heavy-set man in his sixties; what he brought to a problem was a skill in accounting and a set of convictions. If you applied the convictions to the figures, you could generally find your answer. It took a lot of sit-down thought. He'd heard about that fellow Secrist's charges. What bothered him about Secrist was that he didn't have one document. If I were going to make charges, I would have Xeroxed something, Maury Rouble thought.

Now he was studying the company's figures, and something definitely looked wrong. There was, for example, the matter of lapses—people who drop their policies. On EFLIC's books the lapses had gotten fewer and fewer until they were practically nonexistent.

If there were bogus policies, the company was not about to pay bogus commissions. So one thing you did was to check with the agents to see what kinds of commissions they'd been paid.

But there was something you did before that. You moved to protect the assets. If these boys had done all they were alleged to have done, Rouble thought, the assets would be gone by now. He knew the liabilities weren't going to disappear.

It was late afternoon in New York City. Yura Arkus-Duntov's anxiety had been building since Jarvis Slade's visit the day before. Now he called Fred Levin. Levin informed him that they were meeting with Ray Dirks at that very moment. He added: "Dirks is neutralized." When Duntov reported the conversation to Larry Williams, it faintly crossed Williams's mind that Levin had chosen a peculiar word.

"What do you think now?" Stanley Goldblum demanded.
"Well, you guys certainly seem to make a strong case," I said. "Your statement has been certified. The examiners have

been in here for a couple of weeks. Your annual statement's due out in a couple of days. If the auditors certify it and the examiners say that everything's okay, who am I to say that what these characters are saying has any validity? I'm a securities analyst. I don't have access to the books. I'm not even an accountant. If you pointed me in the direction of the books and said why don't you look at them I wouldn't know where to start."

"That's right," they all said.

"By the way," I said, "where are the examiners?"

"They're right down the hall," someone said.

I thought about dropping in to shake hands with them but quickly discarded the idea. I was eager to get away from the company. I felt terribly uncomfortable there.

They seemed just as eager to be rid of me.

As lunch adjourned, Stanley said, "What are you planning to do next?"

"I don't know. I'm in a muddle," I said. "I think I'm going to go back to my room and think about it." I honestly didn't know what I was going to do.

"When you came in this morning, you seemed very concerned, but it looks as if you're neutralized," Levin said.

He walked me to the elevator. I wondered about calling a cab. He told me not to bother. There were plenty of cabs a block away, at the Century Plaza Hotel. I got the feeling he didn't want me waiting around for a cab.

We said good-bye. I took a cab back to my hotel. There was a message to call Bill Blundell of *The Wall Street Journal.*

Calling *The Wall Street Journal* had been one of my first thoughts during Ron Secrist's visit. Because Secrist seemed wary of the regulators, I had asked if he would object to my telling the story to a *Journal* reporter. I told him I thought reporters could be trusted to protect their sources. Secrist said he'd rely on my judgment. I had tried to reach Herb Lawson, the *Journal's* San Francisco bureau chief, on March 12th, but it wasn't until March 19th that I talked to him on the phone. I had met Lawson at a party in August 1972. He told me at the time that he was an investigative reporter. The statement had stuck in my head. But, when I talked to him on the nineteenth and told him about the allegations, he'd said he'd like to get on it but had an annual meeting of Bank of America to cover the next day. That seemed to me a fair indication of how strong he thought the Equity Funding story was. Lawson was also concerned about jurisdiction over the story. He wasn't supposed to handle a Los Angeles story unless there was a San Francisco angle. Apparently, the activity in Equity Funding stock had now impressed him to a point where he had alerted the Los Angeles bureau chief, Blundell. Blundell asked if he could see me. I told him to come right over.

When I checked in with my office in New York a few minutes later, my boss, Walter Delafield, asked to speak to me. He had just received an upsetting call from Jarvis Slade of New York Securities. Slade had told him that a Bankers Trust analyst had said I was alleging fraud at Equity Funding.

I denied it absolutely. I told Delafield I had simply related to three institutions what three former employees had told me. My denial appeased Delafield only slightly. The implication to me was that Equity Funding had just begun its counter-attack, with a veiled threat of a libel suit.

Bill Blundell and I sat for two hours in the Hideaway Bar. He had several drinks and I joined him. I told him the whole story. I gave him people's names and phone numbers. The conversation rambled. I had the impression that he didn't take the story seriously. What I didn't know was that he was incredulous. He couldn't fathom a scam of that size; the administrative problems alone seemed insurmountable. Moreover, he couldn't comprehend how they could fool the auditors.

But two factors worked in my favor. The first was a dissatisfying encounter Blundell had once had with Equity Funding. A few years earlier, the company had acquired Diversified Land Company, only to rescind the deal several months later. The falling out occurred after a grand jury had indicted Diversified's president for selling land in violation of restrictions, conspiring to cheat property buyers and executing false deeds. When Blundell called Equity Funding for a comment, the best he got was, "We didn't know." Equity Funding had been on his suspect list ever since.

The second factor in my favor was his inability to answer a question to his satisfaction: Why would I lie?

Stanley Goldblum called me at 8 A.M. for the second day in a row. "There are rumors around that you're alleging fraud at Equity Funding," he said.

"That's not so," I replied. "You know that isn't true. We went over this whole thing yesterday. I've told three other people exactly what I've told you, about allegations on the part of ex-employees of the company."

"In that case," Stanley said, "do you mind if I tell the New York Stock Exchange that you're not alleging fraud?" He was leaving that night for New York and an appearance the next day at the Sixth Annual Institutional Investor Conference.

It was an oblique threat, but a threat, nonetheless. It was threat number two. If the Exchange got the idea that I was saying something false about one of its listed companies, it would end my investigation.

"Stanley," I said, "you are welcome to go to the Exchange and say that I am not alleging fraud at Equity Funding."

My associates Allen Gorrelick and Gerald Lewinsohn were in Hartford. I was in California. The only man left in my division at the office was Fred Hackenburg, a senior analyst. That morning, the twenty-second, he received a call from a public relations consultant whose company represented Equity Funding. The public relations man asked for me. Fred said I was away. "We're aware that Ray is doing something with Equity Funding," the PR man said. "I'm sure if we can talk to him we can straighten it all out."

Yura Arkus-Duntov was beginning to crumble. All he could talk about was the stock. He was getting phone calls from all over the Street. He, in turn, was calling hourly to the West Coast. He kept reminding Larry Williams, who sat with him in his office, that he had loans guaranteed by his stock. He kept asking Williams, "Is it possible for such a thing to happen?" The two men agreed that the company would have had to compile phony reserves to offset the insurance allegedly in force. "How can the auditors not find out something like this?" Duntov asked almost rhetorically.

Both men were agreed on several points. Neither had put much faith in the company's cattle or oil ventures, because such investments produced a type of earnings that wouldn't necessarily recur. But insurance was solid: its income was predictable; the earnings were constantly recurring.

At that point in their discussions, they would look at one another and shake their heads.

By this point, the calls from clients in the East were flowing into my room at the Beverly Wilshire. It was hard to call out. I finally managed one call to Denver. It made my day.

Ron Secrist had given me the name of Gene Thibodeau, a former Equity Funding employee who had worked in the computer area. I found him at the Western Farm Bureau, where he was the manager of the systems department. "Why did you leave Equity Funding?" I asked.

"I didn't especially care for the way things were running," he said.

"Did the company create 'Y' business?"

"I believe it did."

"Why?" I asked.

"It made them money."

"How did you become aware of this fake business?"

"I ran across it accidentally. Then I did some snooping around."

He told me that the fake policies had been blended into the real ones on the master record of the computer. He wouldn't say how many policies were fake, exactly, but he said there were definitely more than 1000 and that at the end of 1970 there had been a big "one-shot deal."

Then I asked if he knew of anyone else who might help me. He gave me two names. One was Ron Ronchetti; the other was Don Goff. Ronchetti had left Equity Funding, but Goff was still on board.

Sometime during the week of March 19, a small marble owl was stolen from the executive corridors of Equity Funding. The theft was reported to Rodney Loeb. Loeb knew that the cleaning people would be blamed, and the thought made him furious. If there's anything cleaning people don't want, it's a marble owl, he thought. Loeb worked late hours; he was on friendly terms with the cleaning staff; he even kept a jar of chocolates on a bookshelf, to which they had permanent access. He decided to investigate, in hopes of averting trouble.

On the evening of March 22, he asked Gardis Holmes, one of the cleaning ladies, "Was anybody up here after hours?"

"You know, there *were* some strange men up here," Gardis replied. "They were going in all the offices. They had keys and equipment and they knew where they were going. They were up in Mr. Goldblum's office and Mr. Levin's office— in that area, mostly."

Loeb immediately associated the strange men with the missing owl. "Next time," he said to Gardis, "you call the goddam cops."

When Ron Ronchetti returned home late that evening,

he found a garbled message from the babysitter. He'd been out looking for work, and he hoped the message had something to do with a prospect. He called the Beverly Wilshire Hotel. "Someone called me whose name I can't read. Ray something or other. The last name has five letters and begins with D."

"That must be Ray Dirks," the operator said.

The next morning, we were at breakfast, and Ron Ronchetti was talking without reservation. While one person could do nothing, in his view, he thought that perhaps someone like myself, coordinating the stories of many people, might be able to do a great deal.

He had heard that Art Lewis had been the "mechanic" of the "Y" business. There were many euphemisms for the business— "Stanley Goldblum's friends," "The Chicago Area Telephone Directory," "Employees' Franchise." He gave me some estimates of the fake policies: 11,000 in 1970; 45,000 in 1971. The numbering of the policies was random. Each policy could be reinsured as many as four times; as long as there was a "policy" on the books, Equity Funding could reinsure it with first one company, and then another, and yet another. He told me of an employee who had removed a computer tape on which the fake business was recorded, and kept it under his bed. The same employee had retained a lawyer and written a letter to be opened in the event of his untimely death because he had once heard boasts about how easy it would be to get a contract on someone's life.

Then Ronchetti told me about the employees on the inside who knew the system so well that they had created policies with cash values. They had then turned in the policies to redeem the cash values. They received some ten or eleven checks. The company was helpless to stop it. The fake policies had been on the books as real.

He wouldn't tell me which employees had managed this rip-off. But we agreed that, in some involuted way, it seemed like a form of justice.

After breakfast, we went to my room. Ronchetti called Don

Goff. Would he like to have lunch over at that Italian place in Santa Monica? Ronchetti would pick him up. Goff said sure.

Herbert Glaser's mother called her son to tell him that she had bought some Equity Funding stock. The executive vice president for real estate told her she'd made a good buy.

Most Americans who purchase securities buy in quantities of 100 shares. A handful of Americans buy blocks of 100,000 shares and more. Most Americans buy on whim or rumor. The handful buy on the basis of "inside information"—special knowledge that passes from the chief executives of corporations to those managers of great masses of capital in a position to do them the most good.

The operating theory is that, if you want someone to take an interest in your enterprise, you have to give him a justification that extends beyond hard analysis, a feeling that he is privy to special inner knowledge you have not shared with anyone else. The money manager to whom a corporate executive confides believes he has an advantage over everyone else on Wall Street.

This goes on all the time. Most often, it transpires in a setting that befits the richness of the talk—a paneled office, a private home, or a ranking restaurant. On this particular morning, the ritual was enacted in the dining room of the Regency Hotel on Park Avenue in New York. There, Stanley Goldblum and Yura Arkus-Duntov met with Laurence A. Tisch, the chief executive of Loew's Corporation, which owned the hotel.

Two days earlier, Loews had purchased 220,000 shares of Equity Funding at $19.25 a share. Three of the leading insurance analysts on the Street had called to recommend the stock; when a block of stock had become available at under $20 a share, it had looked to Tisch like a very good value. Now he wanted to check up on this purchase.

Tisch had met Goldblum before. Each had flown from his

respective city to Chicago for a birthday party of the wife of a mutual friend. On this Friday morning, Goldblum did most of the talking. He assured Tisch that everything was fine. Business was excellent, earnings would be up. Later in the day, Loew's bought another 53,100 shares at $19 to $19.75 a share.

The last thing Larry Williams did before leaving New York for Boston was to call his brother. The brother owned 200 shares of Equity Funding, and had bought another 200 for their father. Now he wondered if he shouldn't buy another 200 in the father's name. Williams thought he should.

That morning, I called Jerry Zukowski in Boston. "I talked to several more people, and I want you to know that, while you may think you got out at the bottom, it may make you feel better to know that the story has been confirmed by all of the people I've talked to."

"It makes me feel worse," he said. "I just found out that Equity Funding stock has been bought by our affiliate, John W. Bristol."

I couldn't believe that one affiliate of the Boston Company could be buying while another was selling." Finally, I said, "If John W. Bristol & Company wants any further information, they can call me."

"We'll tell them," Jerry said. "I'm sure they'll be in touch with you."

After his breakfast with Larry Tisch, Stanley Goldblum went to the Sixth Annual Institutional Investor Conference, where he was a featured panelist in a discussion of the financial services industry. He was both verbal and knowledgeable on such subjects as variable life insurance and the future of the financial supermarket concept.

"Stanley certainly seemed subdued today," an acquaintance

of his remarked to another panelist after the meeting. "Usually, he's a wild man when he starts talking on this subject."

Goldblum might have been preoccupied with his meeting later that day with officials of the New York Stock Exchange. He needn't have worried about it. When Kathleen Ross of the Exchange talked to Rodney Loeb afterward, she said she had found Goldblum "a perfect gentleman—charming and dynamic."

Lawrence Baker of the California Insurance Department took a call from Bill Blundell of *The Wall Street Journal.* Blundell wanted to know whether the Equity Funding examination was routine or nonroutine. Baker gave a guarded reply: it was a "regular convention exam."

"Are you aware of the rumors?" Blundell asked.

"Of course."

"Are you checking them out?"

"Of course."

"Was the exam prompted by the rumors?"

Baker hesitated. "You'll have to ask Illinois," he said.

At first, Brian Tickler said on the phone, he hadn't known what he was doing. He was given a big group of files to process at the end of 1970, and all of them were out of sequence.

Datair, the computer services software company he worked for, had contracted to set up an information system for Equity Funding. He figured there must be something wrong with those files, so he began to prepare material to correct them. The corrections would be duly ordered, but then the same mistakes would appear again and again. It was obvious that the Equity Funding people didn't want the mistakes corrected.

Tickler had been a part owner of Datair. He and the other Datair people were in a quandary. They suspected what Equity Funding was doing, but lacking concrete information and having beaten out IBM for the contract, they were in an ambiguous position. Tickler had checked with Datair's lawyer, who advised him, "If they give you the work, you do it."

"Maybe I should have done something," Tickler said over the phone now from his new office in San Francisco. He paused. "I'm delighted to hear from you," he said. Then, abruptly, he said good-bye.

The last three hours have got to be the most surprising in my life, Don Goff decided. He was standing on the concrete terrace at 1900 Avenue of the Stars, where Ron Ronchetti had just let him off. Three hours earlier, Ronchetti had called to invite him to lunch, and when he'd driven by to pick him up, some fellow from New York was in the back seat. They'd gone to Anna's, an Italian restaurant. Ronchetti had placed him in a booth against a wall and sat on the outside. The man from New York sat across from him. "Well, we've got you trapped, Don," Ronchetti had said.

Within a few minutes, Don had realized that the moment he had avoided, and had also wanted, was suddenly upon him. God knows, he'd had a good enough excuse to keep silent—a house full of kids and a tough divorce, and now a new marriage and a new baby due any day. It was rationalizing, and he knew it, but he'd had to accept what was happening in order to stay on the payroll. He'd changed jobs to stay out of the problem area. He wasn't forging the fake insurance; but he knew something about it.

And, suddenly, here was his opportunity to be responsible. He had never believed that an individual could go to an investigative body merely with suspicions. Worse, he would have had to go to a state insurance department, and he had absolutely no faith in the investigative ability of a state insurance department. But this fellow Dirks, with his connections, might get a lot of heat on before the company could cover up. It was only after he'd told the story that Don realized he was the first man still with the company to whom Ray Dirks had talked.

What if word got back to the company? What if Dirks didn't pull it off? Don Goff knew the answers to those questions. He'd be out of a job. He sighed, and started for the building. There was only one thing to do now, he knew. He would have to tell his boss.

"Oh, shit," Jim Smith said.

Bill Gootnick, the head of Management Information Services and Don Goff's boss, had just told Smith and several other EFLIC executives about Goff's luncheon with Ray Dirks. Smith and the others had thought they'd convinced Dirks that nothing was wrong.

"Tell Goff to stay out of it," Smith said now. "Tell him we'll handle it."

Don Goff considered Bill Gootnick a good and honest friend. They had often discussed their suspicions about what was going on. One reason Don had told Bill was that Bill had protected him in the past. Some of the EFLIC brass had been campaigning with Gootnick to can him, but Bill wouldn't hear of it. "The shit's about to hit the fan," he'd told Gootnick. It was the least he could do to warn him.

When Bill told Don Goff on Friday afternoon that he had taken his story upstairs, Don wasn't too put out. Don had not told Gootnick everything. He'd said only that Dirks seemed to have the story that they had been trying to put together. He had verified only that he'd heard the same things. He wasn't a person volunteering information. He was a person saying, Yes, he'd heard these open rumors. Don hadn't told Bill that he'd expressed to Dirks his belief that the rumors might be true.

Don Goff wasn't buying the party line Bill Gootnick had brought back from the sixth floor. Ray Dirks, according to the brass at EFLIC, was a "scalper" trying to drive the price of the

stock down; he had a client who wanted to take over the company. There was a big commission for him if his client could
buy enough shares for the takeover.

Once Goff made up his mind about someone, good or bad,
it took a while to drive him from that position. He had to admit
now, though, that Bill Gootnick's trip upstairs had weakened
his trust.

Sometime during the day of March 23, First National City
Bank of New York (Citibank) returned stock certificates rep-
resenting 100 percent ownership of Northern Life Insurance
Company of Seattle to Equity Funding in Los Angeles. Equity
Funding had paid $40 million for the shares represented by
those certificates.

The stock certificates had been given to Citibank as part of
collateral on a $50 million loan that Citibank and three other
banks had arranged for Equity Funding.

The shares were returned by H. C. Brewer, Jr., the Citibank
vice president in charge of Equity Funding's account, at the
request of Fred Levin.

Bonnie Craig and her colleagues were sitting around the
table, doing nothing, when several men rushed in and started
packing files into boxes.

"Things are going to be changing. You're not going to be
working with files any more," one of the men said to them.
"If the auditors should come by and ask about the files, you
never saw any files. You were doing some reinsurance work."

"We really appreciate the way you've worked," another of
the men told them.

Immediately after he dropped me off, Ron Ronchetti had
driven back to Equity Funding, found Don Goff, and taken
him to a bar in the basement of 1900 Avenue of the Stars for a
couple of beers. Now Ronchetti accompanied Goff to his third-

floor office and returned once more to the elevator. As the door opened, he saw Art Lewis. Lewis froze.

"Art, nice to see you," Ronchetti said.

Bob Ochoa wiped the ink from his hands and gave a little sigh. The last of the night work was over; forty-five extra hours. He'd asked his boss if he could get a little extra money; his boss told him Jim Smith was bringing some over.

Smith arrived. "That's it," he said. He handed Ochoa an envelope.

"Incidentally," Ochoa said, "I'm thinking of buying some stock in the company. Is everything okay? Should I buy it?"

"Everything's fine," Smith said. "But let things cool off for a while. Then in a couple of weeks buy all you want."

When Smith had gone, Ochoa opened the envelope. Inside was $200. Ochoa shrugged. Not much for forty-five hours of overtime. But he didn't let it bother him. He had to believe that rubbing elbows with the honchos wouldn't hurt his standing at the company.

All publicly held companies are accountable to the Securities and Exchange Commission, a federal agency with headquarters in Washington and branches in key cities throughout the country. Federal law requires corporations to file annual reports with the SEC concerning their operations, as well as special reports, known as prospectuses, whenever the corporations wish to offer shares or debentures to the public.

The heart of the SEC is its enforcement division, a small unit spread out through the cities whose job it is to investigate reports of securities frauds. The last several years have been busy ones for the SEC investigators. They have moved in to sift through the debris of such downed high-fliers as Westec, National Student Marketing, Four Seasons Nursing Homes, and Commonwealth United.

In 1970, the SEC had transferred Gerald Boltz, one of its top investigators, to Los Angeles from Dallas to be regional director. Boltz is a thin, high-keyed attorney who joined the agency for a brief period after law school and never quit. He was at home recovering from a virus on Friday, March 23, when he received a call from Stanley Sporkin, the SEC's chief investigator in Washington. "There might be information available through Bill Blundell of *The Wall Street Journal* of something wrong at Equity Funding," Sporkin told Boltz.

Boltz said he would check it the first thing Monday morning.

By this point, Ron Secrist, Pat Hopper, Frank Majerus, Gene Thibodeau, Ron Ronchetti, Brian Tickler, and Don Goff had all told me versions of the same story. They had all put the finger on the same people, all described the same process, all given first- or second-hand accounts that fitted precisely together. It was time for me to do something.

My job was to get the stock suspended before the company could cover the fraud. There was only one way to do that, and that was to call the auditors. If the auditors tell the New York Stock Exchange that they can't certify a company's figures, trading is automatically halted; if they tell the SEC, the stock is suspended. The process should be instantaneous.

Equity Funding's current auditor was the firm of Seidman & Seidman. Before calling directly, I talked to an old friend who had once worked for the firm. Was contact a good idea? I asked him. Yes, he said, but do it through a certain senior partner. I finally tracked him down in Jamestown, New York. He said he would call Bob Spencer, a senior executive in Los Angeles. A few minutes later, Spencer called me, and we made a date for the next day.

It was 4:59 on Friday afternoon. I decided to call Mike Balint, the man I had talked to at Equity Funding's former auditors, Haskins & Sells. He listened quietly while I told him the story.

"Where are you staying?" he asked.

"At the Beverly Wilshire," I said.

"How many people know you're there?"

"A lot of people," I said.

Then he said, "If I were you, for your own personal safety, I would move out right now."

"What do you mean?" I said.

"They know you're there. I think you should move."

That really scared me. I hung up and walked to the street and up the block to the Beverly Rodeo, a small hotel on Rodeo Drive. I checked in under the name of Allen Gorrelick.

But I kept the other room.

Don Goff was having second thoughts. The night before, he'd called me and pressed me to say once more that a number of investigative bodies had been notified. He hadn't been happy with my answer. So he'd started calling around the country— to Ron Secrist, Brian Tickler, Gene Thibodeau. What had they told me? he asked them. What had I told them?

He had just finished a call when Bill Gootnick called him. "I've been calling around," Don said.

"So have I," Gootnick said. "Look, let me do the calling. You get out of the middle."

"Okay," Goff said.

Then Gootnick brought up Ronchetti. He didn't like him. He considered him a blabbermouth and troublemaker who told stories out of school and blew things out of proportion. That's what was happening now, Gootnick hinted. Goff didn't agree, and said so.

Gootnick's next question stunned him. "Do you know what we can do to shut Ronchetti up?"

Bob Spencer was a medium-sized man who appeared to be in his late fifties, distinguished looking with white hair, well-dressed but wearing a sport shirt because it was Saturday. He looked like the kind of man who was accustomed to dealing with top executives. He seemed cool, almost aloof.

I told Spencer and his associate, Joe D'Armas, that I hated to be the bearer of bad tidings, but I was doing so in an effort to help them. I started speaking from my notes. Spencer listened in silence. He didn't make notes. He didn't seem too interested in the story. What really interested him was where I'd gotten the information. I felt we were on the same side, so I gave him the names and phone numbers of those I talked to. Then he asked if they could copy my notes on the Xerox machine. It seemed like a sensible way to save time. I felt I could trust him to keep the notes in confidence.

Before I left, I told Spencer and D'Armas that I had talked to Mike Balint of Haskins & Sells, and that he had advised me to move out of my hotel for my personal safety.

At the elevator, I said, "Look, I'm sorry I have to do this."

"It's all right," he said. "If this is what these people are saying, it's your duty. We appreciate your coming in."

Then Spencer asked what else I had done with the information. I told him I'd given it to *The Wall Street Journal.*

"You went to *The Wall Street Journal?*" he asked.

When we said good-bye, he didn't offer his hand. I put mine out, and he took it.

My dinner partner that Saturday evening was Mike Balint. We talked for six hours. I took him through the entire story. He seemed incredulous.

"How many people know the story?" he asked.

"Forty or fifty," I said.

"I can understand how, if all the top officers of a company are in collusion, they could fix the books so we would be fooled. But I don't understand how so many people could know about it, and not one of them would come and tell me."

I began to reel off some names. Balint didn't respond. Then I mentioned Frank Majerus. He looked at me in surprise. "Frank Majerus? I know Frank well. He was coordinator in charge of the audit for the life insurance company. Why, I just talked to Frank last week."

"How far do you intend to proceed with this?" Stanley Gold-blum asked me on the phone. It was just after noon on Sunday. Before I could answer, he said, "What are your motivations?"

"I have a responsibility to my clients," I said. "I have a responsibility to the people who told me these things to see whether they're true. And I have a responsibility to the insurance industry and the investment industry to make sure that these alleged activities don't exist—or don't continue to exist."

"I hope you understand the implication of these continuing activities," he said. "There are rumors floating all over the place. There are policyholders who have heard about these rumors and might turn in their policies. There are mutual fund shareholders who have heard about these rumors and might turn in their mutual fund shares. Even the savings and loan depositors are concerned. They may turn in their passbooks. This whole thing has far-reaching implications. I don't know whether you are aware of what you have created. There are hundreds of liquidation stories everywhere. People have been calling me from all over; some people are saying that I sold all my stock."

He paused for a moment. "I want to meet with you one more time," he said then. "I want to meet with you alone. I don't want to discuss this over the phone."

"When do you want to meet?" I said.

"Tomorrow afternoon. You could come to the office. You don't have to come there if you don't want, although I have a big office and we can talk privately. You could call me at the office. I'll be there all morning."

"All right, I'll call you," I said.

"Jesus Christ, this is really a difficult situation," he said.

Hide and Seek   151

The moment we rang off, I tried to call Frank Majerus. His wife told me he was with Pat Hopper, talking to Bill Blundell at Blundell's home.

I didn't know how to reach Blundell. I wished I'd been invited.

All afternoon and into the evening, I waited nervously for Majerus to get home. Finally, he arrived.

"How do you feel?" I said on the phone.

"I feel great," he said. His doubts were gone. He wasn't afraid. He sounded like a man reprieved.

"Now that you've told Blundell, do you think that you should call Mike Balint?" I asked.

Majerus hesitated only an instant. Then he said he would. I gave him Balint's home phone number.

An accumulation of conscience had pushed away Frank's fears. He dialed Balint's number at once. "This is Frank Majerus," he said. "I understand you were with Ray Dirks last night. In connection with the subject of bad business, I can confirm that there is some bad business on the books."

"Oh, is that right?" Balint responded. It seemed to Majerus that he sounded surprised.

Half an hour later, I called Balint. "Did you hear from Frank?"

"Yes," he said.

"Is there anything else you want to know?"

"No," he said.

"Okay," I said. "Take it from there."

The former controller of a life insurance company had told the former auditor that there was fraud on the books. There was only one thing an auditor could do with information like that: call the SEC and get the stock suspended. I went over to the dining room of the Beverly Wilshire Hotel and ordered a big steak.

8.

Exposure

Ilie Nastase of Rumania won the Second Annual International
Equity Funding Tournament in Washington, D.C., on Sunday,
March 25, 1973. The tournament, for the benefit of the Vincent
T. Lombardi Cancer Research Center at Georgetown University, was under the general chairmanship of Bill Riordan, Mike
Riordan's older brother. President Richard M. Nixon had been
honorary chairman of the first tournament in March 1972, won
by Stan Smith. Fred Levin, executive vice president of Equity
Funding, presented Nastase with the winner's check before a
national television audience. The check was blank. The real
check was to be issued several days later.

Those who knew Levin said he did not look himself.

At 7:41 P.M., Stephanie Bland, the administrative assistant
of Equity Funding's legal department, finished work on a rush
project and signed out on the department's call sheet. She
walked to the bank of elevators in the twenty-eighth-floor
reception hall. In the stillness of the empty floor, she could
hear the hum of the rising cabin. Moments later, the elevator
door opened. Stephanie Bland jumped. There were four men in
the elevator. They filed out, carrying cases.

She recognized one of the men—Jim Banks, EFLIC's attorney. "Oh hi, Jim," she said. She stepped into the elevator,

turned and saw them opening a door to the executive offices. "Oh, can you get in?" she said. Before anyone could answer, the elevator door closed. As the elevator dropped to the garage, Stephanie Bland wondered what those men were doing there—and what was in those packages and briefcases.

Just after eight o'clock, Rodney Loeb pulled into the garage of the 1900 Avenue of the Stars building for his habitual Sunday evening stint at the office. He started the turn into his assigned parking place, then braked short. A car was there. Loeb parked in the space alongside, walked over to the guard and demanded, "Who's parking in my space?"

The guard checked the license against his list. "A guy named Collins, on the sixth floor."

Equity Funding's life insurance company was located on the sixth floor. Loeb knew Collins by name but had never met him.

About 10 P.M., he walked down the empty corridor to the men's room. A door slammed. He made a perfunctory tour but found nothing. When he finished work, he went to the garage and checked the guard's list. No one had signed in for the twenty-eighth floor.

I did not expect Equity Funding to trade on Monday, March 26th. I was wrong.

A little before 7 A.M., I received a call from John Kornreich of Standard & Poor's Intercapital in New York, who had tried to reach me at my office a week or so earlier about another company. I started to tell him about Equity Funding when a voice came on the same line: "This is John W. Bristol."

John W. Bristol manages money for many of the large endowment funds—colleges and universities in particular. He almost never talks to analysts. I had never talked to him in my life.

It was a double connection. Both Bristol and Kornreich were trying to talk at once. "This is Ray Dirks," I said desperately. "Hello, Mr. Bristol. John, would you please get off the line?" Then I panicked; they were both named John. "Not you, Mr. Bristol," I said quickly. "Mr. Kornreich, I can't talk now."

"I'll get off," Kornreich said.

I promised to call him back. He hung up. I said, "Mr. Bristol, I heard that you own some Equity Funding."

"Yes," he said, "we own more than Boston Company Institutional Investors did."

I winced, Boston Company Institutional Investors had sold almost 400,000 shares—nearly 5% of the outstanding stock. Meanwhile John W. Bristol & Company's clients' investment exceeded $10 million.

"What can you tell me that I haven't heard before?" Bristol said.

"All I can say is that I talked to both of the auditors over the weekend and I don't know if the stock is going to open today. Last night, the former controller of the life company called the partner in charge of the audit for Haskins & Sells and told him there was phony business on the books. The auditor's name is Mike Balint. If you want, I'll give you his home number."

Bristol said he would like it. Normally, people don't call auditors at their homes at 6:57 A.M. to check on corporate figures.

I don't believe Bristol called Balint. I don't believe he had time. He had called me at 9:55, Eastern time. At 9:59, just before the market opening, he called Salomon Brothers and said he wanted to sell 446,000 shares of Equity Funding. They traded at 10:17—which has to be record time for a block of that size. By coincidence, Salomon Brothers had a buyer—Loews Corporation. Salomon was the brokerage firm that had arranged the meeting between Tisch of Loews and Goldblum of Equity Funding. Loews took some of it, assorted buyers took some, and Salomon took the rest.

*   *   *

"This is no time to sell," Larry Williams told Yura Arkus-Duntov for perhaps the twentieth time.

They were seated in Williams's office, looking south across Century City to the old 20th Century Fox Studios and Hillcrest Country Club. Duntov, who had flown in from New York the day before, was collapsing. From the moment he had arrived at the Beverly Hills Hotel, he had been besieged with calls from members of the investment community, demanding explanations. Stanley Goldblum had personally reassured him, but Duntov was no longer convinced. "Can there be any truth to this? Could it be possible?" he kept asking. "What happens if they stop trading? I'm wiped out."

Abruptly, Duntov picked up Williams's phone, called his secretary in New York, and told her to sell 39,725 shares of Equity Funding in his name and another 5520 shares held by his brother, a cousin, and his ex-wife.

Rodney Loeb walked into a vacant executive office, just down the corridor from Stanley Goldblum's—the office that was occupied now by investigators from the Illinois Insurance Department. He was still puzzled about that banging door on Sunday night.

"Do you guys work late at night on the weekends?" he asked.

They laughed in unison. "Look," one of them replied, "we work weekdays from nine to five whether we're in Illinois or California."

That morning, Stanley Goldblum placed an order to sell 50,000 shares of Equity Funding stock through the New York firm of Dishy Easton & Co. The shares constituted approximately twenty-one percent of the 233,189 shares Goldblum had held at the end of January. At that time, with the stock selling at about $35 a share, Goldblum's shares were worth in excess of $8 million.

As required by law, Goldblum duly filed a report of his intention to sell with the SEC.

The phone rang. I picked it up. Ron Ronchetti told me a story I could scarcely believe: that Bill Gootnick, the head of MIS, had asked Don Goff what it would take to get Ronchetti out of the picture. While we were talking, Goff called him on another line. "Call me back," I said. When he did, it was with the worst news I had ever heard.

"It's a bloody business," Ronchetti said. "The notes you must have given Seidman & Seidman over the weekend are in the hands of company officials. And Don Goff is shaking like a leaf."

The combined revelations were too much. "Tell Goff to get out of there," I told Ronchetti, "and I'm getting out of this hotel." I ran from my room to the street. I looked for a cab and couldn't find one. I ran into an office building and found a telephone and called Pat Hopper. "I'm in a state of absolute shock. I need help. Can you come over?"

"I'll be there in forty minutes," he said. "Where are you?"

I had to ask a young girl where I was. It was a Bank of America building.

I stayed by the phone until he got there, calling everyone I could think of. One call went to Bill Blundell of *The Wall Street Journal.* "You should know that a good reporter never turns over his notes," Blundell said.

Bill Blundell had been busy. A few days after his meeting with me, he had rented a room at the Sheraton-West Hotel; there, he had begun a series of interviews with past and present Equity Funding employees who might find the *Journal*'s offices intimidating. He had spoken by phone to Secrist, and to several people Secrist had suggested. At first, he had been dubious. He had no illusions about corporate fraud; it happened all the time. What threw him was the magnitude of this one. He didn't understand how it could physically be accomplished.

After several interviews, he knew something was there. The only problem was that most of the information he had was useless for his purposes. It was second hand; he couldn't print it. Here were all these widows and orphans and pension funds and college professors buying the stock, he moaned inwardly. Who can put on the heat? Who can stop trading? The cops.

So, on Friday, he'd called Stanley Sporkin, the SEC's chief investigator in Washington, and today, Monday, Jerry Boltz, the SEC's regional director had called on him at his office. He'd told him what he knew.

Now, Blundell decided, it was time to get Ray Dirks to Jerry Boltz.

In midmorning, Stanley Goldblum told Rodney Loeb that Seidman & Seidman had asked for a meeting at 2 P.M. The accountants had requested the presence of the corporation's general counsel. Loeb said he would be there. A few minutes later, Goldblum called again. Now Haskins & Sells, the former auditors of EFLIC, had asked for a meeting on the same terms. That meeting would be at 4 P.M. Again, Loeb said he would attend. Then Loeb called Larry Williams. "Why don't you sit in with me?" he said. "I have a gut feeling it would be a good idea."

Promptly at two, the meeting began. Bob Spencer informed the Equity Funding officers that he had met with Ray Dirks on Saturday. Dirks had told them he had talked to a number of former employees and one current employee. He had even permitted the auditors to make a copy of the copious notes he'd shown them. It was his conviction, Spencer said, that Equity Funding should be in possession of this information. He handed a copy of the notes to Goldblum.

Goldblum did not say that he had received a copy of the

notes earlier that day from Sol Block, Equity Funding's long-time accountant who now worked for Seidman & Seidman.

Then Spencer outlined the charges. It was the first time either counsel had heard with any specificity what the charges were. When Spencer finished, he apologized. He said he didn't believe there was substance to the charges.

Normally, Goldblum would take command of any meeting he attended. But now, he listened, strangely subdued, while Loeb and Williams cross-examined the auditor. At every meeting, Goldblum would sit behind his long, gleaming desk. On this occasion, he came out from behind the desk and sat in a chair near the couch.

As the several stories unfolded, Loeb's impatience mounted. "Well, goddamit, we've got to get to the bottom of this thing," he exploded at last. "We've got to conduct an investigation immediately."

Spencer proposed an investigative audit and asked for Equity Funding's full cooperation.

"I don't care if you put on ten, twenty, fifty, a hundred people," Loeb said, "we're going to find out about this."

At this point, Goldblum summoned Levin, and briefly informed him of the charges. When he showed the notes to him, Levin said, "Yeah, I've already seen them." Levin said his people would cooperate.

Loeb turned to Williams. "Larry, you're going to have to oversee the auditors. In the meanwhile, the legal department will begin its own investigation. I want you to interview Lewis, Edens, Smith, and Levin."

Spencer had one other thing to tell Goldblum: that Mike Balint of Haskins & Sells had urged Ray Dirks to move out of his hotel, and why.

Pat Hopper arrived and did what he could to calm me down. Finally, I was in shape to call my office. It was then that I learned that Loews Corporation had bought between 500,000 and 700,000 shares of Equity Funding—even more than the Bristol block. I also learned that Wallace Bowman, the portfolio manager of Loews, had called me. I had lost Bowman a lot of money on the Los Angeles Life stock fiasco; I hadn't heard from him since. I was glad to hear from him now. I called him at once.

"What do you know about Equity Funding?" he asked.

"Where do you want me to start?" I said. "I'll tell you the same thing I told John Bristol this morning." Here I was, talking to a man who had just bought the block from a man I had talked to that morning—who had bought his block from a man I had talked to earlier. This block was just trailing around the Street, and I was getting a phone call every time it changed hands.

It wasn't easy to tell a man he had paid $8 million a few hours earlier for something I considered worthless. Nonetheless, I plowed in. When I finished, I said, "I have Pat Hopper here. He was an investment vice president at Bankers National. Do you want to hear what he has to say?"

"I might as well," Bowman said.

Hopper talked to Bowman for fifteen minutes. When I came back on, I said, "What do you think, Wally?" I was sure he would be devastated.

"I think it's absolutely hilarious," he said.

"What?" I said. I couldn't believe it.

"Larry Tisch bought this stock, not me."

Several weeks earlier, Loew's public relations people had persuaded *The New York Times* to do a story on Tisch and Loews Corporation. *The Times* had shown no interest in Loews' theater operations, cigarette company, real estate, or hotels; its interest was in Loews' portfolio. So Tisch had told the paper that he was running the portfolio—which had made Bowman look bad.

He didn't look bad now. He said, "I'll have to call Larry and tell him."

No sooner had the men from Seidman & Seidman departed from Equity Funding than the Haskins & Sells men arrived.

"Did you tell Dirks that I had Mafia connections and could put a contract on him?" Goldblum asked Mike Balint.

"I told Dirks that, if there was truth to what he was saying, he ought to be careful," Balint answered.

"Why did you say that to him?" Goldblum demanded. "That's the silliest, stupidest thing I ever heard."

"If there's fraud, you don't know what's behind it," Balint insisted. "It was my duty to Dirks to tell him so."

"That's the silliest, most stupid thing I ever heard," Goldblum repeated. He was mortified.

Loeb broke in. "Mike, you audited EFLIC for four years and you had dinner with Ray Dirks for three hours. Did anything he say strike a familiar note?"

"No," Balint answered. But, on the strength of what Dirks had told him, he had to go to the SEC.

"We want to go to the SEC, too," Larry Williams said swiftly.

Late that afternoon, Loeb received a call from Stanley Goldblum. "Were you talking to those guys from Illinois?" he demanded. Loeb said that he had been. "I don't want you to talk to them," Goldblum said. His voice was unpleasant.

"Stanley, I don't know why you're so upset."

"I don't want you to talk to them," Goldblum insisted.

Then Loeb explained about the theft of the marble owl, and how he had been trying to find out who had been on the floor the previous night.

"You stay the fuck out of this," Goldblum exploded. "Those people were up here by my authority. They had my key and you stay the fuck out of it."

Pat Hopper finally coaxed me back to my hotel. Rest was out of the question. The calls from the East kept coming in. One was from Equity Funding's largest shareholder.

Harold Richards is the president of Fidelity Corporation of

Virginia. His company owned 579,000 shares of Equity stock—received in exchange for a thirty-six percent interest in Bankers National, a Fidelity Corporation affiliate. He wanted information; I gave it to him, just as I had so many times in the previous days to anyone who asked for it. Halfway through, he said, "Would you mind if I put this on a tape recorder?"

He caught me unawares. For all I knew, he might have been working with Goldblum and Levin. Perhaps he knew the whole story. Perhaps he was one of the conspirators. Perhaps this was an attempt at entrapment. Nonetheless, I said, "Go right ahead. If you want to tell Stanley and Fred, go ahead and tell them. They know the allegations."

"Are you coming back to New York?" he asked then. "I'd like to see you."

"I'm out here doing this investigation. Why don't you come to California?"

"I don't fly to California," he said.

It seemed incredible to me that the president of Fidelity Corp., Equity Funding's largest stockholder—which stood to lose $24 million if a total fraud were proven—wouldn't fly to California, no matter how great his fear of flying.

After two weeks of trying, Jim Steen of the Illinois Insurance Department had finally put himself in the same room with Ron Secrist. He'd had to fly to Washington to do so. Secrist had gone there on business.

They were in Room 626 of the Hotel Washington. As Secrist told his story, both Steen and Tom Conneely, an insurance department lawyer, took notes. They had tried to get a court reporter; there wasn't one to be had in Washington.

The phone rang. Secrist answered. He put a hand over the mouthpiece and said softly, "It's Jim Smith."

Smith came on. Secrist listened. He paled. "That's your prerogative," he said after a minute. Then he hung up.

"He told me it was a mistake for me to talk to anybody," Secrist said to Steen and Conneely. "He said if I continued to talk, they would take steps to discredit me." He seemed nervous and distraught.

Victor Kramer, Equity Funding's marketing director, had returned to Los Angeles that day from the East to confront a printer's deadline on Equity Funding's annual report. At 7 P.M., he finally spoke to Stanley Goldblum, whom he'd been trying to reach all day. Goldblum's voice was curt. "We'd better hold up on the report," he said. "There've been some additional questions raised by the auditors."

By itself, the development wouldn't be alarming; an annual report crisis was par for the course; there was always some last-minute negotiating on wording. What bothered Kramer was the way everyone was suddenly unavailable. The air of normalcy had disappeared.

Shortly after 7 P.M., Rodney Loeb, a habitual late worker, walked from his office to Fred Levin's. He opened the door. There, in a circle in front of Levin's desk, were Goldblum, Levin, Lloyd Edens, Art Lewis, Jim Smith, and Jim Banks. Each man was holding a copy of my notes.

Levin looked up and said sharply, "Get out of here. We're busy."

For an instant, Loeb caught Goldblum's eyes. He saw daggers.

Late in the day, Bill Blundell called me. "Would you be willing to go down to the SEC?" he asked.

I said I would.

He gave me Jerry Boltz's home phone. Boltz had just left Blundell's office near downtown Los Angeles.

Pat Hopper calculated the amount of time it would take Boltz to reach his home in Santa Monica. Then he called and made a date for the two of us to testify the next morning.

After dinner, Hopper and I drove down to the Sheraton-

West Hotel to meet with Bill Blundell. We talked for several hours. I decided that, inasmuch as I was to testify at the SEC in the morning, I would sleep at the Sheraton-West, which was close to the downtown area.

That night I had three hotel rooms.

In Washington the next morning, Milton Kroll, an attorney who had represented Equity Funding for eleven years in matters relating to the SEC, went calling on Stanley Sporkin, the SEC's chief investigator. Rodney Loeb, he informed Sporkin, had requested a meeting at SEC headquarters involving himself, officers of Equity Funding and auditors of the company.

"It appears the Los Angeles office has already begun an investigation," Sporkin said. "The proper place for the investigation is Los Angeles."

When Kroll informed Loeb of this development, Loeb concluded that the SEC wasn't taking the matter seriously. A serious investigation would have emanated from Washington.

Loeb did not believe the accusations. To him, the matter sounded as though an irresponsible analyst named Ray Dirks had talked to some disgruntled employees. What made him uneasy was the passive role suddenly assumed by Stanley Goldblum.

Early Tuesday, Loeb cornered Goldblum. "Can these allegations conceivably be true?" he asked.

Goldblum did not speak for a moment. Then he said, "Anything is possible. This could have happened. I don't know."

"They're doing it, Don! They're covering it up!"

The warning from a colleague were the first words Don Goff heard as he arrived at work on Tuesday morning.

"What are you talking about?" Goff demanded.

"Go look for yourself. It's on the computer."

Goff hurried to the data processing center on the third floor. Briefly, he hesitated. Systems men were not allowed in the computer room. If EFLIC was doing something sneaky, he didn't want to be caught. But it was early; none of the managers were there yet. He sauntered inside, walked over to the lead operator and said, "What have you got running?"

"A big run of letters," the operator said. "It's been running for thirty hours." He was tired and irritated; he'd been pulled in on short notice to work on the weekend.

"What does the letter say?" Goff asked.

"Take a look," the operator offered.

Goff went to the rear of the computer, where the letters had come out of the printer and were being folded. The folding went so fast that he could only catch phrases like "unique offer" and "free life insurance" and "assigning you policy number"—followed by the number. He wrote down as best he could what was on the letters. Then he hurried from the room.

Don Goff had never been certain that the phony business existed. Based on what he had seen and heard, he had figured there was a forty percent to fifty percent chance that it did. Now he was certain.

The last days had been a muddle. Elements of himself were warring against one another. He wanted this thing exposed, but he had to have his job. Now, finally, some kind of bottom line seemed to be shaping in his mind. Here are a bunch of guys fooling around with a section of the business, he reasoned. Whatever kind of monkey business they're fooling around with is keeping me from doing a good job. But it's a huge corporation, a conglomerate. If we can wipe out those bad guys, I'm going to have a chance to do well in this organization.

Don Goff went looking for his boss.

"I saw that bullshit they're running on the computer," he told Bill Gootnick at 10 A.M.

"I don't know what you're talking about," Gootnick said.

Between Friday and Tuesday, Don Goff had felt his relationship with Bill Gootnick slowly skating downhill. Now, finally, he concluded that they must be on opposite sides.

"What I'm talking about is an attempted coverup," Goff

said. "Look," he pleaded, "you can't let that letter go out. If there's been nothing else conclusive about something wrong going on, this letter is an absolute admission of guilt."

Half an hour later, Bill Gootnick told Don Goff that he wanted him to take a vacation.

"Why?" Goff demanded.

"So you won't be in the position of having to talk to an auditor."

Ed Lucas of the New York Stock Exchange's market surveillance department telephoned Jim Steen in Illinois to tell him about wild rumors on the floor of the exchange. Was there anything to the story? Steen told him the same thing he'd told everyone: "We don't operate in a vacuum."

In New York, Gerald Lewinsohn of my staff took a call from a client, Roger Collier. Collier said he had heard of our involvement with Equity Funding through Wertheim & Company, a brokerage firm with which he also did business. Wertheim had told him that they were bulls on the stock, and Ray better be right, that's all. If he wasn't right, he was finished.

Two weeks after they had started, the examiners from Illinois still hadn't found a single phony policy or indication of fraud on the books. Nonetheless, the Illinois Insurance Department had heard enough to figure out how the fraud—if it existed—might have been accomplished. The Department decided to act.

First, EFLIC was put on notice that it was under investigation. Second, EFLIC was ordered to divest itself of Northern Life, acquired with its assets, and to return those assets to EFLIC. Third, EFLIC was ordered to return all books, records and operating personnel to Illinois or face revocation of its charter. Fourth, EFLIC was ordered to discontinue the sale of new insurance policies for a minimum of ninety days.

In addition, EFLIC's officers and directors were ordered to

a meeting on April 2 at O'Hare Field in Chicago. The meeting place had been deliberately chosen. When a company is in trouble, you don't go to them, you make them come to you.

That morning, Larry Williams received a call from his old SEC friend, Jerry Boltz, the chief of the Los Angeles office. "What's going on out there?" Boltz asked.

"I don't know," Williams replied.

Later that morning, after it had been determined that there would be no meeting in Washington, Williams called Boltz to request a meeting either the next day or on Thursday. Boltz countered with a demand. He wanted affidavits from Goldblum, Levin, Lowell, Smith, Edens, and Lewis. He wanted them to answer "yes" or "no" to the question of whether there had been phony business on the books. And he wanted some officer of the corporation to say not only that the alleged fraud hadn't occurred, but that it couldn't have occurred without his knowledge.

Larry Baker of the California Insurance Department was getting worried. His man Maury Rouble had been on the job five days and found no hard information indicating the existence of phony policies. He wondered if the fraud was a reality.

Then Jerry Boltz called. Several informants had come forward, the SEC investigator said. One of them had indicated that tapes were being erased in the computer room.

Baker immediately called Christy Armstrong, his chief examiner. "Get Rouble down to the computer room to find out what's happening."

Armstrong called Rouble. Rouble went to a pay phone at the garage level and called Armstrong back. The chief examiner explained the situation. If EFLIC tapes were being erased, he was to order them stopped.

Minutes later, Rouble rushed into the computer room. "Is there erasing going on?" he demanded.

"Yes," one of the operators said. "We do it every week. It saves us money on tapes."

"How can you tell what's being erased?" Rouble demanded. He couldn't comprehend the answer. He was a pencil-and-paper accountant. There was only one way to handle the situation. He ordered all erasing to stop.

"You mean just the insurance company," the operator said.

"No, I mean all the erasing."

"But we've got nineteen subsidiaries."

Rouble called Baker, who put him through to Commissioner Payne. "Maybe you're an ex–insurance commissioner," Rouble said. He explained what he had done. "Here's your opportunity to rescind my order," he said. Tige Payne told him to stand pat.

When Rouble met with Art Lewis, the chief actuary, and Bill Gootnick, the computer chief, Gootnick said he knew of no erasing except for the normal eight-day cycle. Lewis pounded a desk. "If there's anything going on, I want to know about it."

Larry Williams walked down the long corridor to Stanley Goldblum's office, to tell him that he had received a call from the SEC. He used the opportunity to ask the question that burned his mind: "Is it possible?"

"Anything can happen in this world, Larry, and strange things have happened, but if it's happened, I don't know anything about it," Goldblum replied.

Williams spread his arms. "Have you asked Fred?"

"Of course."

"What does Fred say?"

"It couldn't happen. Impossible."

At this moment, Levin walked in. Williams asked him about the charges.

"Laughable," Levin said.

Williams returned to the law offices, passing Rodney Loeb. Loeb drew up. Consciously or unconsciously, his associate had chosen to wear what Loeb always referred to as "Larry's SEC investigator's suit." It was a black suit, with a vest.

The New York Stock Exchange halted trading in the shares of Equity Funding Corporation of America at 12:45 P.M., EST, March 27, 1973.

That afternoon, Gerald Lewinsohn of my firm received a call from a Mr. Manning of the firm of Manning & Napier. He wanted to know if reports that Ray Dirks had a story on Equity Funding were true. Lewinsohn had never heard of Manning. Moreover, he was under instructions from my boss, Walter Delafield, to say nothing other than what had appeared in *The Wall Street Journal.* That morning's edition had carried an article reporting a possibility that accounting statements might not be accurate.

"The reason we want to know is because we have some overseas clients that have the stock," Manning explained.

"You can't trade it. Trading's been halted," Lewinsohn said.

"That doesn't matter," Manning replied. "There's a black market in Europe."

Lewinsohn hesitated. "Just for academic purposes, I'd be interested in a quote," he said then. "See if you can get me a quote."

"Okay," Manning said. He never called back.

The officers of Equity Funding filed one by one into the elaborate board of directors room, looking east to downtown Los Angeles. The board room also functioned as an executive dining room. But this was no luncheon gathering. It was a meeting called by Herbert Glaser, the executive vice president in charge of the company's real-estate division. Glaser, a Harvard Law School graduate, had represented Equity Funding almost since its inception, and had been a director of the company since 1962. He had given up his private practice in 1968 to join Equity Funding as corporate counsel; in 1969, he had selected Loeb, a Harvard contemporary, to succeed him when he took over the new real-estate division.

Outsiders invariably assumed that Glaser was the heir-apparent to Stanley Goldblum's job if Goldblum were ever to step down. They were wrong. Glaser didn't want the job. He knew nothing about the insurance business; he was content to run the company's growing real estate and savings and loan business; and he had other consuming interests. He was active in the Jewish community and worked long hours to raise money for Israel. He was a deeply religious Jew and, incongruously, something of a jet setter who would drive his Jaguar to temple on Sabbath—a blasphemy winked at in spacious Beverly Hills. He skied in Klosters and Vail, maintained a big stucco and tile home in Beverly Hills, which he self-deprecatingly called his "Jewish hacienda." Verbal, musically skilled, a member of Los Angeles's Jewish elite, he epitomized everything an ambitious younger man like Fred Levin might admire, or envy.

Stanley Goldblum, it was said, was not "born to the purple." Glaser was. He had called this meeting because his estate, consisting mainly of 50,000 shares of Equity Funding, had diminished sizably in the previous week—but also because events were underway in which he hadn't participated, and he felt left out. The meeting was one way to get current.

Goldblum took his customary place at the northern end of the vast table. Glaser sat on his right. "We know that Ray Dirks has been spreading rumors about Equity Funding," he began. "I want to know if these rumors are true. I want this for the record. I'm going to ask Stanley and Fred and Sam if they're true—because *I* know nothing."

Now Glaser turned to Goldblum, who was sitting ramrod straight in his chair, and carefully phrased his question: "Are the charges true that are contained in this rumor?"

Goldblum turned away from Glaser. He looked out the window. Then he lit a cigarette. You could almost hear the tip ignite. "Well, you know, Herb," he said, "I just don't know. Anything is possible. I don't know what the rumors are. And I just can't tell you."

For a moment, Glaser contemplated Goldblum. Then he

turned to Levin. "What about you, Fred? What is your answer to my question?"

Levin puffed on a cigar. "It's a bizarre story and there's not anything to it whatsoever. And I wouldn't dignify these bizarre accusations by talking about them."

He's lying, Larry Williams said to himself. That morning, he had read part of the Dirks notes. Also, he knew that Mike Balint had spoken to Frank Majerus, and that, most of all, had impressed him.

Now Glaser turned to Lowell. The portly financial officer seemed to be in another world. Hours earlier, before trading had stopped, he had been asked by his bank to put up more collateral against his loan, or be sold out. He had sought assurances from Larry Williams that the bank couldn't do that because of Section 16b of the Securities Exchange Act of 1934. Williams had laughed. "Sixteen-b is *your* problem, not the bank's problem," he'd said.

"What's your answer, Sam?" Glaser asked.

"I don't know anything about it," the financial officer replied.

Midway in the meeting, Larry Williams was summoned from the room to take a call from Jerry Boltz. Williams is a short, high-strung man who does a lot of shouting. When he returned, his manner jolted Rodney Loeb for the second time that day. He seemed no longer like the house counsel· he was, but the SEC investigator he had been. As he spoke, he began to slap the back of one hand into the palm of the other. What had changed him was a new and hard Jerry Boltz on the telephone. Unconsciously, he was expressing the feelings of the man to whom he had just spoken.

"He wants affidavits," Williams said, "and he wants the six people down there—Goldblum, Levin, Lowell, Smith, Edens, and Lewis."

Levin and Lowell were incensed, and shouted out objections. But Goldblum remained composed. "The written word is such an inflexible thing," he said calmly. "A better way is to go down there and give a deposition under oath and let them examine you."

The meeting concluded with a reaffirmation of Larry Williams's authority to continue his in-house investigation.

All morning, Victor Kramer had been after Stanley Goldblum to issue a statement to the effect that Equity Funding was preparing to purchase one million shares of its own stock. Finally, Goldblum agreed to the release. As Kramer was leaving, he said, "Let's keep my name out of it."

Kramer rushed off to prepare the release. But Goldblum's remark gnawed at him. It was the first time in Kramer's memory that an Equity Funding press release would not begin with Goldblum's name.

That morning, I began four days of testimony at the SEC. At noon, I told the investigators that I had an imperative lunch date. Ron Ronchetti had told me that he and Don Goff were meeting with Bill Blundell. Goff had insisted that I be there.

I was filled with remorse for having turned over my notes to Seidman & Seidman and said so to Goff when I saw him. For an answer, Goff pulled a piece of paper from his pocket with his lawyer's name and phone number on it. "You'll be hearing from him," he said.

"I don't blame you, Don," I said.

Blundell asked questions and took notes throughout the luncheon. I just sat there, listening. As we finished, I said to Don, "Did you tell Bill about the statement Gootnick made about getting Ronchetti out of the picture?"

"What was that?" Bill asked.

"Wait a minute!" I said suddenly. "How the hell would the company have known that Ron brought you and me together?"

Goff smiled at me queerly. "When I got back from lunch, I told the company everything that had happened."

I was greatly relieved. It wasn't my notes that had com-

promised Don Goff. He'd compromised himself. I had to hand
it to him: he'd shrewdly protected himself against the possibility of being exposed as an informer.

At 4:10 P.M., my associate Gerald Lewinsohn spoke to
Dwight West, an analyst at Chemical Bank in New York. West
had a dozen reports on his desk from firms that were bullish
on Equity Funding. The reports had been written within the
last six months. One broker who said he was a technician had
called when Equity Funding hit $19; he recommended that
Chemical Bank buy the stock because it was "bottoming out."
He could tell from the charts. "Okay," West had told him, "I'll
put you down for that."

Three of the men Larry Williams was supposed to investigate
had broken their appointments. He had made four calls to Jim
Banks alone. Each time he was told that Banks was out of the
office. When Banks finally returned his call, he said he was out
of the building. But Williams could hear voices in the background. They belonged to Fred Levin and Lloyd Edens.

At that moment, Larry Williams had become convinced that
the rumors were true.

Williams had always had a queasy feeling about many Equity
Funding people. He thought Sam Lowell, in particular, was a
doubletalker. But about Stanley Goldblum he had never had
the slightest doubt; in fact, his feeling for Goldblum was
close to that of worship. Goldblum was a businesslike man,
never emotionally involved or upset. He was also a man of a
certain righteousness, typified by his service on the business
ethics committee of the local chapter of the National Association of Securities Dealers. Goldblum had been one of the major
factors in Williams's decision to leave the SEC for Equity
Funding. Joining the firm had seemed like the best way for him
to become economically sound. The shares and options he had
received were the basis of his estate. Now the shares were

held by the bank as collateral on a loan—and shaky collateral they were.

Filled with emotion, Williams approached Goldblum, a man of whose innocence he was certain. "How do you save a corporation?" he asked rhetorically. "You get to the bottom of this. You get rid of everyone involved, right up to the top."

"But if I fire them who's going to run the company?" Goldblum responded.

Then Goldblum sent Williams reeling. "I don't think I'm going to go to that meeting at the SEC," he said idly.

Williams did something he hadn't done in years. He began to stutter. "If you don't go, it's all over," he managed. "I don't understand you."

"Look," Goldblum went on, "they're all going to point a finger at me." He shook his head. "No, I don't want to go down."

Williams was frantic. "They can get subpoena power and serve you, and you'll be down there in ten minutes. What are you going to do then, take the Fifth?"

"No," said Goldblum, "I'd never do that."

While at the SEC offices, I heard for the first time from the New York Stock Exchange. Equity Funding stock had fallen from $28 to 14-3/8 in less than three weeks. Trading had been halted because the sellers were overwhelming the buyers.

"We would like you to come back to New York right away," said Jim Davis, manager of the stock watch division of the Exchange. We'd like you to testify regarding Equity Funding and Rule 435. That's the rumor rule."

"I know the rumor rule," I said, "but I don't see the application here. Besides, I'm at the offices of the SEC right now, and I have to testify before them."

"Oh," Davis said, "I didn't know you were at the SEC. Well, we'd still like you to come back here as soon as possible."

I went to the office of Jerry Boltz, the SEC branch chief,

and said, "I just heard from the New York Stock Exchange, and they want to talk to me about Rule 435."

"What the hell is Rule 435?" Boltz demanded.

"That has to do with spreading rumors," I said.

"From what you've been telling us, I don't think you have to worry about that," he said.

"You know," I said, "I don't have a very high opinion of the New York Stock Exchange."

"You're not alone," said Boltz.

LOS ANGELES, March 27, 1973—Equity Funding Corporation of America today issued the following statement:

Rumors have been circulating recently in the financial community regarding the accuracy of statements by a subsidiary, Equity Funding Life Insurance Company, related to the amount of life insurance sold and in force as reported in previous years. The company knows of no basis for such allegations.

These rumors, furthermore, suggest a connection between these allegations and the routine examination of our subsidiary currently being conducted by the Illinois, California, and Mississippi Departments of Insurance. This is entirely without basis in fact. The examination, which has been in progress for the past three weeks, is the previously scheduled, regular triennial examination normal for all insurance companies and, in fact, required by state insurance regulations. No findings have been issued in connection with the state examination.

In response to the rumors which have led to extraordinary activity in our stock, Equity Funding Corporation of America has instructed its independent auditors, Seidman & Seidman, to perform an expanded audit of our subsidiary. The company also has requested the Securities and Exchange Commission to extend the time for filing and publishing the Company's 1972 Annual Report until the auditors have completed their work.

We are confident that the voluntary inquiry being per-

formed at our request by our independent auditors and the
triennial examination currently in progress will confirm our
previously reported financial and insurance results.

The company intends to initiate a program for the purchase of up to 1,000,000 shares of its common stock in the
open market to take advantage of the currently depressed
price of the Company's stock.

When the Securities and Exchange Commission had ruled
in 1962 that Equity Funding's funded programs were securities
requiring registration—a ruling that paralyzed the company
for eighteen months—Herbert Glaser had called an old Harvard law professor, Louis Loss, for advice. Loss, the nation's
leading authority on securities regulation, had called in Milton
Kroll, who earlier in his career had been an associate general
counsel of the SEC. Kroll had represented Equity Funding in
its dealings with the SEC since that time.

Now Rodney Loeb felt desperately in need of help. He
needed someone with muscle who had the respect of the
Equity Funding executives. Kroll was not only an Equity Funding counsel, he was, by this time, an old friend of Stanley
Goldblum's. Moreover, he was an expert in life insurance.

Loeb called Kroll at his home in Washington. "I'd like you
and Peter Panarites to pack an extra shirt and get on the 4
o'clock plane tomorrow. Peter will help Larry, and you can
help me."

Kroll protested. He did not want to come to Los Angeles.

"I'm an important client," Loeb said stiffly to the man whose
legal fees from Equity Funding were $300,000 a year. "I want
you here because I need advice and guidance from someone
I can trust." His voice was hard. He was angry, and he let
it show.

"Those people are too smart to steal in that crude a way,"
Maury Rouble of the California Department said to the other

men in the office. He, Larry Baker, and Jack Doyle of Illinois had gone downtown to meet with Jerry Boltz and Les Ogg of the SEC.

Rouble was convinced that something was strange. The company was not operating in a normal way. But the idea of phony insurance made no sense. "If they were going to manipulate, that's a hard way to do it," the examiner said. It would be a lot easier to manipulate through one of the company's banks, or its subsidiaries, or its cattle program, or one of its foreign ventures. "I've been in the Insurance Department for thirty years. I've never been in a situation where a fellow of the Actuarial Society has falsified a statement. These people are fellows of the Society."

No one had come forward and said, "This policy is bogus," Rouble reminded the others.

Jerry Boltz, the dedicated SEC veteran who had joined the commission for a short period in 1959 and never left, was convinced that something was wrong. A lot of people were coming forward, he said. He had some advice for the examiners. The room in which they were working was in all probability bugged.

Boltz didn't know whether he was witnessing an attempt to manipulate the market downward—known on Wall Street as a "bear raid"—or whether he was witnessing some awful kind of fraud. It had to be one or the other. Conceivably, it was both. Whatever it was the public needed to know.

The company was screaming that suspension could wreck its stock. Nonetheless, that day Jerry Boltz urged the SEC to suspend trading in Equity Funding.

"Those guys were up here again, Mr. Loeb," Gardis Holmes, the cleaning woman, told the general counsel.

"What guys?" he demanded.

"Those guys installing equipment."

"Gardis, what the hell are you talking about?"

"Come with me, Mr. Loeb."

She led the general counsel down to Stanley Goldblum's

office, and then to his private bathroom. On the toilet was a tape deck with a wire going up to a transom. "They had some of the vents out," she said.

"Where else?" Loeb demanded.

"Well, they went down to the empty office."

"Anyplace else?"

For an answer, she led him down to Fred Levin's office. Under the executive's desk, Loeb saw another tape deck.

Loeb went home that night, mystified. He did not know what they were doing. It did not occur to him that they were bugging the office in which the insurance examiners worked.

The phone rang at 6:20 A.M. in Rodney Loeb's bedroom. It was Milton Kroll in Washington, calling to inform Loeb that the SEC had suspended trading in the stock of Equity Funding.

While the New York Stock Exchange can halt trading for a variety of reasons, only the SEC can suspend trading in a stock. What that action told Loeb was that the SEC had hard information, and plenty of it. "You got that extra shirt?" Loeb asked.

"Yes,"

"You'll be on that plane?"

"Yes."

"Good," Loeb said. He hung up, still piqued over Kroll's refusal the evening before.

An old friend called Larry Williams early that morning. He told him that the insurance examiners had been down to see the SEC. He was calling as a favor, he said, and he warned Williams not to say anything. Not only was he, Williams, not supposed to know, but no one else knew.

Rodney Loeb walked down the corridor to Fred Levin's office and opened the door. Jim Banks was seated at Levin's desk, wearing a pair of headphones. Larry Collins was with him.

Loeb closed the door. My God, he thought. He remembered
a luncheon conversation several months earlier in the company's executive dining room. Tom Neff was there, the head
of Ankony Angus, the company's cattle breeding division,
regaling them with stories about his years at ITT, where it
was rumored that the offices of ITT executives had been
bugged with their own equipment.

"Maybe *I* should do that," Stanley Goldblum had joked
that day.

It was no joke any longer, Loeb reflected now. With all the
rumors floating around, Goldblum now seemed paranoid.

Fred Levin passed Larry Williams in the hallway. "The
Illinois Insurance Department has been in touch with the
SEC," he said.

Williams stopped and stared after Levin. How, he wondered,
could Levin know that?

Mike Balint of Haskins & Sells was in the law library with
Larry Williams when Stanley Goldblum walked in. Balint had
just served Williams with a letter demanding that Haskins &
Sells be permitted to audit the books of EFLIC.

"That's like auditing yourself," Goldblum said. He paused.
"If this turns out to be true, we're going to sue Haskins &
Sells."

The monthly meeting of Equity Funding's marketing vice
presidents and sales directors was already underway in the
law library later that morning when Fred Levin arrived. He
surveyed a group of obviously disturbed executives. "The
company has a problem," he admitted. "The auditors are now
in here, and there's no way that they're not going to find it
out. We're in for some rough times—and we'll pull out of it
together."

Levin paused for a moment. "I told Carol about it last night.
I never want to do anything like that again." Carol was Levin's
wife.

Levin shook his head. "The thing that hurts most is that in another year we would have been in the clear."

All the men in the room took Levin's remarks as confirmation that there was some truth to the rumors and that Levin was somehow involved—but not to such an extent that it would impair his role with the company. He offered no further clarification, and they didn't ask him for any.

At 1 P.M., Rodney Loeb walked into the executive dining room for lunch. Stanley Goldblum handed him a message he had received from Bill Blundell of *The Wall Street Journal*. Goldblum asked Loeb to return the call in his behalf. After lunch, Loeb did so.

"Is there any truth to the rumors?" Blundell asked.

"If there is—if this expanded audit shows something—we'd be the most surprised guys in the world," Loeb replied.

That day, Equity Funding began discussions with First National City Bank for a loan of between $17 million and $20 million with which to purchase 1 million shares of company stock.

The company also announced that it was considering legal action against the perpetrators of the "vicious" rumors.

During the afternoon, Loeb told Goldblum that he had asked Milton Kroll and Peter Panarites to fly to Los Angeles. Goldblum was upset. He called it an unnecessary expense.

A few hours later, Loeb and Williams picked up the Washington attorneys at the airport. On the drive back to Beverly Hills, Loeb gave the men a rundown. He indicated his own conviction that the rumors were false. The allegations contradicted everything in his experience. What disturbed him, though, was the manner in which Equity's top officers were responding. Goldblum, in particular, was not being vigorous or forthright, and Loeb couldn't understand that. "You've been with him six years longer, Milton. You've been through a crisis with him. You know him better. But I gotta tell you, I don't like the way he's responding," Loeb said. He made it clear he wasn't questioning the top officers' integrity. It was their business judgment he faulted.

The four men talked for several hours at the Beverly Hilton Hotel. At last Kroll said, "It's 2 A.M. Washington time. I'm sixty years old. Get out of here."

The four attorneys, all alumni of the SEC, met again the next morning in Stanley Goldblum's office. Kroll reminded Goldblum that they had been through crises together before and that they would weather this one.

"I wonder if I shouldn't hire my own lawyer," Goldblum mused.

The remark visibly upset Kroll. "Why do you need your own lawyer?" he asked. "You've got nothing to worry about."

On the way back to Loeb's office, the jowly Washington attorney shook his head. "I don't like the sound of it," he said. "I don't like the sound of it."

"Of what?" Loeb asked.

"Stanley talking about getting his own counsel. It'll look like you're guilty if you go into the SEC with your own lawyer."

At 11:55 A.M. Stanley Goldblum called Rodney Loeb. "Frank Rothman has been meeting with me since 10 o'clock. He wants to see you."

Rothman, a member of the firm of Wyman, Bautzer, Rothman & Kuchel, was a prominent Beverly Hills attorney. He walked in moments later and sat in a chair in front of Loeb's desk. "Rodney," he said slowly, "I've been meeting with Stanley for two hours, and he has told me a story, and if one-tenth of the story I've heard is true, it's a very serious and grave situation. Now I know that you have been preparing an affidavit for Stanley Goldblum and I'm telling you that Stanley has asked me to represent him and I will not let my client sign an affidavit. Furthermore, I will not let my client go down to the SEC tomorrow."

Loeb couldn't comprehend what he was hearing. It made no sense at all. "If you don't let him go, they'll have a subpoena out and he'll still be answering at 10 o'clock."

Rothman shook his head. Then he said evenly, "If my client is subpoenaed to give testimony, my client will take the Fifth Amendment."

Loeb's jaw dropped. For a moment he couldn't speak. "Frank," he managed at last, "do you realize what you've just said?"

"Absolutely. I have heard a grave story."

Now Milton Kroll spoke. "Frank, I know you're a good lawyer, and I know you're protecting your client. But if your client takes the Fifth Amendment, the SEC will put this company into receivership."

"Milton, I have told my client that this is an inevitable result—and I advise you that my client will still take the Fifth Amendment."

Rodney Loeb walked from his office and stood in front of his secretary's desk. "As secretary of this company, I'm calling a special meeting of the board of directors for Saturday afternoon. Call every director this moment. Keep the calls coming. I'll take each call as it comes."

Stanley Goldblum walked into Loeb's office at 12:15 P.M., a sheepish look on his face. He fell onto the couch and stretched his long legs and put his head against the backrest. He drew deeply on a cigarette.

"Stanley," Loeb said, "do you realize that if you take the Fifth Amendment the SEC will put this corporation into receivership?" He had heard the answer from Rothman, but he wanted to hear it from Goldblum.

Goldblum regarded Loeb for a moment. Then he said: "If there's one thing I've learned in my years of association with lawyers, it's to take the advice of my lawyers."

The lights on Loeb's telephone console began to flicker. He stepped outside to take two calls, the first from Judson Sayre,

the other from Nelson Loud. He informed both directors of
the special meeting in Los Angeles on Saturday. As he finished
the second call, Herbert Glaser approached his office. Loeb
took Glaser's arm and propelled him through the door. "Come
in here, my friend, I want you to hear something."

The first person Glaser saw was Rothman, whom he had
known for years. The lawyer's face was heavy with worry.
"Frank, what are you doing here?" Glaser said. He glanced
hurriedly at Goldblum, who had moved to the far corner of
the office. Then he sat next to Rothman.

"I want you to know that I've met with Stanley Goldblum,
and with several other officers of Equity Funding. I have advised those officers that they should obtain counsel, and I
have made some suggestions," Rothman said. He had agreed
to represent Goldblum—and he had advised his client not to
sign an affidavit demanded by the SEC.

Glaser turned to Goldblum. "Why won't you give the SEC an
affidavit?"

Once more, Goldblum reiterated his trust in the advice of
counsel.

"You'll hurt thousands of people if you don't sign an affidavit," Glaser said. "You're going to ruin lives. The employees
will lose their jobs. The stockholders will lose their money."

As Glaser spoke, Goldblum walked across the room, and
stood against a large cabinet at the north wall. Glaser rose and
approached him. "Why can't you sign an affidavit? *I* can sign
an affidavit," he said.

Goldblum nodded. "I can make an affidavit that you can
make an affidavit that you don't know anything about it."

Glaser sank into a chair. For a moment, no one said anything. The only sound was the rattle of keys Goldblum was
tossing in his hand. Then Goldblum turned his head sideways
and looked at Glaser from under his brow. "I guess you think
I'm a prick," he said.

"Yes," Glaser replied. "I do. You *are* a prick."

Rout

That private showdown finished Equity Funding, as the world of finance had known it. From that moment, the fraud, effectively, was exposed. Not a phony policy or bogus asset had been discovered. The company had collapsed from within. It might fool or stall the insurance examiners, but it could not answer the demand for affidavits from the SEC that phony business was not on the books. The SEC had entered the case after the stock began to fall apart. Ronald Secrist's strategy had worked—not precisely as he had envisioned it, but with the same devastating effect.

Yet, only the few men in that room knew that the game was up. The SEC didn't know it, the insurance departments didn't know it, the auditors didn't know it, and I certainly didn't know it. There remained four days before the fraud would become common knowledge. They were days of maneuver, bluff, threat, attempted coverups, and stunning discoveries—days when men had to confront the knowledge that their lives had changed forever.

It was nearly midnight in Brussels on March 29 when the telephone rang in the hotel room of Professor Robert Bowie, director of Harvard's Institute of International Relations.

Bowie had arrived that day to deliver a lecture on Saturday at the Royal Institute of International Relations.

Quickly, Rodney Loeb informed the professor of the special meeting of the board of directors, and the reason for it.

"But I'm scheduled to give a lecture on Saturday," Bowie said. He wondered aloud whether he could catch a plane after his lecture and, profiting from the time zone change, still arrive in time for the meeting.

"Bob, if it will help any, I'll change the meeting to Sunday," Loeb offered.

He just didn't know if he could make it, Bowie said. He knew nothing of the flight schedule from Brussels to Los Angeles. And the concierge had gone off duty.

"Bob," Loeb insisted, "put on your bathrobe, go down to the lobby, and get the airline schedules. You've got to get here for that meeting."

After Loeb completed his call to Bowie, he stepped back into his office. The talk was hard and bitter. Moments later, Goldblum left the room. Glaser followed him down to his office. Goldblum sat at a table in one corner of the room. A secretary served him lunch.

"Are you trying to protect somebody?" Glaser asked.

Goldblum looked up. His eyes welled with tears. "Someday you'll see that I'm innocent," he said.

"Now is the time to save the company and tell the truth. Don't try to protect anybody," Glaser begged.

Goldblum didn't reply.

Within the hour, a trembling Larry Williams was confronting the man he had worshiped. To his disbelieving ears, Goldblum was verifying that he would not appear before the SEC the following day, on the advice of counsel. Nor would Fred Levin, Sam Lowell, or the others. There was no point for him to pursue his investigation further, Goldblum told Williams, because no one proposed to talk to him.

Williams returned, dazed, to his office. He felt that the last four years of his life had been wasted. He knew that he had been taken—by Goldblum most of all. He felt abandoned. The meeting with the SEC, where all the top people from the company were to appear, was one he would attend alone. His investigation was a farce; he was powerless to conduct one. He thought about all the opportunities he had passed up for Equity Funding, a partnership in a prestigious Washington, D.C., law firm among them. He thought about all of his highly paid Equity Funding colleagues—men in their late twenties and early thirties who had been voted units of stock worth $50,000 annually—who were now under suspicion. He thought about the shares of stock he had been given and had put up as collateral against loans, shares that were now worthless.

"I have something to show you," the young file clerk told Rodney Loeb. She led the corporate counsel into Equity Funding's vault, across the corridor from the law offices. She pointed to the ceiling. One of its squares was missing.

"If the square came loose, then it would have fallen to the floor, and it would be here. But there was nothing here when I came in," she said. "Someone removed that square."

Loeb's eyes darted to the far wall. He realized that it backed onto the law library. He had thought the wiretapping extended only to one executive's office; he saw now that it was far more extensive.

"I want you to tack some thin wire across that opening," he told the file clerk. "If anyone reaches through that space, he'll have to break the wire."

"I'm calling you from outside the building. I have two guys who know about fraudulent insurance. They want to talk. But they won't come to the twenty-eighth floor."

The voice on the phone was William Raff's, a young attorney whom Loeb had installed in the life insurance company more than a year before. Loeb said he would work something out.

Then he summoned Williams, Glaser, Kroll, and Panarites; the five attorneys agreed that the two informers should tell their story, in Raff's presence, to the auditors, Seidman & Seidman. "Milton," Loeb said, "give me the key to your hotel room." He then called the auditors and instructed them to have a trustworthy man at the Beverly Hilton late that afternoon.

Hours later, Loeb and Joe D'Armas of the accounting firm met Raff and the two men, Sandy Enslen and Kiyofumi Sakaguchi. Both were frightened. They hung back, while Raff did the talking. The attorney demanded D'Armas's driver's license. He studied it, then said, "It's not you."

"I just got a new hairdo," D'Armas explained.

It was many minutes before Loeb could convince Raff that D'Armas was on the level. Then Raff insisted that another Seidman & Seidman auditor be present. They waited an hour for him to arrive. Finally, Enslen and Sakaguchi began to tell their story.

Sakaguchi was an actuary. His suspicions had first been aroused when the expenses he projected for EFLIC hadn't come close. Invariably, the projections were higher than actual expenses. For the life of him, he couldn't find the answer. Then he heard the rumors about phony policies, and that gave him his clue. The expenses weren't higher because the company didn't need to pay commissions on the business it had "written."

Enslen's story was even more specific. He had joined the company in January as chief administrative officer for Equity Funding Life, in charge of policy issues, policyholder service, and premium accounts. Jim Smith had told him that, because of the company's rapid growth, administrative procedures were weak. They weren't simply weak, Enslen quickly established, they were deplorable: controls were nonexistent; where master files were wanted, compartmentalization was used. But every time Sandy Enslen would go to Jim Smith with suggestions, Smith would say, not now, they were tied up with year-end business. Once, when he had asked for permission to correct the commission accounting system, Smith had flatly said no. "I'm going to back off now, but I'm going to come back at you tomorrow," Enslen had said.

Then, one day, Enslen came upon a case of out-and-out embezzlement.

Whenever EFLIC received a request to surrender a policy for its cash value, the company would send a notice to the sales agent who had sold the policy. In theory, this gave the agent an opportunity to conserve the business; but ninety-nine times out of a hundred the notice went in the wastebasket. On one recent occasion, however, the sales agent had called the policyholder, only to learn that the policyholder had let his policy lapse. Even then, most agents would dismiss the matter as another home office snafu. This agent called the home office.

The policy had indeed lapsed, Enslen found, but the computer records had been adjusted to indicate that it hadn't. Premiums were being paid, according to the records, which gave the policy cash value. It was that value that someone was trying to retrieve.

The embezzler had to be someone on the inside, Enslen reasoned, someone who had access to the computer.

Enslen ordered a check of computer runs on the date the records had been changed, as well as the days before and after. He found two dozen instances of policy record changes. Then he pulled their files. Two cash-surrender checks had already gone out. Two others were in the works.

Sandy Enslen took his findings to Jim Smith. He proposed that auditors be brought in at once. Smith said he would take care of it.

Added to all the earlier evasions, the answer just didn't hit Sandy Enslen right.

On March 29, the California Insurance Department got hold of a report that changed its strategy completely.

A week earlier, insurance auditors had made an inventory of the contents of a safety deposit box maintained by EFLIC at Wells Fargo Bank in Century City. With the stock certificates of Northern Life and some $500,000 in miscellaneous bonds were two certificates of deposit, one for $3 million, the other for $2.5 million. Such certificates can be cashed by whoever possesses them. Now the SEC had just advised the insurance department that sometime earlier in the week those certificates of deposit had been removed from the safety deposit box, taken from the bank for several days, and then abruptly returned by Fred Levin.

To the California Insurance Department, it was no longer simply a matter of proving or disproving fraud. It was a case of $5.5 million in corporate assets that might suddenly leave the country.

Herbert Glaser returned home late that evening from a meeting with Milton Kroll. He found a message from Stanley Goldblum. A few hours earlier, Glaser had learned from Rodney Loeb that several offices on the twenty-eighth floor had been bugged. He was appalled. "What kind of monkey business is this?" he demanded of Goldblum.

Goldblum denied that he had installed bugging equipment and offered to take Glaser to his office then and there.

"There's no point in going," Glaser replied. "I wouldn't know what to look for. And whatever's there will be gone before we arrive."

When Rodney Loeb returned to the Beverly Hilton late that evening, the five men were still talking in Milton Kroll's room, and the Washington attorney was testy. "Get those guys out of my room," he said.

Loeb went upstairs, told the group they would have to move, called the housekeeper, supervised the housecleaning, emptied ashtrays, and tipped the maid $4. Then he went home.

At breakfast the next morning, Kroll and Panarites informed Loeb that they were not going down to the meeting at the SEC. Inasmuch as the corporation's officers would not be present, the two Washington attorneys didn't see why they should be. In addition, they had to return to Washington for an urgent meeting of the law firm's partners.

Loeb was furious. He drew from the two attorneys the admission that they didn't want to be involved in what had become a horrible mess. "We've been fucked," Kroll said. "We've been fucked and we haven't been kissed."

"You've been fucked and you have been kissed," Loeb retorted. "You've been paid a million dollars."

When Loeb got to work that morning, he went to the vault. The wires across the ceiling opening were broken.

By Friday morning, Larry Baker was convinced that the California Insurance Department should seize Equity Funding Life Insurance Company in a quick takeover maneuver. It was the only way to safeguard the $5.5 million in certificates of deposit being held at Wells Fargo Bank. California statutes enable the commission to effect such a summary seizure. The power had never before been exercised, but to Baker it seemed warranted now—and he so stated at a meeting attended by Jerry Boltz of the SEC, and Art De Goede, a deputy attorney general of California.

Late that morning, Maury Rouble called. The company was running out of computer tapes and wanted to start erasing old ones.

"Forget it," Baker snapped.

"It will cost them $1500 a day," Rouble said.

"Great. Tell them to spend it," Baker said.

Jim Steen of the Illinois Insurance Department was having his troubles. He wanted to examine EFLIC's account at Ameri-

can National Bank and Trust Company in Chicago. The bank's
George Metzger was willing, but wanted to wait until Monday.
No, Steen said, he had to do it today. "All right," Metzger
said, "but you'll have to have a subpoena."

Shortly after one, a lawyer for the department in Spring-
field dictated a subpoena order to Commissioner Fred Mauck's
secretary. At 1:30, Steen and two associates served the subpoena on Nicholas Ranallo, second in command of the bank's
internal audit unit. Ranallo informed them that, as of March
29, 1973, the preceding day, there was nothing in the EFLIC
account. Steen asked whether the auditors, Seidman & Seidman, had requested confirmation in the preceding months of
the contents of EFLIC's safekeeping account—bonds worth in
excess of $20 million.

No, Ranallo said, there was no record of such a request. Nor
was there record of a reply.

Odd, Steen thought. He knew that his examiner, Jack Doyle,
had seen the reply.

Then Steen asked Ranallo whether EFLIC had had any assets on deposit in the bank at year-end 1972.

"That would require a special computer run," Ranallo said.

"Then that's what I want," Steen said.

"Only the chairman of the board can authorize that," Ranallo said.

"I've really got to have it today," Steen said.

"I really could learn to dislike you," Ranallo said.

At 2 P.M. in Los Angeles, Larry Baker made his recommendation to California Insurance Commissioner Tige Payne. He
realized that the company had a lot of status in the community,
he said, and that if the insurance department was wrong their
necks were out a mile. But even if they *were* wrong it wouldn't
be a disaster; they would have some personal problems, but no
one else would be hurt. The consequences if they were right

and didn't seize the company were infinitely greater than if they were wrong and did seize.

Payne gave Baker the green light.

Baker instructed a department attorney to call Wells Fargo Bank in Century City, inform the bank manager that they were seizing the company, and order him to let nothing out of the bank. Then he called for a number of investigators to help take control of the premises.

A few minutes later, the attorney reported back. The bank manager said he had no authority to prevent officers of Equity Funding from removing anything they wished to remove.

Baker called the bank manager. "I'm going to hold you personally responsible," he said. "If you let anything out of that bank, I'm going to string you up by the thumbs and prosecute you from hell to breakfast."

Sam Lowell threw himself onto a couch in Rodney Loeb's office. "I don't know what to do," he said. "Those guys have done stuff that I wasn't involved in. When I sat with Fred listening to the stuff Fred had done, I couldn't believe it."

When Lowell left, Loeb slipped from his office, took the elevator to the lobby and walked outside and around the building for a late lunch at Hamburger Hamlet with Herbert Glaser. As he turned the corner, he saw Fred Levin walking toward him.

"Hi, Rodney, how are you?" Levin said.

"Things could be better, Fred."

The two men stopped. "I've been a naughty boy," Levin said then. "I've done some things I shouldn't have. I've told Citibank about it and I've told Harold Richards about it." He paused. "Do you hate me?" he asked. He looked destroyed.

Loeb sighed. "No, Freddie. What's done is done. You need love and affection, not hate now, and, besides, I don't feel it in my heart."

Levin nodded, and walked on.

In midafternoon, word reached the California Insurance Department that records either had been or were being moved out of 341 North Maple Drive and into the garages of Larry Collins and Bill Symonds. A lightning strike was imperative.

After his joust with Ranallo at the bank in Chicago, Jim Steen returned to Director Fred Mauck's office. Mauck telephoned the chairman of American National Bank and explained the situation. The chairman authorized the special run.

Then Steen called Jack Doyle in Los Angeles and had him read off the list of $20 million in corporate bonds that an officer of American National had confirmed as on deposit with the bank as of year-end 1972. The confirmation had been signed by Joseph S. Phillips, a second vice president. When Doyle finished reading the list, Steen's secretary called the bank to verify Phillips's position.

"We have no Joseph S. Phillips," a bank switchboard operator replied.

Steen rushed to Mauck with the news.

"You mean we've got a fraudulent confirmation?" the commissioner said. His mouth flew open; his face grew red.

Steen and his associates rushed back to the bank, knowing almost certainly what they would find. As of December 31, 1972, there was no balance in the Equity Funding account: no cash, no stocks, no bonds. The last transaction had occurred February 15, 1972. There had been nothing in the account since that time.

By way of formality, investigators later drilled a hole in the safety deposit box maintained by Equity Funding Life. As expected, it, too, was empty.

Just before 5 P.M., Tige Payne signed the order to seize Equity Funding Life Insurance Company. Baker passed out certified copies to the assembled investigators. Then, accompanied by police, they sped out to Century City.

Larry Baker didn't know exactly where to go. He walked hurriedly through the corridors of the twenty-eighth floor, opening doors as he went. Finally he came to the legal offices and marched up to Rodney Loeb. "Are you an officer of Equity Funding Life Insurance Company."

Loeb, an officer of the parent company, said no.

"I'm Lawrence Baker of the California Insurance Department. We're taking over Equity Funding Life Insurance Company. We're going to secure the floor."

Baker handed seizure orders to everyone who looked like an official. He ordered all locks changed. Within hours, a force of private security guards was on all floors, in the computer room, even at the company's dead storage room in an adjoining building.

An investigator entered Fred Levin's office to look for the key to the safe deposit box at Wells Fargo Bank. He opened Levin's secretary's desk drawer. The first thing he saw was a key with a tag labeled "safe deposit box."

When Jim Steen reported his findings to Fred Mauck, the director began a series of attempts to block the possible flight of Equity Funding's officers from the United States. First, he contacted the Illinois Bureau of Investigation. The bureau said it couldn't help him because the corporation's officers were in California. Then, Mauck called the Justice Department's Immigration and Naturalization Service. The service said it could do nothing without warrants for someone's arrest. Finally, Mauck called the FBI. Sorry, the FBI said, not in our jurisdiction.

"Goddamit," Jim Steen exploded, "those bastards can't get away with it."

That evening, Fred Mauck decided to seize EFLIC. His department would pull a "quick take": it would serve the offi-

cers with seizure orders at the O'Hare Field meeting it had
scheduled for Monday.

When Mauck called the West Coast, he learned that California had beaten him to it.

Steen, exhausted and nervous, returned to his suburban
home and mixed himself a soothing dry martini. Basically, he
reflected, he was not a physical man. He liked to run an adding machine and play with numbers, but heroics were not his
bag. He'd heard those stories about the Mafia. He wanted this
thing out in the open; he wanted the whole world to know all
about it.

Steen picked up the phone and called Bill Blundell in Los
Angeles and began to tell him what they had found that day in
Chicago.

"Oh, my God!" *The Wall Street Journal* reporter exclaimed.

Twenty-three hours after awakening in Brussels, Professor
Robert Bowie landed at Los Angeles International Airport,
stepped immediately into a pay phone and called Rodney
Loeb. He said he was going to the Century Plaza Hotel. Would
Loeb meet with him there?

Mindful of Bowie's sixty-four years, the general counsel
pointed out that Bowie was on European time. He wondered
if Saturday afternoon would be better. He couldn't make it
on Saturday morning, Loeb apologized, due to a long-standing,
unbreakable appointment.

No, Bowie replied, he'd just like to wash up and get to work
at once.

At 9:30 that evening, Loeb and Stuart Buchalter, a bankruptcy attorney retained hours earlier by Equity Funding, met
Bowie at the hotel. They worked until 1 A.M.—at which point
the professor had been up for thirty hours.

Commissioner Tige Payne went to the executive offices of Equity Funding early Saturday morning. The hallways were empty. He began to open office doors. In one office, he found a big man cleaning out his desk. "What are you doing here?" the big man demanded.

I'm from the California Insurance Department, and I'm looking for some of my people."

"Who are you?"

"I'm the commissioner. Who are you?"

"Stanley Goldblum."

Payne started. Then he said, "Have you been served with the takeover papers?"

"You're making a terrible mistake," Goldblum replied. He hesitated. "I'll ask only one thing of you," he said then. "I want my men to continue selling insurance. I'm sure you wouldn't take food from the mouths of their children."

Larry Baker pulled into the garage at 1900 Avenue of the Stars, his head aching from lost sleep, and looked around for the commissioner's car. Then he saw a Rolls-Royce pull into the slot marked Fred Levin. Levin emerged with his attorney. "Come on up to the twenty-eighth floor," Levin said to Baker. "The commissioner's there, talking to Goldblum."

They took the elevator together to the executive offices, and found the two men.

"You're making a terrible mistake," Goldblum said again.

Baker held up a hand. He warned Goldblum to stop talking. Then he recited Goldblum's rights under the Fifth Amendment. That done, he said, "Now, will you tell us where the assets of the company are?"

Goldblum looked at the floor. Finally he said his attorney had advised him not to respond to questions. Levin refused, as well.

"So you're refusing to reveal the whereabouts of the assets," the deputy commissioner said. At that moment, he knew the seizure had been correct. Larry Baker relaxed.

Rodney Loeb kept his long-standing, unbreakable appointment that morning. He took his daughter to see *Charlotte's Web*.

I had wanted to leave Los Angeles on Friday afternoon, after four days of testifying at the SEC, but I had stayed over to see Harold Richards. Richards had called me on Friday to tell me that he was coming to California after all. Fred Levin was to pick him up at the airport: they would spend a few hours together; then Richards would call me.

By then I had moved back to the Beverly Wilshire. That evening, I remained in my room, waiting for his call. But I didn't really expect it. I figured he and Levin would have too much to say to one another. I was right. He didn't call.

The next morning, I went to the hotel barber shop. Richards reached me there. He wanted to see me, he said, but first he had to go to the company, and then he had to ascertain from his lawyer that it was all right for him to see me. We made a conditional date for noon.

A few minutes later, I returned to my room. Pat Hopper called. For once he sounded excited. "The California Insurance Department has taken over Equity Funding Life," he said. Bill Blundell had just told him. Moreover, $24 million worth of bonds were missing in Chicago. And, Hopper added, Fred Levin's safe deposit box had just been opened; in it were millions of dollars in cash and securities.

I was astounded. I hadn't figured on anything like this. Suddenly, I thought, my God, Harold Richards is going over to Equity Funding at 9 o'clock. I looked at my watch. It was 9:02. I said, "Pat, let me get off. I've got to call Harold Richards at his hotel."

He was still in his room. "Harold, I advise you to go to your lawyer immediately, and don't go to the company," I said.

"Why?" he demanded.

"I can't really tell you. Take my advice. Please go to your lawyer."

"I'm going to the company," he said.

"God damn it, don't do that," I shouted. The only way to stop him was to tell him what I had just heard from Pat Hopper. I did. I feared he would somehow be implicated.

Richards assured me he would go to his lawyer's. A few minutes later, I called my attorney at his home. He hit the roof. "You goddamned idiot, get yourself out of town. If it turns out that Richards goes over there and tells Levin and they take off for Rhodesia or someplace before the FBI gets to them, then you're implicated in aiding and abetting a criminal."

"I think I'll go to Las Vegas," I said.

"That's the worst place you could go. Get back to New York where you belong."

"Okay," I said, "that's where I'll go."

I had come to California without a suitcase. Now I needed to buy one. I had no cash. My credit cards had been stolen two months earlier. I had a cashier's check for $500, but the store wouldn't accept it. The manager finally accepted a personal check. In three weeks' time, I had dropped 8 million shares from a market value of $250 million to zero, but it had taken an apologetic plea to buy a $60 suitcase.

I took the suitcase to the hotel, packed, went downstairs, found a taxi, and said, "American Airlines." Then I looked at the empty seat and realized I'd forgotten my overcoat. I hadn't worn it once in Los Angeles, but it was still winter in New York. For once in my life, I had turned in my room key when paying a hotel bill. The room clerk wouldn't give it back. A bellhop took me up. I found my overcoat, as well as some laundry I'd forgotten. I was just getting into the cab for the second time when a voice said, "Ray Dirks." I turned around. It was Harold Richards.

I had been so eager to leave town that I'd forgotten our appointment. But I was equally eager to learn what had happened.

"Did you see your lawyer?" I said.

"Yes," Richards said. "And he tells me you could be in trouble."

"Over what?" I said.

"For spreading inside information."

"What difference does that make?" I didn't expect an answer.

"And furthermore," Richards went on, "Levin and Goldblum don't have any safe deposit boxes."

"How do you know?" I asked.

"Because I asked them."

I knew then that he had told them everything. "Let's get out of here," I said.

We drove to the Beverly Hills Hotel, went to the Polo Lounge, and ordered drinks. "I got the straight story," he said, "but what you told me is absolutely ridiculous. Fred gave me assurances."

I couldn't believe it. I had tried to help him and he had gone straight to the company. My attorney had been right.

"I made a great financial deal," Richards said. "I proposed that Fidelity Corporation take over Equity Funding."

"On what terms?"

"This is really brilliant," he said. "The terms are we will take them over, and after we take them over we will tell them what the terms are."

"That's a brilliant deal from your standpoint," I said, "but the board of Equity Funding is certainly not going to accept it. Why would anybody be willing to sell out a company for a price to be determined after you take them over?"

"That's the point," Richards said. "If they accept the deal, I'll know that they've been lying."

I had never heard anything so ridiculous. I was tired and ex-
asperated. I said, "Harold, will you please get out of town?
I'm through with this. I'm going to New York."

The meeting with Seidman & Seidman was scheduled for
1:30 on Saturday in the small conference room of the law firm
of Buchalter, Nemer, Fields & Savitch, twenty floors below the
executive suite of Equity Funding. The firm's main office was
downtown; its lawyers used this one when they had an afternoon appointment in the west end of the city, where many of
them lived.

Only a small group had been invited to this meeting—the
auditors, Loeb, Professor Bowie, Yura Arkus-Duntov, and two
investigators from the SEC.

Exactly on schedule, the auditors began to relate what they
had discovered in their investigation. Their account left the
directors restless.

How many phone calls had they made? one of them demanded. The auditors couldn't answer. Had they verified the
material they had been given on Thursday evening by the two
EFLIC informers, Enslen and Sakaguchi? Again, the auditors
couldn't answer. They could offer no concrete numbers.

Robert Bowie became increasingly upset. "Look," he said,
"you met with Dirks last Saturday. You read his notes. You've
had men on the job for a week. You talked to these men on
Thursday evening. Can't you give us more verification than
this?"

As the directors pressed the auditors, Herbert Glaser appeared unexpectedly. At the sight of him, Loeb, Bowie, and
Buchalter rose together and backed him out the door. It was
imperative that he not hear things he didn't already know,
they told Glaser. Glaser grasped the point at once and left the
building.

It was almost with relief that the directors learned of concrete developments from the SEC's Jerry Boltz. He appeared

late in the afternoon with his investigator, Les Ogg, Jack Doyle of Illinois, and Larry Baker of California.

"We know that this is more than fake insurance," Boltz said. "We know that it goes back further than 1968 or 1969. The financial statements have been inflated all the way back."

After the meeting broke up, Loeb and his wife took Mr. and Mrs. Buchalter to dinner at Le Quai, a French seafood restaurant on Wilshire Boulevard in West Los Angeles. "I haven't been drunk in years," Loeb announced. "Tonight, I feel like getting drunk." Only when they were seated did they discover that the restaurant had no liquor license.

That evening, two stalwarts of the Century City sales force, George Friedland, vice president and resident manager, and one of his top salesmen, Munro "Money" Silver, took their wives to dinner. "I know what I'm gonna do," Silver said. "I'm gonna take some money out of the bank, wait for the rise after trading resumes, then a reaction—and then I'm gonna buy the stock."

Silver had good cause for optimism. In the past four months, he and a colleague had gone prospecting among employees of companies that supplied Equity Funding. They were now ready to write Equity Funding programs that would net each man $25,000 in commissions.

Friedland was equally optimistic. A day before trading halted, he had bought 200 shares of Equity Funding at $17 a share. He'd just bought a $500 refrigerator. The rebound, once the stock reopened, would easily pay for the refrigerator.

That the stock would trade again neither man doubted for a moment.

While other dinners were underway around the city, Herbert Glaser was meeting at the Century Plaza Hotel with Harold Richards, Equity's largest stockholder. Richards had called Glaser at his home late that evening and summoned him to the hotel. He had met with Fred Levin, Richards said, and Levin had told him the whole story. He wanted to buy Equity Funding. He calculated the real value of the corporation at $6 a share. He was willing to pay $6 a share, subject to an audit.

Glaser told Richards that any offer he made would have to have the approval of both the SEC and the board of directors.

Richards asked Glaser to arrange a meeting for him with the board of directors. Glaser said he would.

Early Sunday morning, Rodney Loeb called John Schneider, a young attorney in Equity Funding's legal department, and instructed him to prepare resignations for Stanley Goldblum, Fred Levin, and Samuel Lowell. Then, once again, Loeb drove to the airport to pick up the attorneys from Washington, who were returning to Los Angeles for the special meeting of the board of directors.

As they settled into the car, Loeb said to Kroll, "Thank God you were out here."

Instead of accepting the compliment, Kroll complained once more about having to wait for the group to clear out of his room on Friday evening.

"You son-of-a-bitch," Loeb said. "The whole world is falling around me, and you're complaining about not being able to get into your room. I don't want to hear you mention it again."

Two good friends huddled in a room of the Century Plaza Hotel on a matter of precipitate business. One was H. C. Brewer, Jr., a vice president of First National City Bank of New York. The other was Fred Levin. The business concerned stock certificates of Northern Life Insurance Company of Seattle worth $32 million.

Until a week before, the certificates had been in the custody of Citibank as collateral for a four-bank, $50 million loan to Equity Funding. But Levin had told Brewer that Equity Funding wanted to transfer eighty percent of its ownership of Northern to EFLIC, so that the two insurance companies could consolidate their tax returns. The savings, Levin estimated, would be $700,000. To make the transfer, he needed the certificates. Brewer had given them to Levin.

Now those certificates were under guard at Wells Fargo Bank in Century City, seized by the California Insurance Department. Without certificates, Citibank's loan for $36 million was imperiled. Worse, the bank was acting as trustee for the three other banks; if the Northern stock was not recovered, Citibank might have to make good on the other banks' losses.

On Thursday, Levin had told Brewer a story that surpassed his worst fears. On Friday, Levin had canceled the old certificates. Now, on Sunday, in his last act as president of Northern, Fred Levin signed and handed over a new set of certificates to Brewer.

The meeting of the board of directors of Equity Funding Corporation of America on Sunday, April Fool's Day, had been scheduled for the small conference room of the Buchalter law firm, rather than the company's own lush board room twenty floors above. There were two reasons for the choice. The first was the suspicion that EFCA's board room had been bugged. The second was a bit of psychological strategy on the part of the group arrayed against Stanley Goldblum. They needed his resignation; Jerry Boltz had warned that, unless he resigned, the SEC would put Equity Funding into receivership the following day. In the Equity Funding board room, Goldblum was accustomed to command. The new setting would put him on the defensive.

But the corporate chief showed anything but insecurity at the outset. To the contrary, the numbers favored him. Of the nine directors, he, Levin, and Lowell represented one force, and Yura Arkus-Duntov, Professor Robert Bowie, and Herbert Glaser represented another. Between them were three directors with little or no knowledge of the events: Judson Sayre, seventy-four, a retired industrialist from Miami, who had made his fortune at Bendix, where he developed the first home washing machine; Gale Livingston, fifty-seven, who lived in a Century City apartment and was president of three divisions of Litton Industries; and Nelson Loud, fifty-nine, one of the founders of New York Securities, an investment banking firm that had managed the first public offering of Equity Funding stock. All three men had close ties to Goldblum and were disposed to side with the president.

As Loeb tried to call the meeting to order, Gale Livingston demanded, "Wait a minute. We've got a chairman here. Who the hell are you?"

"And I don't know who all these people are," Goldblum said, waving at the half-dozen outside lawyers in the room.

Loeb introduced Richards Barger, the former insurance commissioner of California, whom he had retained the day before to represent the corporation, and Stuart Buchalter and Jerry Nemer from the law firm that specialized in bankruptcies.

"You're not authorized to hire counsel," Goldblum said to Loeb.

"Not true," Loeb countered. "It's inherent in my position. I don't need your authority."

Irritability was the keynote. Not only had the men been summoned abruptly from various corners of the world, but it was a Sunday, the air-conditioning was off, there were seventeen men in the room and the smell of smoke was stifling.

Of all the men, the most irritated was Livingston. He had planned to be in Palm Springs for the weekend and had called Loeb at home to demand if it was really necessary for him to be at the meeting. There was a reason for his seeming indifference to the rumors. He had encountered them once before. Two years earlier, Jack Warshauer, an officer of the Indonesian Development Corporation, had been on the premises to consummate a joint venture for oil exploration with Equity Funding. One day, he had lunch with Bill Mercado, who had been in charge of Equity Funding's computer group but was now work-

ing on the twenty-eighth floor. Mercado told Warshauer that
there was fake insurance on the books. After lunch, the official
wrote a memo to Livingston, the director with whom he was
dealing. Livingston forwarded the memo to Goldblum, along
with a covering letter asking for an explanation. A few days
later, Goldblum replied that he had called Fred Levin and Art
Lewis and had received a satisfactory explanation. He did not
elaborate, but his reassurances had been sufficient for Livingston. Now Livingston listened with mounting impatience while
Jerry Nemer of the law firm questioned Goldblum.

"Stanley, would it be a fair statement that public confidence
in Equity Funding will be at its lowest ebb tomorrow?" Nemer
asked.

"Yes," Goldblum replied.

"Would it be a fair statement that conditions will continue to
deteriorate until something is done?"

"Yes," Goldblum said.

"Well," Nemer went on, "I think it's your obligation to tell
us what you know, whatever that may be."

This time Goldblum said, "If there's one thing I have
learned, it's that you don't make any statements unless you
have spoken with your attorney."

At this point, Livingston's impatience mastered him. He
turned to Goldblum. "Stanley, did you put your fingers in the
cookie jar? That's all I want to know. If you answer no, I'm
leaving."

Goldblum looked at Livingston. "I won't answer on the advice of counsel."

Livingston paled.

Abruptly, the room exploded. You had to shout to be heard.
Several directors cursed Goldblum. Only Fred Levin remained
silent. He bit frantically on his nails.

Professor Bowie then laid down an ultimatum. "If you're not
going to give an explanation to this board," he said, "there's
a method by which we can remove you." If Goldblum, Levin,

and Lowell refused to agree to give testimony to the SEC, they must resign.

"You can't run the company without us," Goldblum replied coolly. "We're the only ones who know how to straighten this thing out."

Bowie persisted. Testify, or resign.

"What about severance?" Goldblum demanded. "What about vacation pay? A fifty-dollar-a-week clerk gets two weeks severance. I've been with the company twelve years."

"These are not matters for negotiation. We're just not going to discuss that," Bowie said evenly. "Whatever rights you have, they will be preserved."

Goldblum had one last suggestion. He would run the company as a consultant for $150 to $200 an hour.

For the first time, Bowie raised his voice. "We will not discuss this at this time and that's all there is to it. We have no question then but to ask and demand your resignation."

Goldblum left the room to consult with his attorney. When he returned, he announced that he was resigning "for the good of the company." The only reason for his resignation, he said, was the SEC's threat to put the company into receivership if he didn't.

Loeb handed Goldblum a resignation statement in which he simultaneously relinquished the presidency of eighty-four different companies. Standing, Goldblum signed it. He did not even look it over.

Levin and Lowell refused to sign. They said they wanted to see their attorneys.

The three men began to file out. The room was so still that the directors could hear themselves breathing. At the door, Lowell hung back. He turned. "I haven't even got a lawyer," he said. "I don't know what you're talking about. I don't know why I'm being lumped with these guys. I'm not part of what they did. The worst I did was play some accounting tricks. I amortized some things when they should have been expensed.

I'm going to be hung by them, and I was not part of what they did. It'll be impossible for me to extricate myself."

The fourteen men remaining then moved to the next order of business. Moments later Bowie held up his hand. Then he rose, opened the door of the conference room, and looked into the outer office. There stood Goldblum, Levin, and Lowell, talking in a corner. Bowie ordered them off the premises.

At 7 P.M., the auditors from Seidman & Seidman gave a progress report to the board of directors on the calls they had made to policyholders in a suspect block of insurance provided by Enslen and Sakaguchi of EFLIC. They had made eighty-two phone calls. Twenty-eight of the calls were to bad numbers. A dozen times, there had been no answer. Of the thirty-five calls they were able to complete, ten of the respondents said they were insured by Bankers; ten said they were insured by Northern; two said they had no policy; and seven weren't sure. Only six of the thirty-five persons listed on the computer tapes as bona fide EFLIC policyholders confirmed that they had policies with EFLIC.

I had missed my flight to New York because of my meeting with Harold Richards. There was nothing else to New York that day; I decided to fly to Las Vegas. Waiting for my flight, I bought a copy of *Barron's*. Alan Abelson's column contained a story of how my investigation had caused the suspension of Equity Funding.

When I landed in Las Vegas, I was low on money. The casino wouldn't cash my $500 cashier's check. Neither would the airline. A taxi driver finally took me to a man who cashed checks for a twenty-percent fee. "How do I know you're Ray Dirks?" he said when I showed him my identification. I shoved the *Barron's* story at him. "Here," I said. "Read it."

He cashed my check for a fifteen percent charge—$75. I was happy to get the money.

In my hotel room the previous Sunday, after Goldblum's call, I had written at the top of a lined page: "What I Would Do If I Were Stanley Goldblum"

1. Go in to the Attorney General in California and tell him you just found out about this yourself. (None of the people I've talked to know of their own experience that you were involved, although they surmise that you were.)

2. Leave the country before Monday A.M.

3. Go in to the Attorney General, tell him you know all, including some things nobody else knows, and you'd like to make a deal in return for immunity. I would, if you did so, say I think you should be absolved of prosecution in return for the complete story, on the grounds that the life insurance and mutual fund industry, the legal profession, and the securities industry would have learned a valuable lesson out of this whole thing—and only you can really tell the whole story.

4. Start writing a book about it.

Now, as I walked around Las Vegas, someone else was preparing to write the first comprehensive story of the Equity Funding fraud. Bill Blundell of *The Wall Street Journal* had gone to his office early Saturday evening, reeling from two days without sleep. As he sat down to his typewriter, the phone rang. It was his wife. "You're never going to forgive me," she said. "I just burned down the kitchen."

"Are you okay?" Blundell asked.

"Yes."

"Good," he said, and hung up. Then he turned to his typewriter, hesitated briefly, and began to type:

> BEVERLY HILLS—One of the biggest scandals in the history of the insurance industry is beginning to break around Equity Funding Corp. of America, a financial-services concern with a go-go growth record in insurance sales.

10.

Chapter Ten

Larry Williams stepped into an elevator at 1900 Avenue of the Stars. It was early Monday morning. He looked away from his fellow passengers; he edged against a wall; he could not bring himself to put his finger on the button for the twenty-eighth floor.

The story was out. He was sure everyone in that elevator knew that Equity Funding, the go-go company with the lush offices on the top floor of the building, was a fraud. His mortification was total. After eight years at the Securities and Exchange Commission running after people just like this, it had gone on right under his nose. "How couldn't he know?" a relative had asked his brother. "He spent eight years at the commission."

"I just didn't know. How could I know? I'm not an accountant," Williams had cried in reply.

Now, he stood motionless, until the other passengers had debarked. Only then did he press the button.

It was 8:55 when Rodney Loeb arrived at the legal offices. Twenty people were waiting for him in the large reception room, a dozen more inside his office. Every department head was there. Every light on the phone console was lit. Most of the calls were from the managers of sales offices around the country, informing the home office that telephone systems were about to be cut off. Landlords had changed locks on office doors. The sales office in Elmhurst, Illinois, had been locked by state authorities; its branch manager had been held up against a wall and searched.

Loeb took a call from Stanley Goldblum's brother, who had been on the company payroll in various capacities for several years. He needed $900, he said now. Would the company lend him $900? No, Loeb said. He hung up, called personnel. "Fire that son-of-a-bitch."

On Loeb's desk was a list of six names: Arthur Lewis, Jim Smith, Lloyd Edens, Larry Collins, Jim Banks, and Bill Symonds. "I want them in my office the moment they show up," he told his secretary.

By 10 A.M., all but Smith were in the waiting room. "Show them in," Loeb said. To the people in his office, he said, "Everybody leave."

As soon as the five men were seated, Loeb told them they were fired. Their response seemed like a replay of the day before.

"What about severance?" someone asked.

"What about vacation pay?" another demanded.

"You can't run the company without us," Art Lewis said. He offered to consult for $200 a day.

"You're terminated," Loeb said. "Get off the premises. You're not to go back to your offices."

When the five men left, Loeb took a call from Larry Baker. "We've got evidence on Mike Sultan," Baker said. "We want him suspended."

Sultan was the corporate controller. It was the first time Loeb had heard his name in connection with the fraud. He called Sultan and told him of his conversation with the Insurance Department.

"I understand," Sultan said. "Don't worry about it. I'll leave."

Bonnie Craig went to work as usual at 341 North Maple. When she got there, the door was locked.

That morning, Equity Funding announced that its chairman and two other top executives had resigned. The company said its operations would be directed on an interim basis by a management committee consisting of Herbert Glaser, executive vice president for real estate; R. W. Loeb, executive vice president and general counsel; and a third member who would be named after consultation with creditor banks.

Tight security measures went into effect throughout the five floors operated by the company. Guards with clubs, some of them armed with pistols, opened the briefcases of all persons entering and leaving their floors. The guards carried photographs of the ten former company officials who had resigned or been fired. The guards were under instructions not to let these men into the premises.

During the morning, the accounting office disclosed that Sam Lowell, who had a monthly nonaccountable expense draw of $1000, had, the previous Friday, drawn an advance on the remaining nine months of 1973.

John Schneider of Equity Funding's legal department had been summoned to the office at 3:30 that morning, after three hours sleep, to help secure the premises. Now, he walked into Loeb's office. His eyes were bloodshot. "There's a check downstairs for $500,000 the securities department got from Stanley Goldblum's redemption of Equity Growth Fund. They want to know what to do with it."

"Hold it," Loeb said. The SEC had ordered him to stop all payments to Goldblum. But this was not corporate money; it was the proceeds of an investment by the deposed president.

Loeb went looking for Peter Panarites, pulled him into his office, and quickly explained the problem. "I can't think of any reason under the Investment Act of 1940 why we shouldn't release the check," Loeb said. "But I have a gut feeling we shouldn't. I need an excuse not to release it."

Panarites suggested he call his office in Washington. "Not

here," Loeb said. If his phone was bugged, he didn't want to make a call that involved Stanley Goldblum.

The two lawyers walked down to John Schneider's office. Panarites called on the speaker phone.

Goldblum, they were told, had put $500,000 into Equity Growth Fund at its founding in 1966. He had promised the SEC that he would not withdraw the money until the fund's initial expenses were amortized. If those expenses hadn't yet been amortized, the money could legally be held.

Another call, however, disclosed that the expenses had been discharged in the first five years. Panarites's firm could think of no reason why the check shouldn't be released.

Loeb and Panarites left Schneider's office and returned to the general counsel's to pursue the problem further. "I still don't want to release the check," Loeb said at last.

"Who's got it now?" Panarites said.

"It's in the securities department," Loeb said. As an after-thought, he called in one of his secretaries and asked her to check with the securities department to make sure the check was still there.

She came back a minute later. "They just released the check to Mr. Goldblum."

"Oh, no," Loeb cried. He called the head of the securities department.

"John Schneider told me to release it," the man explained. Goldblum had called five times that morning. The moment it was released, he had personally carried it upstairs.

Shaken, Loeb went looking for Schneider.

Based on what he'd heard, Schneider said, he'd authorized the check's release. Loeb was dismayed, and said so. Schneider insisted that, as he understood it, it was okay to release the check once the Washington law firm waived objections. He was removing himself from the matter.

Herbert Glaser, Jerry Nemer, and Larry Williams were sitting in Jerry Boltz's office, working on papers for a consent decree, when Stanley Sporkin, the SEC's chief investigator, called from Washington. He had just learned from Panarites's office that Stanley Goldblum had collected his check. The speaker phone in Boltz's office broadcast a stream of curses. Sporkin demanded that payment on the check be stopped.

Williams relayed the news to Loeb. Loeb asked to speak to Boltz. Boltz, shaking, near exhaustion from overwork, shouted, "I won't talk to Loeb. He's violated our instructions."

He *hadn't* violated instructions, the general counsel thought bitterly as he hung up. There had simply been insufficient communication between men who were tired, pressed and under unbelievable strain. He had assumed Schneider would hold the check; Schneider had concluded he should release it.

Now Loeb called Goldblum, who was clearing out his office. "I want that check back," the attorney said.

"It's my money," Goldblum replied.

Downtown, Boltz called Frank Rothman, Goldblum's attorney, and demanded the return of the check. Rothman then called Goldblum. A few minutes later, Goldblum marched into Loeb's office, stood in front of his desk, and said, "Get the SEC on the phone." Loeb asked for Boltz. Boltz was busy. Larry Williams came on. Still standing in front of Loeb's desk, Goldblum yelled into the speaker phone, "You tell Jerry Boltz I commit I will not negotiate that check."

In the background at the SEC offices came Jerry Boltz's voice. "I'm holding Loeb personally responsible."

After Loeb's call, Larry Williams volunteered that he knew the president of United Missouri Bank in Kansas City, on which the check was drawn. At Boltz's behest, Williams called the president, Charles P. Young, and asked him to stop payment on the check. Young was reluctant to do so. Boltz came on the phone. "This is Gerald Boltz, a representative of the Securities and Exchange Commission. I'm telling you to stop that check right now."

Young asked for something in writing.

When the call was finished, Boltz turned to the men in the

room who were working on the consent decree—a feature of which was the appointment of Glaser and Loeb as interim co-managers of Equity Funding. Boltz's face was red. He quivered. "Take Loeb off this thing," he said. "I don't want Loeb on it."

That day, the two certificates of deposit, one for $3 million, the other for $2.5 million, turned up not in EFLIC's safety deposit box—but in a "safekeeping account" set up the previous Friday by Fred Levin. The certificates, it developed, had been purchased in mid-March, and delivered by Brinks to Equity Funding on March 19. Sometime during the week of March 26, Fred Levin took possession of the $3 million certificate, Sam Lowell the $2.5 million certificate. But then Levin's wife and brother-in-law implored him not to do anything foolish. It was not like 100 years ago, they argued. A man might hide then; he couldn't hide today. Levin's wife did not want to spend her life running from the authorities.

Levin then went to Lowell, and they returned both certificates to the bank, and placed them in the special safekeeping account so that no one else could touch them.

That afternoon the SEC office was filled with attorneys representing the banks that had made loans to Equity Funding. The attorneys were insisting on their clients' right to retain all the money in Equity Funding checking accounts as an "offset" against the outstanding loans. If the banks were to seize these deposits, Equity Funding would have no money to operate.

Boltz was adamantly opposed to this. The banks, he said, were acting in bad faith. It violated the whole spirit of what one tries to do with a wounded corporation—mend its wounds so it doesn't die.

Jerry Nemer threatened the banks with court action. Based on recent court decisions, offsets, he said, weren't legal.

The banks demanded to know what additional collateral

Equity Funding had. Herbert Glaser said they would review the situation and respond to the banks the next day. To demonstrate their faith, they would redeposit in the lender banks a check for several hundred thousand dollars that they had placed in another bank.

Both sides agreed to meet again the following day at the SEC, and to do nothing pending the next meeting. Equity Funding wouldn't draw down money; and the banks wouldn't call the loans.

All day negotiations had been under way as to what kind of a consent decree the directors of Equity Funding would sign in response to the complaint against the company the SEC planned to file on Tuesday. Now the entire board had assembled at the Federal Building, in an office made available by Boltz. As a group, they were bewildered, stunned, and frightened.

It was a stiff decree they were being asked to sign. Like most such documents, it entailed an admission by the board of directors that certain unacceptable events had occurred, and a promise on their part to see that such things wouldn't happen again. But there was an added ingredient in this decree—a tacit admission by the board's members that they had somehow been responsible.

"I won't consent," Robert Bowie said emphatically. "I wasn't culpable."

"This is the best we can do," Stuart Buchalter said.

Gale Livingston had brought his attorney, Brian Manion, with him. "I won't accept for my client," Manion said now.

Buchalter turned on him. "You stupid ass. The SEC is dictating. If you don't accept, the SEC is going to put the company into receivership."

"I can't believe the SEC can be so irrational," Robert Bowie said.

Both Jerry Nemer and Herbert Glaser told him that they couldn't move the SEC any further. They had tried. Nonetheless, Bowie was determined to see Boltz. He did, along with Brian Manion.

An hour later, the two men emerged with a compromise.

By Monday night, Equity Funding had been sued in various courts for a total of $10 billion.

Among the calls Rodney Loeb took that evening was one from a woman who said she had placed the entire estate left by her husband into Equity Funding stock.

On Tuesday morning, Herbert Glaser went to the chambers of United States District Court Judge Harry Pregerson, where Jerry Boltz presented him as the SEC's nominee to run the company on an interim basis.

"How come you selected Mr. Glaser?" the judge asked Boltz. "Is he the only clean one left?"

There was no evidence to indicate Glaser's involvement, Boltz replied. But he cautioned that the investigation was still underway.

A Wall Street Journal News Roundup

The Securities and Exchange Commission filed suit in federal district court in Los Angeles against Equity Funding Corp., charging the company with fraud and other violations of federal security laws.

The filing was immediately followed by a court order consented to by Equity Funding. The order granted a permanent injunction prohibiting the company from fraudulent acts in the future, and provided for a plan of operation outlined by the SEC. Equity Funding, in consenting to the court order, didn't admit to any wrongdoing.

In New York, Loews Corporation announced that it had requested its broker to refuse delivery of 216,900 shares of Equity Funding the investment house had purchased in the several days preceding suspension of the stock. A spokesman for the company suggested that the sellers might have had inside information on Equity Funding's troubles. "If they had, they had an obligation to disclose this to us, and they didn't make any such disclosure," the spokesman said.

While no definite seller could be established, it was felt that most of the 216,900 shares had been sold by John W. Bristol & Company.

Loews did not mention that it had succeeded in selling more than 100,000 shares of Equity Funding stock the day trading was halted.

Herbert Glaser and Jerry Nemer returned to the SEC at 2 P.M. for their meeting with the banks. No one was there when they arrived.

By 2:45, the bank representatives still hadn't shown. Nemer called to find out where they were. He was told they had been tied up in traffic but were on their way. They would be there at 3:30 P.M.

By 3:45, no one had arrived. Nemer called once more. This time he was told that the banks were seizing Equity Funding's deposits.

The phone rang early in Rodney Loeb's Westwood home on Wednesday, April 4. It was Ron Hall, the man placed in charge of Equity Funding's accounting operations when the controller, Mike Sultan, was fired. He had documents to show him, Hall told Loeb. He was afraid to discuss them on the phone. If Loeb couldn't see him within an hour, he'd have to go to the authorities.

Loeb rushed to the office. There, Hall told his story to the general counsel and Larry Williams.

Immediately after his assignment, Hall had begun to check the books. On the company's year-end statement for 1972, he had found notations of purchases of commercial paper in December totaling $8 million. There were two slips in the file noting the transactions, but when he'd looked for a bank transfer receipt he couldn't find it.

Normally, in such transactions, the bank purchases the commercial paper in a client's behalf, charges the client's bank account, sends a confirmation and debit advice, and then holds the documents. Under normal procedures, the documents would be in a safekeeping account at the bank.

Hall had telephoned the bank. The bank had no record of the transactions.

Larry Williams took the documents from Hall, put them in an envelope and sealed it. Then he gave Hall a receipt for the documents.

Now the two lawyers knew it was no longer just a matter of fake insurance. There were fake assets on the parent company books, as well.

Herbert Glaser walked through the five floors of Equity Funding offices on Wednesday morning, introducing himself to employees. He smiled, shook hands, patted people on the back. "Things are going to work out," he kept saying.

Few of the employees were working. They appeared listless and demoralized. Many were reading newspaper accounts of the fraud. Glaser returned to his office and took a call from a sales manager in Chicago. *The Chicago Daily News* had reported that the sales manager had been fired. People thought he was part of the scandal; it was ruining his life. Glaser called *The Chicago Daily News,* confirmed that the salesman had not been fired, and asked for a retraction. The newspaper said it would oblige.

Later, word reached Glaser that Don McLellan, the man who maintained the figures on the funding program, had refused to discuss the program with authorities. "Fire him. Get him out of here," Glaser said.

By late morning, Glaser knew the company couldn't operate. There was no money in the till. Creditors were closing in on all the Equity Funding offices around the country. Lights were going out. Telephones had gone dead. Landlords were threatening eviction. It was clear that the company had to file for bankruptcy or be dismembered.

When a corporation gets into financial difficulties, it has three basic options. The first is a straight bankruptcy, in which the company, recognizing it cannot operate further, sells its assets, distributes the money and disappears. The second option is known as a Chapter 11 proceeding. This option is used normally by corporations in which there is no large public financial interest. The debtor proposes an arrangement to satisfy its creditors; only when no arrangement is accepted by the creditors is the company declared to be bankrupt and its assets sold.

The third option is known as Chapter 10. It is invoked where a substantial public interest is involved. A trustee selected by the court takes over the company.

When a company has no chance of remaining in business, the choice is generally for a straight bankruptcy proceeding. The assets are sold, and the money is used for payment of claims.

But under Chapter 10 a company may continue to exist even though it cannot pay its creditors. The purpose of the chapter is to maintain the life of the corporation, so that it may eventually be rehabilitated. The reasoning is that for its own sake and the sake of its creditors, the corporation is better off alive than dead.

There had been no thought on the part of the officers and directors of Equity Funding to put the corporation into bankruptcy. To a man, they had believed that the corporation was sufficiently solvent to make good on whatever fraud was disclosed. Now, with their working capital immobilized by the banks, they had no other choice.

Bob Ochoa went home after work and sat at his kitchen table, a pencil and paper at hand. That morning he had seen the names in *The Los Angeles Times* of all the men who had resigned or been fired. Several sounded familiar; they were the men for whom he had done that special printing job.

Now, from memory, Ochoa wrote out a list of all the securities he had created. Beside them, he listed the number of certificates he had printed. Then he multiplied the number of certificates by the average price of the securities. He drew a line, and added the products. Then he dropped his pencil and stared. "Jesus Christ," he said aloud. "One hundred million dollars! *One hundred million dollars!*"

It was early, Thursday, April 5, when Rodney Loeb returned from downtown Los Angeles, where the Equity Funding officers and their attorneys had worked together on the petition for bankruptcy. Jerry Nemer drove him home. They sat talking until 1:30. Then Loeb walked up the steps and slipped quietly into the bedroom where his wife, Bunny, lay sleeping. She awakened as he undressed, and asked him how he was.

"I've just finished working on the petition for bankruptcy. The company's going down the tubes," he said. Then, abruptly, he faltered. He felt a welling of emotion he could not suppress. Once before, he had been counsel for a company in disgrace— Commonwealth United. "I'll never be able to get a job as a lawyer," he blurted. "I don't know what I'll do." For the first time in twelve years of marriage, he wept.

Thursday morning's *Los Angeles Times* disclosed a curious transaction between Equity Funding Life Insurance Company and its parent, Equity Funding. Documents on file with the state insurance department showed that EFLIC had earned a net profit of $3,056,724—and paid $3,535,000 in dividends to

EFCA. No one could recall a previous case where a life insurance subsidiary had paid its parent company more in dividends than it had earned. All of the profits from the fraudulent reinsurance program had apparently found their way to Equity Funding.

The records showed further that executive vice president Jim Smith's salary had increased from $28,500 in 1971 to $58,716 in 1972; that Arthur Lewis, vice president and actuary of EFLIC had had a jump in salary from $23,417 in 1971 to $44,291 in 1972; and Larry Collins, vice president, had gone from $19,500 in 1971 to $34,162 in 1972.

The story did not say that, in addition to their salaries, all three men had been voted shares in those years worth $30,000 to $50,000.

That morning, Herbert Glaser, accompanied by Jerry Nemer, went to the clerk's office of the United States District Court and filed a petition for bankruptcy under Chapter 10 of the Federal Bankruptcy Act. Witnesses said Glaser looked stunned.

"There are two lines forming at the U.S. Attorney's office. One is for those who tell all they know. The other is for the jail house."

Larry Williams was working on Don McLellan. He had been working on him ever since McLellan had refused to cooperate with investigators. He was afraid to talk to the SEC, McLellan explained, because his attorney had warned him not to. Now, with imminent dismissal hanging over him, McLellan, on Williams advice, called his lawyer once more. His lawyer told him to give his story to the SEC and to Williams, as well.

McLellan had joined the funding department in early 1972, under a man named Dave Capo. One day, when McClellan was preparing figures to send up to Larry Williams for a prospectus, he noticed that the total figure in the presentation was 40,000 active funded programs. He marched in to Capo. "I know we have only 20,000 programs."

Capo stalled him. McLellan persisted. The next day, Capo told him the additional numbers were included to solve a minor problem that would last a year. But the next year they did it again on an even grander scale.

Larry Williams had entertained several escalating theories about Stanley Goldblum. The first was that he was innocent. The second was that he knew but had only lately learned. The third was that he knew, had been involved, but hadn't originated the idea. Now, on learning that the funded program figures were fraudulent, Larry Williams decided on a fourth theory—that Stanley Goldblum had known from day one.

The one thing Goldblum knew was the financial side of the company, Williams reasoned, because he had to know how much the company had in order to know how much it could borrow.

When Bonnie Craig got her check that day, it included amounts for back pay, severance, and vacation. The woman who gave her the check said, "You probably won't find another job like this again."

That week, Bill Riordan, Mike's older brother, realized that there would be no check from Equity Funding to cover Ilie Nastase's winnings at the second annual Equity Funding International Tennis Tournament. He had to pay $23,000 in remaining expenses out of his own pocket—including Nastase's $2000 first prize. It was doubly galling for Riordan: he was Nastase's manager.

As the worst week of his life was coming to an end, Herbert Glaser received a call from his accountant, Roy Horn. Horn, once an agent of the Internal Revenue Service, had worked for Wolfson, Weiner on the Equity Funding account, then quit to set up private practice. His clients included most of the top

brass at Equity. Now Horn explained he had an urgent need
to see Glaser.

In Glaser's office late that afternoon, Horn told of a call
from Sam Lowell the previous Friday, March 30. Lowell had
decided to commit suicide. He wanted Horn to take care of
his family. He had borrowed heavily against his stock. "Friends
are as good as the market is," he said, "and Stanley won't per-
mit bankruptcy. He'll fire me."

Horn got Lowell's secretary on the phone. "Don't let him out
of the office," he said. "I'm coming over there."

Horn calmed Lowell down, then urged the financial officer
to unburden himself. Lowell said he had been lulled into many
of the schemes, most of which were accomplished fact when he
encountered them. He said the man who had lulled him was
Goldblum. The story about false insurance was correct, he
went on, but Herbert Glaser and Rodney Loeb had no idea
what was going on. They had been kept in the dark.

On his way home, Horn had made a recording of his encounter. He had a transcript of the confession, he said now.
He didn't know what to do with it. He trusted Glaser, and
wanted his advice.

"Now that you've told me this, I'm obliged to call the SEC,"
Glaser said.

It was after working hours. The SEC's switchboard was shut
down. Glaser obtained Jerry Boltz's night number from Stuart
Buchalter and finally reached the SEC's regional chief.

Boltz listened to the story, then told Glaser that he could
not use the story unless Lowell had been assured of his consti-
tutional rights.

As the new week began, Rodney Loeb made an early afternoon visit to the United California Bank on Wilshire Boulevard
to discuss his unsecured $75,000 loan. The meeting lasted an
hour. When it ended, Loeb took the narrow stairway from the
bank to the parking lot. On the stairway, he met Stanley Goldblum.

In the week since the two men had spoken Loeb had managed to come to terms with the calamity but not with the embarrassment he had suffered as a consequence of the delivery of the checks to Stanley Goldblum. There had been two checks, it developed, one to Goldblum for $458,849.70, the other to Goldblum's wife for $72,637.80.

"Stanley, what did you do with those checks?" Loeb demanded now.

"I tore them up," Goldblum said.

Loeb was overwhelmed. "Thank you," he said. "I appreciate it."

When Loeb returned to his office, he learned the day's big revelation—that Goldblum had arranged for someone to put a man on an airplane to Kansas City, that the United Missouri Bank had cashed the checks, that $355,753.57 of the proceeds had been used to repay a loan the bank had made to Goldblum, and that $175,733.93 had been put into a new account and removed the following day. (Goldblum's attorney would later place the remaining money in an escrow account, pending litigation.)

Paul Conrad's editorial cartoon in *The Los Angeles Times* of April 11, 1973, was a drawing of the Brooklyn Bridge. On the bridge was a sign. It said: FOR SALE. CONTACT EQUITY FUNDING.

That day, Robert M. Loeffler, forty-nine, a smallish man with a diffident manner, arrived in Los Angeles to take charge of Equity Funding. Loeffler had been appointed the day before by U.S. District Court Judge Harry Pregerson to reorganize and rehabilitate the company under federal bankruptcy laws. Loeffler, senior vice president and general counsel of Investors Diversified Services Incorporated of Minneapolis, had resigned his post in order to take the trustee's job. His fee was $12,500 a month, living expenses in Los Angeles, and paid travel to and from Minneapolis every weekend.

The choice of Loeffler had culminated a frantic week of search for a top man. Everyone knew it was a killing job. Loeffler's acceptance had been conditional; if he didn't like it, he could quit. Without a trustee, the organization of Equity Funding could not get underway. Everyone was worried that Loeffler would take one look, turn around, and go home.

The moment he arrived in the office, he was besieged by people. Jerry Nemer pulled him into an office and talked to him for fifteen minutes. "Take your time," he said to Loeffler. "Let's get the thing organized."

Loeffler took his time—but not on organization. On Friday, the thirteenth, Equity Funding paychecks, bearing the signatures of Stanley Goldblum and Samuel Lowell, began bouncing all over the United States. The corporation put a man on a plane to Rochester to pick up a new signature plate. In the meanwhile, Bob Loeffler spent most of the day signing new checks by hand.

That day, Rodney Loeb walked into the office of James Murdy, a young but experienced business executive who had just been appointed chief financial officer of Equity Funding. Murdy had a visitor—Bill Blundell of *The Wall Street Journal.* Two weeks earlier, Loeb had told Blundell on the phone that the executives of Equity Funding would be "the most surprised guys in the world" if the rumors turned out to be true. Now, Murdy introduced Loeb to Blundell. Grinning, Blundell said, "Surprise."

A sign went up in the computer room at Equity Funding early in May. It said: THANK GOD FOR WATERGATE.

As Watergate preempted Equity Funding on the front pages, Bob Loeffler got to work. He looked in on Stanley Goldblum's old office, said it was a fine place for conferring sainthood, and installed himself down the hall where Fred Levin had been. Early in May, Loeffler exposed his first project—a lawsuit against Stanley Goldblum.

Sometime before 1969, Loeffler charged, Stanley Goldblum began a scheme to defraud Equity Funding of his salary and other compensation totaling more than $1 million. The false reports the corporate president had given directors and stockholders made sales, revenues and profits look far greater than they actually were. As a consequence, the company paid Stanley Goldblum exorbitant compensation.

"The services of Stanley Goldblum as president and chief executive," Loeffler charged, "were worthless and in fact positively damaging to Equity Funding."

As he dug further into the shambles he had inherited, Bob Loeffler could scarcely believe what he found. The company, he concluded, had spent so much time on the fake books that the real books were worthless. There was, for example, no record of incoming checks. To try to construct a balance sheet for April 5—the date Equity Funding went into bankruptcy— seemed all but impossible. Loeffler began to wonder if Equity Funding had ever been profitable.

But there were some hopeful notes. There might be $120 million in bogus assets, but there were real assets whose condition was unchanged. The cattle operation was intact; the cattle were there. The real-estate and savings and loan operations were solid. Both Bankers National and Northern Life were legitimate insurance companies. By June, Loeffler concluded that Equity Funding could be salvaged without liquidation. On June 4, he reported his preliminary findings at a hearing for creditors and stockholders held before Judge Harry Pregerson. "I am reasonably confident," he told the court, "that once accurate balance sheet figures are available they will show assets at least equal to liabilities. Other than falsification of accounts to create profits, the fraudulent activity was without effect on the company's real customers." There was no evidence of bogus assets or transactions at Equity Funding's forty main and second-line subsidiaries. "There can be no question that, except for Equity Funding Life and the books of the parent firm, the assets that are supposed to be there are there."

Through the summer, Loeffler, Glaser, Loeb, a crew of lawyers from O'Melveny and Myers, and Jim Murdy, the chief financial officer, labored over the reorganization. By fall, they thought they had the outlines of a small but salvable company. It would own two insurance companies. Everything else was for sale; some of the properties had already been sold.

Two banks—Liberty Savings & Loan in Beverly Hills and Bishops Bank in the Bahamas—netted $24.3 million. The company's real-estate properties netted $4 million. Ankony Angus, the cattle breeding operation, went on the market. Oil and gas exploration operations, a casualty operation, and assorted international assets were also about to be sold. The company's sales force had been reduced from 4200 men in 152 offices to 1250 men in fifty-seven offices and rechristened Independent Securities Corporation. In EFLIC days, there was no control on the sales force; now it was tightly budgeted.

Downstairs on the sixth floor, J. Carl Osborne, a rangy, leathered, occasional rodeo rider from Ketchum, Idaho, who had been lured from an early retirement to take charge of EFLIC as a special deputy of the Illinois Insurance Department, had halved his staff, reduced monthly expenses from $250,000 to $100,000. To his delight, two-thirds of EFLIC's 33,000 legitimate policyholders continued to pay their premiums.

Osborne had two choices: to attempt to put EFLIC back on its feet or to sell EFLIC's policies to another insurance company. Because of the tremendous handicap the company would have operating with its new, ineradicable reputation, Osborne finally decided to sell. Equity Funding was to be given first priority to assume the business in behalf of Bankers National or Northern Life. That failing, EFLIC's assets would be sold to an outside company.

"I'm not going to go out and have a fire sale," Osborne warned. "I don't want any liens on these policies. Everybody's cash value is good, everybody gets full up." The caretaker sighed. "This was a real good company. It had over $10,000,000 in premiums annually, $1.05 billion of insurance in force. If you have a company with a billion dollars insurance in force, you've got a darn good company."

By November, the trustee's projected reorganization of Equity Funding was complete. It envisioned a company earning between $7 million and $8 million after taxes a year. There would be 5 million shares—1.25 million issued to the old stockholders, the remainder issued to creditors. The company would earn about $1.50 a share. At ten times earnings, the stock would sell for $15 a share. Each stockholder, in effect, would have shares worth approximately seventeen percent of the value he held on the day Equity Funding stopped trading. Thus, his old Equity Funding stock might be worth about $2.50 a share.

Even this low price for Equity Funding's stockholders could be achieved only by the grace of the creditors, who would be disposed to settle for far less than what they were owed only in order to wind up their affair with the company. For Bob Loeffler's initial report to the court on June 4th had been too optimistic. By 1974, the trustee calculated that liabilities exceeded assets by $42.1 million. The creditors would consider a settlement for two reasons. First, the great majority of shareholders of Equity Funding were unlike shareholders in other bankrupt companies; they had clearly been defrauded, and they might assume the status of creditors in a legal proceeding. Second, everyone wanted to resolve the complicated legal question if possible.

Was Equity Funding ever worth anything? To find out costs more than the knowledge is worth. One living man could answer that question if he chose. But, as his and his co-defendants' trial approached, no one knew if he would.

11.

Who, What, When, How, and Why

One day in 1969—a theory concerning the origins of the Equity Funding fraud had it—two executives of EFLIC found out that a third was getting rich on a scam deal he had invented. First he would create a phony life insurance policy. Then he would sell the policy to a reinsurer. After a while, he would kill the "insured."

The EFLIC scammer would forge a death certificate and send it to the company that had reinsured the phony policy. A check from the unsuspecting reinsurer would be sent to the executive at EFLIC, who would cash the check and pocket the money. The two EFLIC executives who learned of the scam deal demanded to be cut in. Then the top brass found out about it and were horrified—until they considered the possibilities.

The story came complete with motive. In 1969, Equity Funding stood to lose money for the first time in its history. The top brass couldn't stand the thought.

The problem with the story, as with reality, is that while method might lend itself to precise scrutiny, motive rarely if ever does—and that, in any case, the two are so inextricably intertwined as to inhibit the examination of either. Only after each strand is isolated can the braid of a crime be woven.

This a federal grand jury in Los Angeles purports to have done. The Equity Funding fraud, it asserts, did not originate in 1969, as almost everyone assumed, but in 1965. The fraud was the result not of a sudden emergency occasioned by a decline in the price of the company's stock, but of a labyrinthine effort to make a great deal out of not very much. Stanley Goldblum, the grand jury further asserts, was not attempting to plug a dike. He was attempting to build one.

On November 1, 1973, seven months to the day after Goldblum resigned as chairman of the board and president of Equity Funding Corporation of America—and, ironically, on the very day that the bankrupt corporation signed a letter of understanding with its creditor banks regarding terms of reorganization—the grand jury indicted twenty-two men, including Goldblum, on 105 criminal counts. The charges: Conspiracy to commit felonies, including securities fraud, mail fraud, bank fraud, interstate transportation of counterfeit securities and other securities obtained by fraud, electronic eavesdropping, and the filing of false documents with the Securities and Exchange Commission. Twenty of the twenty-two defendants were former executives and employees of Equity Funding. The other two were members of Equity Funding's independent accounting firm, which had done the company's books since its inception. An essentially similar indictment was issued on the same day by the DuPage County Grand Jury in Illinois, where Equity Funding Life Insurance Company was chartered.

A surprising—and ironic—feature of the federal indictment was the inclusion of Ronald Secrist and Frank Majerus as "Unindicted co-conspirators." It was Secrist's decision to expose the fraud that led to the indictments. It was Majerus who first gave critical confirmation of Secrist's charges to the authorities.

The grand jury's findings were based on a prolonged investigation undertaken jointly by the Securities and Exchange Commission, the Federal Bureau of Investigation, the Postal

Inspection Service, the Illinois and California Departments of Insurance, the United States Attorney's office in Los Angeles, and the Attorney General's office in Illinois. The most conspicuous strand of this raveled tale bore the marks of Stanley Goldblum.

In the language of the indictment, Goldblum "would set periodic standards for growth in income, assets and earnings of EFCA [Equity Funding Corporation of America], which growth he did not expect to be achieved and which growth was not achieved, through the conduct of legitimate business operations." According to the indictment, he would then arrange for various officers and employees of EFCA and its subsidiaries to make fictitious bookkeeping entries that would give a false portrayal of the income and assets of the company. It was Stanley Goldblum who directed his employees to use computers to create fictitious insurance policies, the indictment alleged, and it was Stanley Goldblum who directed that counterfeiting be undertaken.

As to motive, "said acts, transactions and practices," the indictment asserted,

> would enable the defendants to continue EFCA's normal business operations, to fraudulently increase the market price of EFCA stock, to acquire assets and companies for EFCA with falsely valued EFCA stock and other considerations, to borrow money on behalf of EFCA, to realize incomes from EFCA salaries, commissions, bonuses, fees and expense allowances, to sell fraudulently valued EFCA stock owned by them, all the while concealing from other EFCA shareholders, the general business community, regulatory agencies and the public the true business and financial condition of EFCA.

The chronology of the indictment weaves the strands of a story unparalleled in the annals of finance:

January 15, 1965: Stanley Goldblum tells one Jerome H.

Evans, at that time the chief financial officer of Equity Funding, to make "fictitious entries in certain receivable and income accounts of EFCA."

March 8, 1965: Goldblum signs the company's annual report. It contains "inflated figures for certain receivable and income accounts, and for earnings per share." (This was Equity Funding's first annual report as a publicly held corporation. If the allegation is true, then Equity Funding never issued an honest annual report to its public stockholders.)

September 30, 1966: Goldblum and Evans sign an application to list shares of EFCA common stock for trading on the American Stock Exchange. (The application, perforce, is based on erroneous data.)

March 15, 1968: Julian S. H. Weiner and Marvin Al Lichtig, representing the accounting firm of Wolfson, Weiner and Company, issue an unqualified certification of the 1967 Equity Funding financial statement. (They know, the indictment asserts elsewhere, that the statement is false.)

January 16, 1969: Goldblum sells 5000 shares of Equity Funding stock—one of many such sales. A few days later, Evans sells 2200 shares.

February 22, 1969: Goldblum instructs Fred Levin that "publicly held companies do not lose money."

September 19, 1969: Sam Lowell tells Levin that the funded loans and other asset accounts are inflated, and that certain liabilities which should have been disclosed on EFCA's financial statement have not been disclosed.

November 30, 1969: David Capo, in charge of the funded loan department, acting on instructions from Samuel Lowell, makes the first in a series of journal entries to an EFCA account known as Client Contractual Receivable.

December 15, 1969: Fred Levin, Jim Smith, Art Lewis, Lloyd Edens, and Larry Collins discuss the "placing in force, and reinsuring, of life insurance policies that are not in force."

December 15, 1969: William Mercado, then the head of

Equity Funding's computer operations, supervises the preparation of a computer printout of funded loan receivable accounts that are intentionally inflated.

February 12, 1970: Julian Weiner and Sol Block discuss the "accounting treatment" to be given to EFCA's client contractual receivable account.

March 3, 1970: Samuel Lowell explains to Mike Sultan, Equity Funding's controller, that, because EFCA's legitimate earnings for the first quarter of 1970 are insufficient, Sultan will be required to make certain journal entries to increase the income reflected on EFCA's books.

May 19, 1970: Stanley Goldblum signs an agreement for the "purported sale to Compania de Estudios y Asuntos of the rights to certain net trail commissions." (The company is a shell, the indictment alleges, with no ability to pay EFCA for these rights. EFCA, nonetheless, would carry the item as an asset on its books.)

June 18, 1970: Mike Sultan makes a journal entry recording notes payable to Loeb, Rhoades & Company and a note receivable from Établissement Grandson. (Again, Établissement Grandson, a shell company, has no capacity to pay such a note—but the note would appear on the books as an asset to offset the liability to Loeb, Rhoades.)

August 10, 1970: Levin, Smith, Art Lewis, Edens, and Collins discuss the "manner and method of creating and reinsuring fictitious insurance policies."

August 20, 1970: Goldblum and Marvin Lichtig, now the EFCA treasurer, sign an application to list shares of EFCA common stock for trading on the New York Stock Exchange.

September 15, 1970: Goldblum and Levin discuss "the creation and reinsurance of fictitious insurance policies."

October 14, 1970: Goldblum and Lowell order $2 million to be sent to Account Number 001-1-821-774 at Banque Cifico-Leumi in Geneva, Switzerland for the account of Établissement Grandson.

November 2, 1970: Computer specialist Mike Keller—at the direction of Art Lewis—writes a computer program for the creation of fictitious insurance policies with a face value of $430 million and a total yearly premium of $5.5 million.

December 4, 1970: Art Lewis sends a memorandum to Mike Keller and Jim Smith "concerning the relationship between EFLIC's fictitious insurance business and its reinsurance commitments."

December 16, 1970: Samuel Lowell discusses with William Mercado, the head of computer operations, the preparation of a computer printout of funded loan receivable accounts that would contain an intentionally inflated total.

January 20, 1971: Smith, Lewis, Edens, Collins—and "unindicted co-conspirators" Francis D. Majerus and Ronald Secrist—fill out and sign forms and "use the forms to create fictitious insurance policy files."

March 24, 1971: Smith explains to Jim Banks that fictitious insurance policies have been reinsured and that Banks will be expected to make death claims on various of the fictitious policies.

April 1, 1971: Sam Lowell informs Roger Coe, manager of Bishops Bank and Trust Company, Limited, an Equity Funding subsidiary, that Stanley Goldblum has directed Coe to cease attempting to confirm a certain $2 million receivable on the books of Bishops Bank.

May 19, 1971: Jim Banks makes "the first in a series of death claims on fictitious EFLIC insurance policies by mailing to Phoenix Mutual Life Insurance Company a letter enclosing documents relating to the death of Fenton Taylor, insured under fictitious EFLIC policy number 7101481."

July 20, 1971: Richard Gardenier, the young man who worked at 341 North Maple, supervises and helps to prepare fictitious insurance files, and Smith, Art Lewis, Dave Capo, Lloyd Edens, and Larry Collins complete the documents in the fictitious files and forge signatures on them.

September 30, 1971: Sam Lowell asks Fred Levin how much income EFLIC can reflect on its books in order to reduce the amount of fictitious business that would need to be inserted on EFCA's books.

November 30, 1971: Levin, Sultan, Smith, Art Lewis, and Edens discuss the transfer of funds from EFCA to EFLIC and the counterfeiting of various documents reflecting fictitious purchases of commercial paper.

December 10, 1971: Stanley Goldblum tells Mike Sultan to "proceed with the counterfeiting of documents relating to fictitious purchases of commercial paper."

December 18, 1971: Lowell and Sultan discuss "the absence of assets in EFLIC and the necessity to transfer funds to EFLIC to conceal the absence of assets."

December 21, 1971: Art Lewis and Dave Capo "discuss creation of a computer printout listing which would contain fictitious funded loan accounts."

December 23, 1971: Sultan, Edens, and Gary Beckerman, then head of communications for EFCA, discuss "the counterfeiting of documents relating to fictitious purchases of commercial paper."

December 23, 1971: Art Lewis and Alan Green, a computer specialist, discuss "creating a computer printout listing which would contain fictitious funded loan accounts."

January 14, 1972: Bill Symonds—acting on instructions from Art Lewis and Lloyd Edens —begins to manipulate computer records "so as falsely to show five thousand lapsed policies to be in force."

February 15, 1972: Fred Levin and Jim Smith discuss "the amount of fictitious insurance business which would have to be created in 1972."

March 1, 1972: Mike Sultan and Sol Block discuss "the making of an intentional mistake in the calculation of EFCA's 1971 earnings per share."

March 10, 1972: Bill Symonds and Rick Gardenier discuss the creation of fictitious insurance files.

March 15, 1972: Goldblum, Lowell, and Sultan discuss "the making of fictitious entries to EFCA's funded loans and accounts receivable account and commission income accounts."

July 14, 1972: Smith, Art Lewis, Capo, Collins, Edens, Banks, Mark Lewis (Art Lewis's brother), and Rick Gardenier help to prepare fictitious hard-copy insurance documents and forge signatures on the documents.

October 26, 1972: Goldblum, Levin, Sultan, Smith, Art Lewis, and Edens discuss the printing of counterfeit bonds.

December 18, 1972: Goldblum, by phone, discusses with Levin the renting of an office in Chicago, Illinois, to be used as a mail drop in connection with the use of counterfeit bank documents.

December 20, 1972: Gary Beckerman—on the instructions of Stanley Goldblum—orders stationery bearing the letterhead of the American National Bank and Trust Company of Chicago.

December 27, 1972: Dave Capo and Don McLellan compile addresses of various persons to whom funded loan confirmations could be sent.

January 5, 1973: Lowell confers with the manager of computer operations, unindicted co-conspirator William Gootnick, concerning the company's fictitious life insurance business.

January 8, 1973: Banks and Smith discuss "the amount of money to be derived in 1973 from making death claims on fictitious life insurance policies."

January 15, 1973: Mike Sultan makes entries on counterfeit bank documents relating to "fictitious purchases of commercial paper."

January 15, 1973: Levin, Smith, Sultan, Edens, and Beckerman meet at EFCA's printing plant and commence the printing of counterfeit bonds.

February 27, 1973: Mike Keller and Al Green instruct un-indicted co-conspirator Aaron Venouziou on writing computer programs for fictitious insurance business.

March 12, 1973: Goldblum, Levin, Sultan, Smith, Art Lewis, Edens, and Banks discuss the disposition of the counterfeit bonds.

March 14, 1973: Stanley Goldblum and Jim Banks discuss the electronic surveillance of state insurance examiners who have begun working on EFCA's business premises.

March 14, 1973: Collins and Banks, with the help of two experts, "make the first of a series of installations of electronic surveillance equipment."

March 22, 1973: Bill Gootnick, an unindicted co-conspirator —acting on the instructions of Smith, Art Lewis, Edens, Collins, and Banks—supervises "the writing of computer programs designed to conceal the existence of EFLIC's fictitious insurance business from auditors and state examiners."

March 23, 1973: Collins, Symonds, and Mark Lewis—acting on orders from Jim Smith—remove all documents relating to the creation of insurance files from 341 North Maple Drive.

March 26, 1973: Goldblum, Lowell, Levin, Sultan, Smith, Art Lewis, Edens, Collins, Banks, and McLellan sell shares of EFCA stock.

March 27, 1973: Collins and Banks, with professional help, try to install electronic surveillance equipment "designed to intercept telephone conversations of state insurance examiners."

March 30, 1973: Marvin Lichtig asks Fred Levin whether Levin wants "any documents destroyed."

Equity Funding, the grand jury asserts, was not the profitable public company it portrayed itself to be. It was a loser.

For the year ending December 31, 1969, the corporation and its subsidiaries reported earnings from consolidated operations before income taxes of $12,590,278. In fact, the indictment states, the corporation lost "not less" than $6 million. In 1970, EFCA reported earnings before taxes of $10,751,366.

In fact, the indictment states, the corporation lost "not less" than $7 million. There were numerous instances of misstated assets, according to the indictment. As one example, Equity Funding's 1970 statement showed a note receivable from Établissement Grandson for more than $9 million. "Said Établissement Grandson was a shell corporation which did not owe EFCA the amount stated and was without the ability or intention to make any payments on the note."

So, too, were there numerous instances of monies received that had not been earned. An example: Of $5,749,000 received from reinsuring companies in 1971, approximately $4.3 million was attributable to the reinsuring of fictitious insurance policies.

The magnitude of the fraud can best be comprehended by comparing the figures filed by Equity Funding with various stock exchanges in 1971, and the figures reported by the Grand Jury.

	Reported	*Real* (at most)
Income from insurance premiums and commissions	$62,482,000	$44,000,000
Income from securities	14,824,000	8,000,000
Earnings before taxes	26,636,000	(400,000) Loss
Funded loans and accounts receivable	88,616,000	45,000,000
Contracts, notes and loans receivable	34,162,000	26,000,000
Cash and short term investments	39,593,000	20,000,000
Total assets	496,695,000	424,000,000
Tangible Net Worth	141,200,000	104,000,000
EFLIC Premium Income	16,839,624	7,000,000

	Reported	*Real* (at most)
EFLIC sales, face amount	$1,780,270,704	$1,100,000,000
Equity Funding programs in effect	41,121	25,000
Sales of Equity Funding programs	13,813	4,000

How did they get away with it for so many years?

The men who investigated the Equity Funding fraud are agreed that it could not have been carried off for so long without the assistance of the company's auditors. The Grand Jury concurs. It contends that Sol Block, Julian Weiner and Marvin Lichtig—a former employee of Wolfson, Weiner who became an officer of Equity Funding—conducted "incomplete and insufficient" audits of the parent company. These audits would serve as the basis for unqualified CPA certifications of the company's yearly financial statement.

The man in charge of the day-to-day Equity Funding audit for four years was Sol Block. He was not a certified public accountant; he did not become one, ironically, until a few days after the fraud was exposed. Although Block was presumably on the premises to scrutinize the company's fiscal morality, he was listed in the company's telephone directory, his office was indistinguishable from any other, and most Equity Funding personnel assumed that he was on the payroll.

A second means of accomplishing the coverup was the utilization of the right kind of personnel in areas where it was needed. An example was the mass marketing unit at 341 North Maple. Some of the young girls employed had scored poorly on Equity's intelligence test—as low as 20, 30, or 40 on a scale of 100. The girls might object to the tedium of creating files that looked just like the ones that already existed, but they would not question the reasons for the work.

There were many employees at Equity Funding who performed mechanical functions on phony papers—but had no
way of knowing they were phony. Others developed suspicions.
Some questioned their superiors and were satisfied by explanations that seemed plausible. Others were not entirely fooled
and shared their deepening mistrust of company officials
with co-workers. Many became convinced there was wrongdoing but avoided confronting it directly. Some surreptitiously
investigated for further confirmation of the rumors. A few
spoke about specific fraudulent activities in an open fashion.
A handful actually went to the authorities.

Few knew of the staggering dimensions of the fraud; those
who did were included among the men eventually indicted.
But many employees or affiliates of Equity Funding had some
inkling that there were illegal activities taking place within
the company. Precisely how many can't be determined, but 100
seems like a reasonable guess.

Why did none of these people give the game away? There
are many reasons, none very appetizing. Many of those who
knew did not want to get involved. Others whose consciences
twitched did not want to lose their jobs. So what if the game
was rigged? They were still being paid—and their pay would
cease if the game stopped. There were some who knew *something* about the fraud—but not enough to make a case. There
were others who knew enough to make them find other jobs—
but not enough, once again, to enable them to approach the
authorities. Last, there were the bright young men, eager to
progress in the corporate world, impressionable, willing, sedu-
lous. Was this the way one made it? Then that is what one did.
Only after they had performed an act did they realize what
they had done.

Consider Frank Majerus, named as an unindicted co-conspirator by the federal grand jury. He was told—not asked—
to "do a file" by one of his superiors at EFLIC. Majerus did the
file. Then he went to a minister. The minister advised him that

his first duty was to protect his job for the sake of his family. He took his minister's advice.

Ronald Secrist, named as an unindicted co-conspirator in the federal case, gives even greater pause. The prosecutors have hinted that Secrist was involved. Secrist did "do a file," and he did sign a confirmation for a funded program he didn't own. He was worried about his career; he felt he had to play the game. But even as he played it he thought of ways to expose it. He began planning how to do the job more than a year before he did it. But it took a firing to propel him.

So a major factor in the coverup was the inertia of the spectators and casual participants.

Then there was Equity Funding's Balkanized corporate structure. Executives of other Equity Funding departments were kept in the dark regarding the operations of the insurance subsidiary and the funded program department. These executives would give reports on their divisions' operations, knowing them to be true—and then listen to reports from the insurance and funded loan divisions, assuming them to be equally true. There was no reason why they shouldn't. "It's not normal to believe that the guys you're working for are criminals," one corporate officer observes.

The men deeply involved in the fraud—the men who made it work—numbered less than twenty. The phony insurance operation, for example, required only a few knowledgeable men when it came time to fool the auditors. When the auditors would ask for files on specific individuals, they would be told that the files were scattered through the premises and that it would require at least a day to pull them together. An employee in on the game would then order the needed files.

There were many computer operators on the premises, but only a few men who operated computers in behalf of the conspiracy.

By themselves, computers are as benign as paper and pencil. But when put to adverse use, computers can do things that were never possible prior to their inception. The key factor is one of compression: what were once a series of step-by-step processes in old-fashioned bookkeeping are now engorged by computers into a single product.

A computer produces printouts; each printout, however, may be a refinement of several printouts. The details, in effect, remain inside the computer. Only the final result appears on the printout—not the many calculations and changes that produced it. All that an auditor sees is the final product. He no longer sees the process by which it was achieved. A superior example of what can happen occurred in the funded program records at Equity Funding—those mutual fund and insurance packages that were the company's flagship product.

There were no phony files for the funded program. The only instruments of deception were the computer and its output. When the auditors wanted to review the funded program, the computer would duplicate the real program a sufficient number of times to reach a total figure equal to the amount of funded programs the company was reporting. The real funded programs bore five-digit file numbers. So did the fake programs added to the new composite tape. But the tape was programed so that its printout would show only the last three digits of each program. If the auditors asked for five-digit numbers, they were told the tape was unavailable.

The owner of a funded program owed money to Equity Funding. This money was supposed to be in the form of a note payable to the corporation and secured by mutual fund shares. Such notes showed on the corporate books as assets. To confirm the existence of the notes, the auditors would select a sampling of funded programs from the three-digit numbers—the only source available to them. Theoretically, the auditors should have then gone to retrieve the file corresponding to the computer number. But, because there were only three digits, they did not know where to look. So they gave the list of numbers to employees of Equity Funding. Had they looked, they would have found one file for several numbers.

Now the computer helped in a second way. The tape had

been prepared so that the computer would reject all duplicate numbers. The good numbers produced the name and address of a bona fide funded policyholder. Duplicate numbers produced nothing. The printout was then taken to a conspirator, who would fill in the blanks with names closely resembling those of Equity Funding employees.

The auditors' request for confirmation would go either to the employee's home address, or the address of a relative or friend. The relatives and friends—whose names were supplied by cooperating employees—were told that the audit requests were part of a computer test the company was running. They obligingly signed the confirmations and returned them to the auditors.

Equity Funding carried on its books as assets $117 million in loans taken out by customers to fund their mutual fund and insurance package combinations. The collateral for $40 million of these loans was held by New England Merchants Bank of Boston. The remaining $77 million in collateral was presumably held by Equity Funding. In fact, it did not exist.

Computers were also used in a grim game of hide-and-seek in the final days before the fraud was exposed. Investigators had been informed by cooperating employees to check "Department 99." The computers quickly put the phony business into another department. Neither the auditors nor the insurance examiners, when told where to look, could find it.

Sometime during the 1920s a man named Ponzi appeared from Italy with a seductive scheme. He would offer to borrow money at a high rate of interest. The word would quickly spread; Ponzi would get more and more money. He would pay the first lenders with the money of the second, the second lenders with the money of the third, and on and on. It was the closest thing to a perpetual motion money machine—until he eventually ran out of investors. Equity Funding's reinsurance scheme was something of a throwback to Ponzi.

The keystone of the operation was the common practice of

one insurance company selling policies to another in order, presumably, to spread its risk.

A legitimate policy with a $1000 annual premium would cost about $1300 to service in the first year. (A life insurance company, due to the first year commissions it pays, loses money in the first year and makes it up in renewal years.) Equity Funding would sell a legitimate policy to a reinsurance company for $1800. The cash profit in the first year would be $500. But for a fake policy there was no $1300 expense. Equity Funding simply forwarded a "premium" of $1000—and received $1800 in return. Its profit: $800.

In the second year, however, Equity Funding would be required to pass along ninety percent of the annual "premium" to the reinsurer—or $900. But there was no policyholder paying the second year premium. The cash loss was $900. So (shades of Ponzi) Equity Funding would create other fictitious policies whose proceeds would pay for the first one.

The Equity Funding conspirators may very well have thought they could eventually pay it all back.

In theory, if Equity Funding forwarded premium payments each year to the reinsuring company, and eventually bought a policy back, the reinsuring company had made a legitimate return on its investment—as illegitimate as the means may have been.

There are some indications that several of the principals to the fraud believed that they were approaching a turning point, and would soon be able to retire whatever bad business they carried on the books. Ironically, the economy move that caused Ronald Secrist to be fired was made to reduce expenses sufficiently so that profits would increase and the reinsuring practice could be phased out.

The principals to the fraud may also have rationalized that it made no difference to investors how Equity Funding arrived at the earnings trend line it was expected to reach, so long as it eventually got there.

A company is evaluated on its multiple of earnings. In a go-

go era, what it makes or doesn't make in the interim makes little difference in the long run — because investors don't evaluate stocks on the *accumulation* of earnings, but on the basis of current and future earnings. The conspirators may have figured, Eventually we're going to make legitimate earnings one way or another. If we can keep the stock going up along with the trend line, we'll have time either to build earnings internally or make acquisitions. As time went on, as a matter of necessity interest in internal earnings lessened and interest in the acquisition of companies increased. Mathematically, it's easy to create earnings if you can keep your company's stock price high enough long enough. You simply acquire companies that are earning money — and then merge their earnings with yours.

Equity Funding came close. If the prosecutor is right, the company had reduced a loss of $7 million in 1970 to just under $500,000 in 1971 by acquiring profitable companies. Maintenance of the price of its stock was Equity Funding's overriding objective. With valuable shares, the company could trade for healthy companies. The acquisition of companies with billions of dollars of insurance in force would have provided opportunities to bury the fraud forever.

There was one further, vital reason to keep the stock price up. The backbone of the company was its marketing organization, which was compensated to an important degree by stock options. If Equity Funding lost money and the price of its stock fell, not only would the company be unable to borrow money or make acquisitions, it could no longer adequately compensate its salesmen.

So the fight to maintain the price of Equity Funding stock was a fight for the life of the company.

That annual report for 1973 never did get published. But the proof sheets, tucked now into investigators' files, can be read as a wish projection of epic and tragic dimension: year-end assets, $737 million; stockholders' equity, $143 million; profits, $22.6 million.

The records of this fantasy are packed now into sealed boxes. For months, many of the boxes were stored in an empty room—the choice corner office once occupied by Stanley Goldblum.

The room is rank with memories. A handsome, old-fashioned telescope stood once at one of the windows, a gift, Goldblum would explain, from his wife. Auditors found an invoice for the telescope dated May 18, 1970, in Equity Funding's accounts. It had been paid by the company. Six months after Goldblum's ouster, a painting still hung above the fireplace, a rendering in vivid colors of an Elizabethan chess match for which Goldblum said he had personally paid $10,000. An invoice for this purchase was also found in Equity Funding's files. When Jim Murdy, the bankrupt company's new financial officer, learned that the painting belonged to the company, he asked an art dealer in to make an offer. The art dealer took one look and said, "It's a piece of varnished crap, and I wouldn't give you $50 for it." Months later, Murdy thought of the appropriate reply: "Would you give $45?"

Goldblum would frequently boast that he was the only executive at 1900 Avenue of the Stars who didn't have to rent a piece of the twenty-eighth floor in order to have a fireplace flue. But he was, and is, a quixotic man. One day, a few weeks before his fantasy world came unstuck, an attorney asked him if the fireplace was real. "No," Goldblum replied, "it's fake— just like everything else in this room."

He was the salesman who had no time for $5000 and $10,000 insurance policies. His market was the $50,000 and $100,000 crowd. He knew where he wanted to go, and he was in a hurry to get there.

Why the hurry? From whence the need? The clue, perhaps, is not in the office he left in disgrace, but in the private $100,000 gym to which he repaired several times each week as he awaited the ordeal of his trial. A visitor asked him why he lifted weights. "For size," the giant said.

12.

Some Out-of-Court Indictments

Equity Funding stands as an indictment of an investment system that deceives and mocks the individual. As that system exists today, the individual cannot operate on a rational theory of value unless he is willing to brave the crowd. His only choice is to follow. Don't bother about what a company does; care only about what it shows. Don't think of a stock purchase as an investment; think of it as a trading unit someone will buy after you do. Your buyer will operate that way, because everyone operates that way. As long as you get in at the right price, it doesn't matter what the values are, because no one else pays attention to them.

There is not a single component of this system that escapes the indictment—not the New York Stock Exchange, not its member firms, not the regulatory agency that supposedly maintains order. The Equity Funding scandal can be understood in its magnitude only when one analyzes the weaknesses on which it thrived. Had even one of the system's components functioned with strength, the fraud could not have occurred.

In 1959, Equity Funding was little more than an idea. Eleven years later, it was one of the most actively traded issues on the New York Stock Exchange. Its rise to prominence in the world's most dominant and exclusive financial trading market epitomized the American dream. Yet Equity Funding had no right to a listing on the New York Stock Exchange. It was this very listing that gave the company the endorsement it needed to perpetuate its fraud. That Equity Funding managed to be listed is only one of the overdue indictments against the New York Stock Exchange. This venerated institution is not the guardian of the free enterprise system it proclaims itself to be. It is an expensive and outmoded monopoly.

The thrust of the Stock Exchange's message is that its listed stocks are the nation's biggest and best companies. The ultimate objective of a go-go corporation like Equity Funding is to interest financial institutions in the purchase of its stock, so that the stock will sell at a high multiple of earnings. The objective focuses on a Stock Exchange listing. There, the presence of legitimate blue-chip stocks presumably rubs off on other listed securities. Moreover, the go-go company profits from the Exchange's incessant proclamations of itself as the bastion of respectability and rectitude.

Equity Funding began as a company whose shares were held by its founders. The first step for an ambitious corporation is to "go public." By selling shares to the public, the corporation raises the money with which to finance its operations and growth. True, the founders dilute their holdings, but the larger the enterprise the larger the salaries and perquisites and the greater the opportunities for expansion. Moreover, the founders' shares are immediately priced at market levels.

Equity Funding made its debut as a publicly held corporation in the over-the-counter market. Some of the nation's most reputable corporations are traded in this market, but essentially the market remains a testing ground for smaller, newer companies in training for the big time.

The next step up for such corporations, frequently, is a listing on the American Stock Exchange. This exchange can be likened to the Triple A minor leagues in baseball—good

sport, but not the big time. After a few years on the American
Exchange, Equity Funding reached sufficient size to apply for
a New York Stock Exchange listing.

The Exchange maintains certain requirements for listing,
and departments whose job it is to enforce those requirements.
The staffs of those departments looked over Equity Funding
and found its application deficient. One objection was that
Equity Funding's board of directors was not large enough and
did not contain enough members from outside the corporation.
A second, more significant, objection was that the auditing
firm employed by Equity Funding had neither sufficient size
nor reputation. These objections contained Equity Funding
for some months, but eventually politics prevailed. The public
interest the Exchange's regulations are meant to guard became
secondary to the interests of certain NYSE firms who found
this new "concept" stock romantic and liked the way it "performed."

Equity Funding's listing was authorized in October 1970 on
the condition that the company would expand its board of
directors and secure the services of a national auditing firm.
The company did expand its board, but its effort to comply
with the auditing requirements was sheer comedy. Wolfson,
Weiner, the firm Equity Funding had used as auditors, simply
used the Equity account as the basis for a merger with a larger
accounting firm. Eventually, it sold out to Seidman & Seidman.
More than a year after Equity Funding went on the big board,
Seidman & Seidman took over the audit. What the New York
Stock Exchange never realized was that the same individuals
who had audited the Equity Funding books for Wolfson,
Weiner were now auditing them for Seidman & Seidman.

Why had the member firms of the New York Stock Exchange
wanted Equity Funding on the big board? Because the stock
was one of the most actively traded on the American Stock
Exchange, which made it ripe for brokers to begin peddling to
large institutions, many of which limit their shopping lists to
companies listed on the New York Stock Exchange.

Allowing Equity Funding to be listed goes to the heart of the question of the New York Stock Exchange's ability to function as the regulator it proclaims itself to be. Clearly, there was a conflict here between the standards of the Exchange—the presumed stockholders' watchdog—and the interests of its member firms. The latter's interests prevailed.

Once the stock was listed, the Exchange should have determined that its requirements had been met. There may have been some effort in this regard, but none vigorous enough to establish that Equity Funding had effectively winked at the order to obtain new auditors. For all practical purposes, the change was in name only.

Such laxity puts the lie to the New York Stock Exchange's proclamations of itself as a self-regulating institution—and yet it is this very status that the Stock Exchange enjoys. Technically, the Exchange comes under the jurisdiction of the Securities and Exchange Commission, but in reality, it operates as an autonomous club.

There is justification for the self-regulation of an industry, if the industry can do the job. But the New York Stock Exchange has not remotely acquitted itself of its responsibilities as a self-regulating body: not only is the Exchange incapable of monitoring its listed companies, it is incapable of monitoring its member firms. It hasn't the mechanism to comprehend the fraud and inefficiency in its own house. The greatest example of this deficiency is the Exchange's failure to foresee the impending bankruptcy of many of its brokerage firms in recent years. On several occasions, the Exchange has failed to take timely action to protect investors against loss. The NYSE may even have failed to prevent various versions of Equity Funding among its own member firms.

On April 2, 1973, the day the Equity Funding scandal was made known to the public on page one of *The Wall Street Journal,* a minor story inside the newspaper related that the New York Stock Exchange was abandoning the practice of requiring independent accounting firms to perform surprise

audits of its member firms. Less than two months later, as I
was testifying at the SEC offices in New York, I overheard one
SEC examiner tell another, "We're taking over a stock exchange firm. There's fraud involved. The New York Stock
Exchange hasn't moved on it, and we're going into court today." And the next morning, *The Wall Street Journal* informed
its readers that the SEC had obtained court approval to close
up Weis & Company. It was alleged that officers of Weis had
created fictitious assets on the company books to deceive
regulators and the firm's customers. Either the Exchange had
known about it and failed to act, or it had failed to discover
the fraud.

Insufficient action has been taken to correct the anachron-
istic conditions endemic to the industry that produce such
failures. The decision to omit surprise audits means even less
policing of dangerous or fraudulent conditions at stock exchange firms.

The charge against the New York Stock Exchange is more
basic than whether the house is safe. It's whether it should
stand. Today, the Exchange is an institution that has outlived
its time. It proclaims itself the hub of the business world, but
its image transcends its reality. The Exchange ought to be
judged, not for its symbolic value, but in terms of whether what
it does is the best way that task can be done.

The Exchange is really nothing more than a physical place
where brokers buy and sell from one another, reflecting the
orders of their customers. It began under a buttonwood tree in
1792 as a central place where stocks could be traded. There
was an obvious advantage in congregating people in order to
make a marketplace. The more people the greater the market
—and the more likely that buyers and sellers would find one
another. For years, the Exchange provided this central mechanism. It grew, prospered, and moved indoors. But its basic
nature remained unchanged. The only major changes were the
telephone, which permitted orders to be transmitted to the
floor of the Exchange rather than carried there; the introduc-

tion of the specialist system, wherein one individual would keep a continuing record of all unfilled orders and use his own capital to try to maintain an orderly market; and the ticker tape, which enabled investors to watch the market action from remote stations. But the manner of buying and selling remained the same. Brokers gathered around one another in a single location. That was the way it was done in 1792, and that's how it's done today.

The system disserves its customers. They pay more when they buy and obtain less when they sell.

The existence of a physical marketplace puts a limitation on the number of brokers who can work there. That automatically limits the market. Moreover, it defines the kind of market that can be maintained. Trading is restricted to an auction market centered around one specialist. There is no room on the floor for others.

There are dealers throughout the United States who can offer to buy or sell securities listed on the New York Stock Exchange at prices that, in many cases, are more favorable than those available on the floor. But brokers who belong to the Exchange are prohibited from seeking better prices away from the floor. What that means, effectively, is that an order given to a member firm for a stock listed by the New York Stock Exchange must be handled on that exchange. That's profitable for the members of the club, but it can be costly for their clients. The clients would be far better served if their order to buy or sell a stock could be offered to dealers everywhere; only then would they be assured of the best possible price.

There is an infinitely more appropriate market, and the technology to produce it. It's called a dealer market. Instead of one specialist standing in one place making a market, there are five, ten, twenty, or more market-makers willing to buy and sell a stock through the facilities of a computerized visual display system that functions nationally. Whereas the auction market is a monopolistic system, the dealer market encompasses everyone. A system called NASDAQ (National Association of Securities Dealers Automatic Quote) tells which dealers anywhere in the country are willing to buy or sell a stock. A seller need only push a button to find the highest bidder for his shares.

If many specialists were permitted to make a market in a stock, the price would invariably be the most advantageous possible to the customer. So would the cost of doing business. Competition would produce smaller price spreads and lower commissions. But, as long as the stocks of the most important companies in the country can be traded only on the New York Stock Exchange, NASDAQ cannot fully function.

The New York Stock Exchange is a monument to monopoly, not a pillar of competitive free enterprise. Such a situation breeds resistance to change. Inevitably, the monopolistic practices on Wall Street have produced inefficiency among its member firms and lack of depth in their work. Wall Street today is the most poorly managed industry in the country. Such conditions immeasurably assisted the rise of Equity Funding.

The Equity Funding scandal would not have occurred had analysts done their jobs. The function of security analysts, like that of investment bankers, is to determine the real worth of a company, so that investors will pay a fair price for its securities. No price was fair for the stock of Equity Funding—but numbers of analysts touted it.

"Why were so many analysts recommending Equity Funding only months and in some cases days before the collapse?" *The Wall Street Journal* wondered in the aftermath of the exposure.

The answer is not reassuring.

Most investors—even professionals who manage large funds —are not really disciplined to arrive at values as opposed to fads and fashions and snap judgments. A lot of them (and I include myself) have a gambler's instinct. They are willing to plunk down money based on swift impressions rather than

solid research work. Few men in the Street dig deeply. Super-
ficiality is the name of the game.

After the Depression, stock analysts paid strict attention to
corporate balance sheets, which reflected the net worth of
companies. But, gradually, as the economy strengthened again,
the money men became increasingly preoccupied with a company's earnings potential and less concerned about its present
financial condition. Earnings can change swiftly, but net worth
changes slowly.

Today, analysts for the most part project prices of stocks
by using an oversimplified measure known on the Street as
"performance." They try to determine what the normal true
growth rate of a company is in terms of its earnings per share
and then determine the degree of confidence they have in that
growth rate. From this calculation they then assign a multiple
of earnings to a stock. If a stock earns $1 a share in a given
year with a projected growth rate of ten percent per year, and
the degree of confidence is high, then an analyst might feel that
the stock warrants a price twenty times earnings, or $20 a
share. If the confidence factor is lower, then the multiple of
earnings figure would be commensurately lower—say, ten
times earnings—and the stock would warrant a price of only
$10 a share.

The keys to the confidence factor are the consistency and
growth of reported earnings. For how many straight quarters
have earnings risen, and what percent? If the earnings have
followed a consistent pattern of quarterly growth, then the
analyst or fund man assumes that the earnings will continue
to grow.

But this kind of analysis is simplistic, and often leads to
trouble. As John H. Allan noted in *The New York Times* in
April 1973:

> In the nineteen-sixties security analysts screened the earn-
> ings of all the companies they could find, trying to discover
> a trend in per share earnings that rose beautifully at a rate

of 15 or 20 percent year after year. When they found a stock
that performed so nicely, they recommended that investors
be willing to pay a high price for it.

If a company earned, say 46 cents a share in 1967, $1.04
in 1968, $1.67 in 1969, $1.84 in 1970 and $2.36 in 1971, its
stock should definitely be worth buying.

There was just such a stock, and it sold at forty-eight times
earnings back in 1968. However, the company was the
Equity Funding Corporation of America, the disgraced
life insurance and mutual fund complex that filed for bankruptcy this month.

There are other problems as serious as the analysts' singular
reliance on "performance." One of the worst habits analysts
have developed is to rely on the reports of other analysts. A
good financial public relations firm will arrange for a friendly
analyst to visit a company and then write a favorable report—
which the public relations firm, in turn, will then distribute
to other analysts.

The easiest way for an analyst to do his job is to copy another
analyst's work. Part of an analyst's function is to read what the
competition is saying; but when an analyst uses another analyst's work to produce his own a line of integrity has been
crossed. This line is repeatedly crossed on Wall Street.

A harried analyst with much work to do receives a twenty-
five-page report from a large firm, written by a prominent
analyst. He makes a few perfunctory checks, which seem to be
in line with the conclusions of the detailed report. He churns
out a report of his own. What the analyst may not know is that
the report has been monitored, managed, or even partially
written by the very company it purports to judge.

It is common practice on Wall Street for an analyst to send a
draft of his report to the company. Such submission, in these
cases, has been a condition of access to the company's inner
sanctum. The company does not say, "We want to censor you."
It says, "We want to read your report to check for inconsisten-

cies. We don't care what you say or what your opinion is, we just want to make sure everything in it is accurate." In fact, the company is exercising censorship; often, it rewrites sections of the report. Most companies think it is their prerogative to see any report an analyst writes about its affairs prior to publication. They will then attempt to correct any negative impressions.

The analyst is not the most powerful man in a brokerage house. He may have a good reputation, but he doesn't have much stature. Suddenly, he is dealing with top management of a major company. As sturdy an individual as he may be, he feels a great deal of pressure. Unless he has an enormous amount of self-confidence, he is going to be persuaded, or intimidated, into doing what the company wants.

There's yet another problem. It's human nature to want to believe in the people with whom you're dealing. Such natural tendencies, however, are contrary to the interests of investors who must rely on the analyst's assessment. I can sympathize with the analysts who came to know and like Stanley Goldblum and Fred Levin. Compounding the problem was a vigorous company effort to cultivate analysts.

> It's known [*The Wall Street Journal* reported] that some Wall Street analysts were friendly with a number of top Equity Funding executives. . . . Other analysts are known to have accepted favors from Equity Funding. And, according to one source, Equity Funding officials kept a written record of favorable and unfavorable analysts' reports that had been released or were *about to be* released. Indeed, it's said that Equity Funding executives actually wrote parts of some analysts' reports.

Conflicts of interests militate still further against hard analysis. A brokerage house earns its money on commissions from the buying and selling of shares. Most "analysts" aren't really analysts; they are essentially salesmen motivated by the need to generate commissions.

There is a Wall Street axiom to the effect that "negative stories don't sell." No one but the man who owns a stock wants to hear something bad about it—and even he is uncomfortable with the revelation because it tells him that he made a bad judgment. All other investors want a positive story, one that tells them about a stock that might make them some money— and the major consequence of this condition is that very few analysts go after negative stories. There is much more money to be made in the recommendation of a buy (which implies the possibility of profit) than in the recommendation of a sell (which usually implies a loss).

The analyst who writes negatively about companies may eventually find himself with no one to talk to. Companies are unlikely to cooperate with an analyst with the reputation of a skeptic. While an analyst must go afield to form his ultimate judgment, his impressions of management are vital to his assessment. Therefore, consciously or unconsciously, the analyst who wants to remain an analyst either doesn't dig deeply enough—or else doesn't disclose with sufficient force the facts that he uncovers.

So the general course of "research" on Wall Street goes about like this: An analyst hears management's story and, if he's favorably impressed, writes up a report. (If he's not impressed, he generally does nothing.) The report is then submitted to management, management corrects it and sends it back to the analyst, the analyst then persuades his firm to send the report out, the report is distributed to the firm's salesmen— who are not analysts—and these salesmen, in turn, distribute the report to their customers as gospel. No wonder the general tenor of most brokerage house reports is overly favorable to management.

Equity Funding was an analyst's darling. In the light of events, their reports make ironic reading. Burnham and Company:

In 1960, Equity Funding began marketing a unique product
—the funding program. This event sparked the birth of an
industry and the inauguration of a virtually unmarred pattern of revenue and earnings gains. An able and imaginative
team, however, views past achievements as merely a model
upon which to fashion future performance. As a consequence, they have assembled a broad array of in-house
financial services which are available to a strong, wide-
spread sales force . . . we consider Equity Funding's common stock to be an attractive long-term investment situation.

Lehman Brothers:

We recommend purchase of this stock as an attractive,
long-term investment. The company, through a sales force
now of major size, markets a consumable service . . . attractive to a segment of the total employed estimated at
over 25 million persons. By virtue of its broad appeal, the
company serves an untapped market, which has shown re-
silience even during recession. The company has an experienced innovative management and significant financial
resources to meet the challenge offered by a unique product
in a vast market. This analysis details our confidence that
the company's exceptional growth record will continue.

(Both the Burnham and Lehman Brothers recommendations
were written by the same individual—who had left one house
and gone to the other.) Edwards & Hanly:

In its first decade of operations, Equity Funding Corporation of America has emerged as one of the most successful
marketers of individual life insurance, with particular
strength in equity linked products. In 1971, including recently acquired subsidiaries, it ranked fourth among stock
companies in the U.S. in terms of ordinary insurance written.

"Equity Funding's inherently conservative approach to business may be viewed as a strong defensive weapon in the hands of a group of uncommonly able executives aggressively seeking and obtaining a growing share of the financial services market," Wertheim & Company noted in a recent report. Its conclusion, the brokerage firm said, was based on Equity Funding's system of internal controls, which was designed to "minimize surprises."

One curious study, by Adams, Harkness & Hill, had its sardonic aspects. Equity's management had made itself so available to analysts that it didn't seem to do anything else, the brokerage firm noted. There were always negative rumors floating around about Equity Funding, the report went on, but the brokerage firm had not been able to substantiate any of the rumors. Despite these reservations, the firm recommended purchase of the stock.

Early in 1972, a group of institutional analysts was asked to vote for its favorite stock out of the hundreds of financial services and insurance securities. The choice: Equity Funding. *Institutional Investor,* one of Wall Street's bibles, carried a story about life insurance companies in its February 1973 issue. Of five money managers and analysts featured in a sidebar to the article, two singled out Equity Funding as one of the likely star performers in 1973.

But the brokerage firm most embarrassed by the scandal was, perhaps, Hayden Stone. One day before the Exchange halted trading, the company issued a report that said: "Several rumors have been circulating which have affected Equity Funding's stock; we have checked these rumors, and there appears to be no substance to any of them." Hayden Stone's analyst said he had checked the insurance departments of Illinois, New Jersey, and Washington, three states in which insurance companies owned by Equity Funding were licensed. "Each man told us that he is not conducting an investigation of Equity Funding or any of its subsidiaries, has no present intention of conducting an investigation and knew of no other insurance department that is conducting an investigation." In the case of Illinois, the man to whom the analyst spoke was Jim Steen—who was directing the investigation.

"There's no way of adjusting for massive fraud in analyzing a stock," Laurence A. Tisch, Loew's chief executive, said after the fraud had been disclosed. "There's just no answer to it. Either you believe the whole system of investing is based on fraud or you do business on the basis of audits, insurance regulation, and other safeguards."

That is absolutely true. So is it true that some of the firms with big positions in Equity Funding took them only after what they thought was careful research. Boston Company, for example, relied on Conning & Company, one of the most reputable and conservative firms in the business of analyzing insurance stocks, to analyze Equity Funding. Four analysts went to Los Angeles, spoke extensively with management, accountants and actuaries. They returned with a recommendation to buy. (Prophetically, the senior man at Conning, Joe Sargent, observed, "I just don't like the feel of this company.")

But clues were available long before the formal investigation of fraud.

One printed clue could have given the game away as early as 1967. The clue is contained in a comparison between what Equity Funding said it had sold in the way of insurance in 1966, and what another company said Equity had sold. In its first years, Equity Funding was an agency. It had no insurance company of its own. Much of the insurance the company sold to clients it placed with Pennsylvania Life Insurance Company. In 1966, according to an Equity Funding prospectus of May 1967, the company sold $226.3 million face amount of life insurance, the "greater part" underwritten by Penn Life. But Penn Life's prospectus one month later stated that it had underwritten only $58.6 million of policies for Equity Funding in 1966. No one caught the discrepancy.

Another clue was the sale of Equity Funding stock by key insiders. Consider Stanley Goldblum, the largest individual stockholder. On the day trading was halted, he owned some 250,000 shares. But several years earlier he had owned close to 500,000 shares. All sales by insiders are reported to the SEC and duly published, but none of the many favorable reports on Equity Funding noted that Stanley Goldblum had been a steady seller of some $10 million worth of Equity Funding stock.

None of the analysts who spoke of Equity Funding's aggressive sales force properly evaluated the sales figures. The salesmen were not selling nearly the amount of life insurance or mutual funds the company's figures indicated. Had even one analyst interviewed a random sample of salesmen, averaged their sales, and multiplied that average by the 5000 man sales force, he would have known immediately that something was wrong. Even granting that all 5000 salesmen were bona fide, the total would not have come close to the figure presented each year by the company. But all of the salesmen were not full time: some worked part time; others produced very little. So the total would undoubtedly have been even further removed from the figure alleged by the company.

In addition to clues like these, there were questions analysts might have asked.

Why should Equity Funding have grown at a far faster rate than any other company in its field?

Why was Equity Funding successful with a product that no one else could sell?

Why, in the recession year of 1970, was Equity Funding able to go against the current and report its customary increase in sales and earnings?

Why, in a period when it was increasingly difficult to sell life insurance and mutual funds, was Equity Funding able to increase the sales of both?

No one asked these questions. I didn't either. I refused to take Equity Funding seriously. The only reference I ever made to the company in my newsletter was a passing one—which I hope, in retrospect, my clients received with the same ir-reverence with which it was written.

In 1971, Equity Funding negotiated a complex agreement with another insurance firm called Kentucky Central. I knew that the purpose of the contract was to increase the earnings of both companies. It seemed ironic to me, as well as relevant to investors in both companies, to know that both manage-ments could, with the stroke of a pen, increase their earnings by signing an agreement with one another. Because I knew the earnings of both companies would increase, I facetiously rec-ommended the purchase of both. It was a putdown that no sophisticated investor could take seriously.

Why didn't I take Equity Funding seriously? Because I never believed in the concept. Borrowing money against a mutual fund seemed like an expensive and risky way to buy insurance.

That, as it turned out, was the most telling clue of all. Equity Funding projected its concept as a modern approach to life insurance protection. Only the means of purchase was new. The product was just as old—and flawed—as what other in-surance companies sold.

The critics peering through the rents in our social fabric for an explanation to the Equity Funding fraud could do worse than contemplate the large object in the foreground—the life insurance industry, itself.

Equity Funding might never have come into being had the life insurance industry provided the consumer with modern alternatives to its outmoded products.

The life insurance industry is the bluest of the chips. It con-trols more assets than any other industry in the country. It is all but immune to change. The great social concerns that butt up against other industries make a detour around the insurance industry. Life insurers do not pollute the environment, nor are they obliged to change their model each year; their customers do not trade in their old policy for a new one every few years, because it would cost them dearly to do so. But what most distinguishes the life insurance industry is that, year after year, it makes settlements with cheaper dollars than those it has been paid.

The life insurance industry, moreover, enjoys a favorable tax position. There is a special tax law for life insurance companies. The industry is one of the few that files income tax reports on other-than a regular corporate income tax form. It enjoys special tax deferrals.

For all these reasons, life insurance companies like to keep things quiet. They broadcast an image of solidity. They build huge office buildings to concretize the image. They give the policyholder the feeling that his investment is as solid as a rock.

The notion is ridiculous.

Most life insurance companies are misleading, at best, in their representations to consumers. This is particularly true of mutual life insurance companies, which are theoretically owned by their policyholders. Prudential Insurance and Metropolitan Life, the largest in the business, are prime examples. Their policyholders may own a minuscule position in the equities of the company, but they are offered none of the perquisites of ownership.

Policyholders may own a mutual company, in theory, but in fact they have no say in the management of the company and no way to exercise their rights as owners. Managements, answerable only to their policyholders, have the power of czars. They control their companies, and there is no appeal from their rule. There is an annual meeting, which policyholders may attend or to which they can send proxies. But policyholders in the bigger companies number in the hundreds of thousands; they are not organized into any cohesive public interest group to determine whether management does a good job.

The motivation of a mutual life insurance company management is actually at cross purposes with that of its policyholders. Management wants to get bigger, in order to command more prestige and pay. Its means to do so are limited; it cannot make acquisitions because it is not a stock company; the investments it makes must be inherently conservative. So the only route to greater size is to sell more life insurance policies. The way to accomplish that is to invest the company's earnings in the hiring of salesmen.

But the policyholder's interest in a mutual company would best be served if the company were to stop selling insurance and liquidate. Then, and only then, would he get the fruits of ownership. There would be no expenses incurred in the search for new business, no commissions, no expansion of offices. Assets could be sold, and the proceeds paid out in dividends. All the company would need would be a sufficient amount of capital to protect the interests of the policyholders. The surplus could be paid out immediately.

Mutual life insurance executives, and their enormous force of salesmen, would find such a thought heretical. Their well-being depends on the maintenance of this gigantic system of accumulating assets.

The life insurance industry began before 1700. Initially, the cost of insurance increased as an individual aged. Over the years, there developed a profession of men called "actuaries." They calculated the risks inherent in the selling of insurance, and the premiums needed to offset those risks. They then formulated the "level premium" policy, wherein the insurance company would charge more than necessary at younger ages in order to fund the higher cost of insuring policyholders in their later years. This type of insurance became known as "whole life."

The concept made seeming sense to the policyholders. They would be protected in their old age without being overburdened with enormous premiums. But the concept also created some socially unfortunate side effects. The first of these was that it thrust the life insurers into the business, not simply of insuring against death, but of acting as investors of premium dollars. The second, which flowed from the first, was to foster an archaic and distorted system of investment.

There are two basic kinds of life insurance policies, term and whole life. Term policies are those in which you pay a premium each year for insurance protection but retain no cash value. Whole life policies are those in which you obtain protection and retain cash value. Term insurance is far less costly than whole life—but whole life offers a system of protection and savings. Premiums on whole life policies remain consistent throughout the life of the policyholder; premiums on term policies rise every several years as the policyholder ages—and the risk of insuring him becomes greater.

From this comparison, it would seem that whole life insurance is much the better deal with its savings and level premium features. Nonetheless, if you've ever owned an insurance policy other than a term policy, the chances are that you've been gulled. You've paid a great deal more than you needed to, and for many more years than you needed to.

The only time you need life insurance is when you must protect your dependents. Between fifty and sixty-five years of age, you don't need insurance nearly as much as you do between the ages of twenty-five and fifty, when you're supporting your wife, children, and perhaps your parents. After fifty, your children are out of school, your parents are most probably dead, and the only person left to support is your spouse.

Supposing you had bought a $100,000 whole life policy at the age of twenty-five, at a cost of $1250 a year. (That amount is not so excessive as it sounds; many young men bought policies in that amount as a form of investment, as well as protection.) By age fifty, you would have paid $31,250. The cash value of your policy would be about $35,000. So, you think, you've done pretty well. You've had twenty-five years of protection, and you've still got your money. Of course you haven't done well at all. Not only have your original dollars vastly depreciated in value, but you have received almost nothing for the use of this money during twenty-five years.

Supposing you had bought a $100,000 renewable *term* life policy at the age of twenty-five. Your premium would have averaged $350 a year. If you had invested $900—the difference between a $1250 premium and a $350 premium—in the stock market each year for twenty-five years, your equity would have increased an average of nine percent a year. At age fifty, you would have had twenty-five years of protection—and about $80,000.

Had you invested the $900 in a savings account each year, you would have had considerably less than $80,000, but a good bit more than $35,000.

The basic principle in the purchase of life insurance is: buy term insurance and invest the difference. But the last person to tell you this is your insurance salesman. For years, the insurance industry has been able to put savings and protection against death under the cloak of life insurance. What you, the policyholder, bought was really death insurance and an inferior lifetime savings plan that may pay as little as two percent a year.

There are two types of whole life policies sold by insurance companies. One is participating, the other nonparticipating. Nonparticipating policies offer a fixed guaranteed return; you get no percentage of any additional profits the company might earn on the investments it makes with your money and the money of others. Participating policies, which are sold primarily by mutual companies, pay you according to how well they do with the money you give them.

Insurance companies mostly own bonds and mortgages. When interest rates go up—as they have in recent years—bond prices go down. A life insurance company that were to sell all of its bonds today could probably not meet its obligations; if all the policyholders turned in their policies, the company might not be able to pay them off. Until the late 1960s, bonds were a horrible investment, averaging a yield of two to four percent a year. These were the bonds that insurance companies bought in quantity. So if you had bought a participating

policy twenty-five years ago, your annual yield on your investment has been roughly three percent—reflected in the increase
in cash value of your policy. To the extent that a mutual company might have invested in stocks, and the stocks performed
well, you might have earned extra money. But it's not very
likely; it's not the nature of the breed.

Any way you look at it, whole life insurance is a terrible
investment; yet insurance companies and their salesmen, with
few exceptions, try to sell you whole life. They say, "Don't buy
stocks until you have a tremendous amount of life insurance
that includes a big savings program." They don't say that if
you buy term insurance they won't get much commission.

People don't like to think about their death. Life insurance,
accordingly, is not something they go out and buy. It has to be
sold. Most life insurance is sold because an agent finds someone and talks him into buying it. Agents receive a huge front
end "load" on any policy they sell. The load may be anywhere
from fifty percent to more than 100 percent of the first-year
premium. Some companies have been known to pay their
agents 120 percent of the first year premium, adding their own
dollars to the money coming in. Each renewal year for up to
ten years an agent generally receives ten percent of the premium.

It's a wasteful system, fraught with deception and oppor-
tunism.

The thrust of any selling pitch ought to be simplification.
The individual should be told what he's paying for in terms of
an investment program. That almost never happens.

Years ago, an old friend looked me up, took me out to dinner, and tried to sell me a policy. "What do I need one for?"
I asked. "I'm twenty-three and single."

"You ought to buy one, to be sure you have it," he argued.
"Suppose you have a heart attack, or a disease?"

My death, at that point, made no difference to the support
of anyone. I simply didn't need a life insurance policy; surely
I wouldn't benefit from it. I tried to explain that to my friend.

"The insurance industry ought to have a policy for a person like myself, guaranteeing me the right to buy insurance when I really need it. I'd pay $100 a year just to be able to buy the insurance should I marry and have a family."

"We don't offer that," he said.

Now, as then, salesmen still swarm around colleges and universities, urging students to sign up before they start to work. Premiums will cost less, they argue, because you're buying at a younger age. They fail to add that you'll pay for more years. Think of the dividends you'll receive, they go on. They don't explain that you're not getting a reward, you're simply getting some of your money back, plus a small return on your investment. Then, the salesmen argue that if you pay in for twenty years you'll eventually get all of your money back. You could do better yourself, avoiding the salesman's commission, plus the overhead and profits of the life insurance company. The salesmen argue that a permanent life insurance policy is an enforced savings plan, that if you don't have a life insurance policy you'll spend the money. That may be the best argument they've got. But there are other forms of enforced savings plans that offer better yields than insurance.

Equity Funding wouldn't have been possible if life insurance hadn't been the poor investment that it was. Somehow the public sensed that it was poor, and gradually their savings dollars began to find their way into savings and loan associations, banks, mutual funds, and the stock market. But they still needed *some* kind of protection. The lure of Equity Funding was that it seemed to overcome these deficiencies. You could put it all in one package, send one check a year that would take care of your insurance and your investments. You didn't have to arrange to borrow money; Equity Funding took care of that. The program didn't affect your credit. Additionally, if the market went up, you would, in fact, come out ahead.

The Equity Funding concept contained the elements the Wall Street money managers and analysts look for—a service, a packaged product of insurance and mutual funds combined into one sales pitch. When to that combination is added leverage, that's a Wall Street dream. Wall Street is populated by men who think they can beat the averages.

But in the long run you don't beat the averages. As Lord Keynes said, in the long run, we're all dead. The concept of leverage embodies the idea that one person can take another person's money and do better with it than he can. It's a tenuous idea.

Equity Funding said to the consumer, The cost of the money you borrow is a lot less than the money we're going to make for you. To illustrate its thesis, initially, the company used a ten-year historical period characterized by low interest rates and rising stock prices.

But trying to project the past into the future can be dangerous. By 1970, Equity Funding had to start using twenty-year projections, because the previous ten years showed such a poor pattern. In the meanwhile, interest rates had begun to climb. By 1970, they had reached eight percent. After a brief falling-off period, interest rates climbed again, until they reached an alltime high in 1973.

Since the average appreciation on stocks has been less than nine percent over the last ten years, leverage doesn't do you much good. The interest you pay to borrow money equals or exceeds the amount you can expect to gain from your investment. If you're lucky, you can win. If not, you lose. If you include the high costs of purchasing an equity program, you'll probably end up in the hole. Paying salesmen, handling the operation, managing the money—all that costs money, and those costs have to be paid for by the client. To those costs, moreover, must be added an assumed profit for the company running the program. You pay for that, too.

At first glance, the concept had appealed to investors because they had come to see the life insurance industry as sleepy, backward, not very aggressive, putting its money into conservative bonds and mortgages. Suddenly, here was a company saying, We're going to take this client's money and invest it for him aggressively. The basic appeal of the product was that you could have your cake and eat it too. You could have your life insurance and that big pot at the end of the ten-year period. You had the element of conservatism and the element of speculation.

But on close inspection, Equity Funding's program didn't fill the investor's needs nearly so well as it had seemed to. There was, first of all, the problem of making money. In the markets of 1969 and 1970, leverage began to look like reverse leverage. The man who bought an Equity Funding program found himself needing to put up additional collateral to secure his loan. By 1970, anything that reeked of risk was suspect— particularly when it seemed somewhat complicated.

"Everybody always says this is a complicated product, when it's really very simple," Stanley Goldblum contended. But Equity Funding couldn't quite simplify it enough. It *sounded* complicated. It put together four different ingredients—in-surance, savings, a mutual fund, and a loan. It was supposed to be simple, but it wound up being complex. The only part that was simple was writing out one check.

But the problem went deeper than that: What was wrong with the whole insurance concept of saving was equally wrong with the funded program offered by EFCA. You were saddled with an antique form of savings, with no special compensation. If you were making money under an Equity Funding program, you would also be making money through your own investment —without the costs of the funded program and the antique form of insurance.

The Equity Funding program couldn't withstand the in-evitable fluctuations in the market and market psychology. Coincidentally, it was in 1969, the first year of bad times for mutual funds and insurance companies, that the company's insurance fraud began. The public had begun to recognize that the Equity Funding program had the inherent weaknesses of any program that attempts to combine life insurance and investment. The program, which had sounded so promising, just didn't fit the needs of enough people.

Equity Funding was a leveraged company in its own right. It borrowed heavily to run its business. It couldn't convince enough customers to do the same. The real reason Equity Funding failed was that people suspected its product.

And so a product of uncertain social value disappoints its creators, the creators issue false reports to a Wall Street disposed to unsubstantiated success stories, and Wall Street kites the stock.

What defense remains to the public if the New York Stock Exchange—or some other Exchange—has failed it? Basically, there are two: independent auditors who must certify the company's figures, and the Securities and Exchange Commission, which regulates financial markets. But because Equity Funding involved an insurance company, there was a third line of defense, the state insurance departments under whose jurisdiction EFLIC operated.

If the Equity Funding scandal proves anything, it is that auditors as safeguards are worthless. The "independent" auditor may not be independent. Paid by the firm being audited, he is worried about keeping the account.

I went to Seidman & Seidman truly believing that I was doing this nationally ranked auditing firm a favor. It was about to publicly certify a report I believed was fraudulent. Instead of reporting the matter to the SEC, the auditor applied the most narrow interpretation to his role and went directly to Equity Funding. When I asked him why he had done so, he replied, "They're clients of mine."

"Aren't you independent auditors?" I asked.

"Sure we're independent, but we have an obligation to our clients."

The two postures are irreconcilable.

Corporate managements understandably want to control their destinies. Our system places a check and balance on this very tendency; it requires a corporation to justify itself to the independent public accountant. The public accepts what this independent auditor certifies. But when an auditor is beholden to a corporation his certification may be worthless. It is unrealistic to expect the auditing firm to function independently. Auditors, paid by the companies they audit, must accept many of management's assessments or they won't keep the business. It is to their economic advantage to do so. Such pressure is scarcely conducive to diligence.

Forgetting for the moment the ambivalent economic position into which the auditor is placed, forgetting the possibility of collusion, there is the additional problem of human inadequacy. If auditors do nothing else, they should determine that the assets listed by a company actually exist. If the assets are there, nothing too serious can be wrong. Equity Funding's auditors either didn't diligently check the corporation's assets —or were hoodwinked when they did.

When the computer expert hired by the Illinois Insurance Department belatedly arrived at Equity Funding as the scandal was exploding, he asked the manager of the company's computer operations if he had spoken to the auditors about his control system. "I never met with any auditors," the manager replied. "At no time did the auditors come down and ask me for tapes or files." Had the auditors done so, they might have found telling discrepancies. There was, for example, no computer file of insurance policies—real or alleged—that reconciled to the amount of reserves the company carried on its balance sheet. Whether anyone would have understood what they found raises yet another question. Few people understand computers.

Much has been made of "computer fraud" since the disclosures at Equity Funding. Computer experts react with legitimate outrage. Computers are just "big dumb adding machines," as Don Goff put it. Only when a human mind puts computers to devious purpose do they become accomplices to fraud. But computers do provide a facility to create impressive-looking printouts that never existed before. A fraud of the magnitude created by Equity Funding is inconceivable without the support of computers. For auditors to be meaningful regulators of corporate morality, they must master the tools of their clients.

A frequently heard comment after the Equity Funding scandal became public was that "routine auditing procedures aren't designed to detect fraud." If routine auditing procedures cannot detect 64,000 phony insurance policies, $25 million in counterfeit bonds, and $100 million in missing assets, what is the purpose of audits?

What can be said of independent auditors engaged by corporations can also, unhappily, be said of another line of the public's defense—the state insurance departments.

New York's insurance department is considered the best in the country. In April 1973, the department concluded a two-year study of its operations with a doleful finding. Under the existing system of insurance examination, Malcolm MacKay, the department's first deputy superintendent, concluded, the department "asks the wrong questions and gets the information too late."

There are 1800 life insurers in the United States today. They write a volume of business ten times what it was in 1945. In 1972, they took in premium income of $23 billion on policies with death benefit values of $1.5 trillion. They are regulated not by the federal government, but by the single states. Some states have ample departments. Others must hire outsiders to perform the examinations on insurance companies that are supposedly mandatory every three to five years. But even the best departments lag behind in their work. California's insurance department did not adhere to the regular three-year audit schedule in the case of Equity Funding. The last full-scale audit of the company was in 1968. The audit of a large insurance company can take as long as two years; the results may not be available for another two years. By the time the audit is published, it's all but irrelevant. If a crime is discovered, it could, by then, be protected from prosecution.

Like the "independent" auditors, the state's examiners lag behind the insurance companies in technological competence. All insurance companies use computers, but few state insurance departments have personnel knowledgeable about computer systems. State examiners were on the job at Equity Funding for almost three weeks before they found a clue. Another problem: The range in which the insurance departments operate is inherently too restricted to detect fraud if a parent company is involved. The insurance department has no charter to inspect the parent company. Consequently, the department can't possibly know what's happening overall. An example: a life insurance subsidiary receives a $600 premium for insurance. It then pays a $600 commission to the parent company. From the subsidiary's standpoint, that's $600 in and $600 out — a wash transaction. Since the companies are owned by the same corporation, it can just be a bookkeeping entry. No check. No cash transaction. Just an entry. When the insurance examiners inspect the books, they have nothing really to examine in such an instance — unless they can inspect the books of the parent company to make certain a customer was there.

The state of New York maintains that its insurance department must look at all the books that reflect the life of an insurance company. Otherwise, the department has no way of knowing what the parent is doing with the assets of the subsidiary. Where other state agencies do not employ such surveillance, corporate hanky-panky flourishes.

"Predatory parent companies can and do siphon millions out

of the insurers they hold, legally or illegally, and effectively thumb their noses at the regulators," Bill Blundell and Priscilla S. Meyer of *The Wall Street Journal* wrote a few months after the exposure of Equity Funding. They listed several ploys:

—The Bum Asset Swap. One of the most common ways of removing money from an insurance subsidiary, this involves a transfer of cash or gilt-edged assets from the insurer to the parent, who replaces it with something of dubious worth (often its own debentures).

—The Shell Game. In this, a holding company milks insurance subsidiaries for cash and other assets. The parent simply concentrates what assets are left in subsidiary A, when it's facing an audit, moves them to subsidiary B when that company is due for examination, and so on. Since insurance subsidiaries in different states usually are audited at separate times, the weaknesses never show up unless one or more of the companies finally goes under.

—The Surplus Slurp. This is used to take cash out of insurance subsidiaries laden with money well in excess of their needs for reserves against insurance claims. The insurance subsidiary declares a hefty dividend to its shareholders—the parent.

The purpose of these ploys is either to disguise a shortage of assets or to swell the assets of the parent so that the price of its stock will rise. Both strategies were attempted by Equity Funding after it purchased Bankers National.

There is a more intrinsic problem still—the coziness of the insurance departments with the industry they regulate.

The relationship of a state insurance department to a resident insurance company is something like that of a hotelier to a paying guest. The companies pay far more for the privilege of operating than the states pay to maintain them. Illinois, for example, takes in $48 million in taxes on the premium income of the insurance companies it regulates. The state spends $3.6 million on regulating these companies. Insurance departments, viewed by their state governments as money-makers, suffer accordingly. In California, where the Equity Funding scandal occurred, the department operates with less men and money today than it did ten years ago.

The flow of manpower between the industry and its policemen is inexorable. Executives of insurance companies are appointed insurance commissioners or deputies. Insurance commissioners resign to become officers and directors of insurance companies. A chumminess develops that cannot assist regulation. In the matter of Equity Funding, two former insurance commissioners, one from Illinois, the other from California, called the respective state insurance departments to ask if the audit begun on March 12 could be postponed.

In June 1973, the insurance commissioners of the fifty states met in Washington, D.C., with the Equity Funding scandal foremost in mind. The commissioners agreed that they should set up a commission to find out what went wrong and how they should fix it. They agreed that the study should be financed by the insurance industry. When regulators ask those they regulate to finance a study on how to better regulate them, something is wrong with regulation.

The ultimate objective of insurance regulation is to protect the policyholders by making certain that companies remain solvent. To achieve this objective, insurance departments tend to fall back on a strategy that protects the inefficient. Insurance commissioners propound rates and policies that enable the weakest companies to survive. This means that policyholders in the strongest companies pay premiums as though they had bought insurance in the weakest companies.

"Informed buyers would avoid about eighty percent of the

companies domiciled in the U.S.," Herbert Denenberg, the insurance commissioner of Pennsylvania, has declared. *Caveat emptor.*

After the Equity Funding scandal, regulators revived proposals for an insurance fund to protect life insurance policyholders against insurance company failures. Only a few states now have such protection. In the past, large companies, most of them mutuals, lobbied in the legislatures against such plans. Their motivations were twofold. One, they would nominally have to contribute to a life guarantee fund. More importantly, they would lose an oligopolistic edge, for the policyholders of the little companies would then seem as safe as those of the big companies.

In Illinois, where EFLIC was regulated, the insurance department's bill to establish a life guarantee fund was defeated just two months after the greatest insurance fraud in history was exposed.

The final line of defense against fraud for the public is the Securities and Exchange Commission. The commission came into being in 1934 under the Securities Exchange Act. The first commissioner was Joseph Kennedy. He was qualified, critics felt, because he had engaged in many of the acts he would now seek to prosecute.

The five Securities and Exchange Commission members, including the chairman, are appointed by the President of the United States. Ultimately, therefore, the quality of regulation of the securities industry reflects the quality of those individuals elected by the people. Richard Nixon appointed three SEC chairmen in the four years and three months that preceded the Equity Funding scandal. His first appointee, Hamer Budge, was in office less than five months when he met privately with officials of Investors Diversified Services, the country's largest mutual fund management company, to discuss an offer to become president of that firm at a salary twice his SEC salary. These meetings occurred during the period when IDS was attempting to deter an SEC proposal, instituted under the preceding chairman, that would severely restrict its sales presentation.

The next chairman was William Casey, a lawyer who had once been linked to an alleged securities manipulation. Casey was in charge when the SEC staff undertook an investigation of the largest merger in corporate history—that of International Telephone and Telegraph Company (ITT) and the Hartford Fire Insurance Company.

The SEC staff, though utilizing the services of only two young investigators, developed thirty-four boxes of evidence demonstrating an ITT attempt to influence state and federal officials. Chairman Casey quashed the SEC staff's recommendation that ITT be charged with fraud for its activities. Then in the early fall 1972, with the election drawing near, Casey deliberately disobeyed orders from the Congressional committee that oversees the SEC to make the thirty-four boxes of files available to the committee. Instead, Casey sent the boxes to the Justice Department until after the election. Later, Casey claimed under oath that a Justice Department official had requested them. This was denied under oath by the Justice Department official.

Nixon's third SEC chairman, G. Bradford Cook, resigned under fire when it was disclosed that during an SEC prosecution of financier Robert Vesco, Cook, then SEC general counsel, had been instrumental in suppressing facts concerning Vesco's contribution to the Nixon campaign. Nixon's fourth appointee to the SEC chairmanship, Ray Garrett, had this to say in 1973 to a group of fellow lawyers:

"The romantic hero of our profession is not the one who fought for what he believed in, for that would be easy, but the one who fought for his client." He added: "Too much conscience on substantive matters is unprofessional."

The SEC is staffed primarily by young attorneys looking for

two to four years experience they can convert into plush jobs in private practice. Presumably, they would then know the career SEC people, as well as the rules of the game.

The backbone of the SEC, its permanent staff of attorneys, can be faulted neither for integrity nor zeal. They have chosen careers in public service at far less money than they could make in private practice. But they are hobbled, first, by political realities and, second, by the literally impossible task of policing the colossal securities industry with a staff of 1700 people—a total that includes every last clerk–typist. There were fewer SEC employees in 1973 than there were in 1941.

If an SEC chairman quashes an investigation of a corporation deeply enmeshed in political intrigue as was ITT, there is little the permanent staff of the SEC can do. But it was the second inherent weakness of the SEC—lack of appropriate manpower—rather than political considerations that led to its dismal performance in the matter of Equity Funding.

On April 5, 1973, *The New York Times* published an interview with a "high official" of the Securities and Exchange Commission. The official, who was not identified, told the reporter that when the commission decided to suspend trading in Equity Funding's shares, it acted "only on the fact of unusual activity in the stock and not on any information that something was amiss with the parent or subsidiary companies." The statement is simply untrue.

The SEC suspended trading on March 28. The previous day, the SEC's Jerry Boltz had told Larry Baker of the California Insurance Department that his office was obtaining "hard information" from primary sources to which it had been led by Bill Blundell of *The Wall Street Journal.* That same day, Boltz gave the commission a "stiff recommendation" for suspension.

In point of fact, the SEC had been informed of allegations of fraud on March 9—almost three weeks before it acted. On that date, Edward Germann, the lawyer for the California

Insurance Department, walked over to the SEC's Los Angeles office and met with Les Ogg, an SEC attorney. He specifically mentioned the possibility of fake insurance policies, fake mutual fund shares, and fake bank certificates. According to Germann, Ogg expressed interest but said a manpower shortage would limit active SEC participation at that time. Ogg later contended that Germann had spent most of his time asking for information on mutual funds and funded programs.

But, if an attorney for the California Insurance Department presents himself to the SEC and so much as utters the word fraud, it seems reasonable to expect the SEC to elicit his story. Not only did the SEC fail to do that on March 9, it failed to do it fourteen months earlier when a former employee of Equity Funding indicated that he could implicate the company in a story of fraud. The SEC in Washington had received anonymous reports about misstatements of assets at Equity Funding. In the course of its investigation of these reports, the SEC's Los Angeles office had contacted the former employee, who had recently been discharged. Twice he asked for immunity, and twice the SEC refused to grant it. Had the SEC been able to come to terms with this informant, it could have had a far more detailed story than the one Ronald Secrist told more than a year later. The informant was William Mercado, once Equity Funding's computer chief, the man whose assertion that fraudulent insurance policies were on the books had reached director Gale Livingston.

The Securities and Exchange Commission would like the public to believe that it would have exposed the fraud if only Ronald Secrist and Raymond L. Dirks had gone to its investigators. But if the SEC wasn't alerted by one former employee to the existence of a scandal in 1971, why would it be alerted by another in 1973? If the SEC didn't take the allegations seriously when they were related by an attorney with the California Insurance Department, why would they have listened any more seriously to the story of a security analyst?

What all of these out-of-court indictments add up to is this: the individual investor is not adequately protected, not by the securities markets or their brokers, not by auditors or regulators. He proceeds at considerable risk.

It needn't be that way.

13.

The Bottom Line

Historians with a sense of humor may remark that in the multiple prosecutions emanating from the champion of frauds, I was the first person charged.

On April 12, 1973, eleven days after Stanley Goldblum resigned as president of Equity Funding, the New York Stock Exchange formally accused me of violating its own rules as well as the antifraud provisions of the Securities Exchange Act of 1934. I had, the Exchange said, spread rumors, transcended the bounds of "just and equitable principles of trade," and failed to adhere to "good business practice." The penalty for these offenses—if proved—was expulsion for life from the Exchange. The Securities and Exchange Commission, in the meanwhile, undertook a prolonged investigation leading, presumably, to its own prosecution of me for allegedly passing along private, material information to my clients.

These two punitive actions encouraged lawyers throughout the U.S. to file lawsuits against me, seeking redress, ironically, in behalf of Equity Funding stockholders—who were suing me for uncovering fraud in their company.

Merits or demerits aside, such prosecutions are unfortunate diversions. I should not be an issue in the matter of Equity Funding. To make me one is to deflect attention from the problems the fraud exposes. The most immediate problem is the survival of the individual investor.

In a stock market dominated by institutions, the individual is the last to know.

Information is the basis of investment. "Inside" information carries the highest price. Its possession guarantees success on Wall Street. SEC or no SEC, the market operates on inside information. This information is parceled out unevenly among investors. Institutions own only thirty percent of listed securities, but they account for seventy percent of trading. Brokers don't get paid for carrying an account. They get paid when people trade. The most active traders, consequently, receive the best and freshest information.

The last thing a man with information on Wall Street wants to do is make that information public. If he has information, he can make money with it. First, he acts. Then he lets the information out in such a way as to help those who will one day return the favor. The broker who hears about a great stock keeps the information totally confidential until he has gained his position. Then he happily spreads the word. Companies give information to analysts like myself in the expectation that we will spread the word—not necessarily recommend the stock, but actively follow it. The analyst's clients just as actively seek information.

Brokerage firms are divided into departments: trading, research, sales, and corporate finance. One department may not tell the other what it's doing. It is not only conceivable, it is likely that the trader in a Wall Street firm will take market action adverse to a security held by a retail client of that firm.

The stockbroker handling retail accounts is the last man in the brokerage firm to receive information. By the time he gets it, its value has been depreciated and may even be worthless.

Everyone gets in or out of securities ahead of the individual investor. Even the brokerage firm with which he maintains his account may act in its own behalf before it acts in his. Many large brokerage firms take positions in securities to make money for themselves. Their advantage is two-fold: they have more corporate information *and* trading information.

The only role left to the individual investor in the stock market is one of speculation. He might as well play roulette. Over the long run, he'll just as surely lose. The house always has the better odds.

What, then, should the individual do? Should he avoid the stock market entirely? Not necessarily. But he should approach it with the trust of a lion.

The principle of investing today remains what it was when inflation became a fact of life—to stay abreast of inflation, to obtain (it is hoped) an edge. For years stocks were bought as a hedge against inflation. But in recent years one of the significant factors driving stock prices down was the fear of inflation. There are good reasons for this seeming inconsistency. First, while corporations charge more for their products, their costs go up, as well. Second, there are the uncertainties that accompany an inflationary economy—the threat of price controls, the possibility of an unequal distribution of price change, the unpredictability of public response, the prospect that corporate profits or the price of the stock won't keep pace with the rate of inflation.

When the rate of inflation is steady, common stocks are a good hedge against inflation. But when the rate jumps up and down, uncertainty results. Investors are very shy when they can't predict with any degree of reasonableness what's going to happen. Uncertainty invariably drives down the price of common stocks.

So the first question for the individual investor is whether he really wants to risk his money on the whims of 30 million strangers. There are, today, some pleasant alternatives, with high yields and no risks. Savings and loan associations are one such alternative. Bonds are another.

When an individual can get an eight-and-one-half percent return on his money in the bond market, common stocks make small sense. Historically, stocks have averaged no better than nine percent a year. In any given year, as most of us know, they may do frightfully worse. The most important question the individual must answer is whether he can do better in the stock market then he can by investing in bonds that yield seven, eight, or nine percent. *Borrowing* money at ten percent to invest in the stock market makes absolutely no sense at all. In that event, a stock must appreciate at least ten percent a year before the investor is even.

Leverage tempts me, as it does everyone else. But eventually, I find, I lose my money. I don't have enought conservatism or foresight to anticipate a bad market. Sooner or later, the leveraged investor will get caught in such a market.

Ten years ago, when bond yields were four or five percent at most, common stocks were the better investment. Today, the best program for the individual investor is one mixing fixed income and equities. Fixed income would be the certain interest on savings accounts and bonds or certificates of deposit. But how does one choose equities? No one can expect to beat the market unless he is prepared to devote considerable time to it or has an inside view of some company. A doctor, for example, might pay close attention to the products he and his colleagues consistently use. In this way he might be alerted to a sound investment. But most individuals aren't in such circumstances; they don't have time to devote to the study of investments or real knowledge to interpret what they find.

The individual with sufficient funds to invest—say $100,000— should find a professional investment counselor. The individual with a smaller amount to invest should purchase a mutual fund, preferably a no-load fund. The no-load mutual funds are particularly recommended because, unlike other mutual funds, they charge no sales commissions against the initial investment. A similar way to diversify is to purchase closed-end funds, publicly traded companies that invest in a broad list of common stocks.

Diversification is a fundamental of investor strategy. It's

extremely hard for the individual to diversify. But diversity is part of what he buys in a mutual fund or closed-end fund.

Individuals and institutions alike owned stock in Equity Funding. But institutions lost less than one percent of their money, in most cases, whereas numbers of individuals lost all of theirs. Had these individuals purchased shares in a mutual fund that owned shares of Equity Funding, their loss—pennies per share in most cases—would have been shared by thousands of investors. Dreyfus Fund, for example, owned 140,700 shares of Equity Funding, but those shares accounted for only .2 percent of the fund's $2 billion in assets.

Large blocks of money, moreover, have a decided advantage over small blocks in the buying and selling of securities. The man with the greatest number of chips in a poker game can place his bets more heavily, overwhelm his opponent when he has a good hand and withstand a run of bad luck. The man with the small stake finds it hard to stay in the game. One bad bet and he's finished.

If an individual is determined to invest independently, he ought to find a stockbroker who understands a narrow segment of the market, works hard, has good sources, is skeptical and conservative by nature, and never risks unduly. I wish I knew a single broker who possesses all those attributes. I certainly don't myself.

The second major problem exposed by the Equity Funding scandal flows directly from the first—the need to obtain parity on Wall Street for the individual investor.

As conditions exist today, there is an unbridgeable chasm between this ideal and the reality of Wall Street.

Section 10b of the Securities Exchange Act and its accompanying Rule 10b-5 prohibits a corporate insider—or anyone he contacts—from trading on the basis of information that hasn't yet been made public. He is supposed to take such information, at a minimum, to the New York Stock Exchange or the National Association of Securities Dealers. But, as *Fortune* put it, in assessing the Equity Funding scandal: "The proposition that an analyst who learns something important about a listed company should bring it to the Exchange will strike many analysts as hilarious."

The operations of Wall Street are in almost total conflict with the letter and spirit of Section 10b. When that many people are in violation of the law, something is wrong with the law, or with its application.

The SEC has long proclaimed that its purpose in regulating the flow of information, such as that given in prospectuses, is to provide the investor with the full facts of a company's position. But SEC requirements have fallen far short of such disclosure. The flow of information has not been regulated, except for periodic intervals. Each corporation must file a statement with the SEC within ninety days after issuing its annual statement. Each corporation must file a nonaudited statement each quarter. But there is no requirement whatever to file anything in the interim. Nor are there sufficient regulations as to how and when and to whom information is made public.

Clearly, the SEC has failed to enforce its provisions for "full disclosure." Nor is Wall Street, by definition, the channel for such information. A fresh solution must be found that makes financial information equally available to all investors.

The solution is voluntary, full, and constant disclosure by the corporations. Every time anything of significance occurs in their operations, corporations should make it public. They should be subject to suit for not doing so if inside information is utilized by any investor in buying or selling stocks. Realistically, there can be no full disclosure until there are penalties for failure to fully disclose. There are no such penalties now.

Equity Funding was an outright fraud in which the company turned out to be worthless. But the individuals who bought stock have no remedy whatever. They are at the bottom of the list of corporate liabilities; if they sue the company they are simply suing themselves.

Every corporation should have insurance against liability for negligence on the part of its officers for failing to adequately disclose information. This insurance should be mandatory—so that in the event of another Equity Funding the investor won't be stranded. If the insurance industry won't provide such protection, then the government should set up an insurance fund and require corporations to pay premiums according to the average market value of their stocks.

The major problem of "full disclosure" would be one of dissemination. A corporation could disclose that its orders went up forty-two percent last month, but the question is whether *The Wall Street Journal* would print it or whether the information would just be mailed to stockholders.

But dissemination does not need to be a problem. We have the technological equipment already to create a storage facility for information that could be made available to any investor who walked into a brokerage house or investment advisory service. Such a facility could parallel and augment NASDAQ's visual price display system.

To the extent that there are so many analysts, it's an indication that there is "inside information" being passed about. It's the job of the analyst to obtain valuable information for his clients. That's why he's paid. Full disclosure would put many analysts out of jobs. The surviving analysts—presumably the better ones—would be able to evaluate all the available information and try to determine which stocks are the best purchases and sales.

It is rare, indeed, when an analyst uncovers a case of outright fraud. But there is another kind of fraud that is just as insidious and infinitely more prevalent. This is the fraud perpetrated on the public by inefficient executives who run companies poorly. Analysts can take their measure.

Analysts can also examine the quality of corporate earnings in ways the lay person can't. What Wall Street wants is steady earnings growth—and many corporations see that Wall Street gets it by resorting to sleight-of-hand. If a company reports

earnings that go up fifteen percent one year and five percent
the next, the average is a respectable ten percent. But to Wall
Street that represents an unacceptable year-to-year drop in
earnings growth, so it drops the stock accordingly. Corporations, as a consequence, manage their earnings—withholding
earnings in a good year in order to fatten them in a lean one.
Such a practice tends to hide the true condition of a company.
Analysts can expose such maneuvers.

Corporations contend that for competitive reasons they must
withhold information. But there are degrees of information.
A corporation need not disclose the ingredients of its secret
new product. But it should be required to say, "We have a
product we're working on and we think it could be significant."

The SEC has said that corporations should make public
five-year projections. That's the best idea of all. The corporation would be required to tell an investor what he most needs
to know when he buys or sells a stock. The investor still takes
a risk. The company may not be right. But at least the odds
aren't stacked against him. As the regulations exist today,
the odds are so heavily stacked against the individual investor
that he has no business investing.

On first reading, this proposal for full disclosure might sound
naïve. What makes it practical is the support it would give to
the very public corporations that might oppose it.

Why are many public corporations so upset today over the
prices of their stocks and the unwarranted fluctuation in those
prices? The basic reason is that so much of the important information is distributed by so few security analysts for the
decisions of so few money managers. By and large, many corporations have encouraged the practice for lack of any alternative. For all but the largest corporations, it's a shortsighted
policy. If managements of public companies don't want their
stocks to be priced by a few large institutions, then they should
strive for more disclosure of their affairs to all of the investing
public.

Only when the public is on an equal footing with the institutions will it return wholeheartedly to Wall Street. Should financial favoritism continue, individuals will gradually withdraw. The consequences would be devastating. Truly private capital would become the scarcest American resource; small corporations would flounder and individual initiative would wither; only the richest would survive.

More serious by far than the consideration of the individual's financial equity is that of his equity in America.

Equity Funding was not simply a computer fraud or an accounting fraud or an insurance fraud or even a business fraud. It was an all-American fraud. Its dimensions cannot be comprehended simply in terms of the thousands of policies invented or millions of dollars of assets faked, or even the hundreds of millions of dollars lost by investors. It can be understood only in terms of the people involved.

They were not special people. They were products of the System. They were not bigtime crooks. They were functionaries of business. It is not the magnitude of their fraud but the distortion of their values that is ultimately so suggestive.

Years ago, the operant American ethic was, "It's not whether you win or lose, it's how you play the game." Today, the American sermon is drawn from the football playbooks: "Winning isn't everything, it's the only thing."

Perhaps one special man took advantage of many ordinary men and, by so doing, exploited the System. But if so, it was the System that supplied his objective.

Wall Street demands big winners. Corporations must "perform." Corporations, in turn, demand performance from their employees—not just loyal and zealous performance, but overloyal, overzealous performance. The requirements set by Wall Street may not be realistic for some companies, but all public companies must answer to Wall Street, so their employees must answer to them. Wall Street is not the villain: it simply expresses the American ethic. The ethic leaves small room for individual choice.

For the American way of life today reflects few of the attributes and many of the deficiencies of team sports. The individual subordinates his will to the group. This is healthy to a point. It becomes unhealthy when the group's objective should be questioned, and isn't.

In government, the operative phrase is "game plan." In the business world, it's the "money game." It's not how you play the game that matters, it's whether your team wins.

Individuals seldom pause to examine either the method or the prize. They simply play the game. Few members of Equity Funding's team joined the company knowing it was crooked. Some committed crimes without realizing the significance of their acts. If the System is corrupt, then corruption is normal and a little corrupt conduct on their part is neither abnormal nor immoral. "These things go on all the time," a man from Boston said early on. It's not the individual's fault. Coach told him to do it.

Even those games played according to the rules are marked by fouls the referees don't call. Corporations project themselves as something they're not. Employees sustain the projections.

A single idea can start a fortune. A few men gather together a small nucleus of talented sales people who go out and push product "Y." After a bit, the founders go to an underwriter and say, "Look at the sales we're generating." "That's terrific," says the underwriter, "just keep on growing. Don't worry about money; we'll get you all you need." After a bit, the underwriter takes the stock public at a price many times higher than the founders' privately held shares, so that the only people risking their money are the public investors.

Everyone cheers the expansion of volume. No one questions the virtue of size. But bigness generates its own problems; the first is a tendency to go soft.

National competence has been one of the assumptions of our culture. We're not simply the biggest but the best. We may have been able to indulge ourselves in this fantasy until recently, but we can't do so any longer. One of the most shocking revelations of the Equity Funding scandal was the slackness of effort it exposed. The scandal demonstrated not simply a failure on the part of the financial exchanges and regulators, but by those who had a stake in the company and stood to lose heavily from irresponsible work.

Underwriters looked the company over carefully. Banks did intensive analyses before lending the company money. Lawyers were paid substantial fees to prepare each prospectus. Consulting actuaries certified the insurance reserves. Auditors blessed the books. Every last one of them failed. Were these men incompetent? Not likely. More probably, they had immersed themselves so totally in technicalities that they ignored the essentials, such as character and purpose.

Equity Funding was not a trip down the rapids by a group of reckless adventurers. It went adrift in the American mainstream. The burden of its story is not that all men are venal. The evidence doesn't support the charge. One thousand men and women worked for Equity Funding; less than thirty were indicted.

There are lessons galore from this repellent event. Auditing processes must change, stock exchanges must democratize, surveillance must be more meaningful, publicly held corporations must become truly public.

But what Equity Funding tells us more than anything is where we have come as individuals in regard to our institutions. What matters most is not that the values of a few men were perverted, but that the consciences of many were stilled.

What is ultimately most distressing is not that some people defrauded others. That has gone on forever, and that alone can't bring down a free society. What *can* bring down a free society is when people do not feel they can live by the rule of law.

Not one of the people whose witness enabled me to expose the fraud had been willing to go to the authorities. They were afraid the authorities might do nothing. They were afraid they wouldn't be believed. They were afraid the authorities would take their information back to the company—thereby exposing them. They were afraid their careers would suffer and that they might expose themselves to physical harm. They were afraid, at the very least, that they would carry the taint of "informer."

When conscience is immobilized, public trust has disappeared. At that point, by default, institutions become omnipotent.

May Equity Funding tell us, at a minimum, that there is work to be done—not simply to police our commerce, but to redeem the efficacy of will.

Appendix

UNPUBLISHED LAST ANNUAL REPORT OF EQUITY FUNDING CORPORATION OF AMERICA

TO OUR STOCKHOLDERS

Over the past five years the company has successfully evolved from a mutual funds-insurance sales organization to a major national corporation whose revenues and earnings are solidly based on life insurance marketing and operations. As a result of internal growth and acquisitions, we have become a major factor in the U.S. life insurance industry, and we expect to further strengthen our position in the future.

To more accurately reflect our continuing evolution into a life insurance-based financial services company, our Board of Directors, at its March 1973 meeting, approved a change in the company's name to EQUITY FUNDING LIFE CORPORATION. The new name will be submitted to our stockholders for their approval at our Annual Meeting scheduled for May 22, 1973.

FINANCIAL RESULTS

After-tax earnings from all operations for the year ending December 31, 1972, increased 17 percent to $22.6 million. This is the tenth consecutive year in which reported earnings from operations increased by more than 15 percent.

On a per share basis, 1972 operating earnings were $2.81, compared to $2.45 in 1971. These per share earnings are based on an average of 8,036,000 shares outstanding in 1972 and 7,883,000 in 1971.

LIFE INSURANCE RESULTS

During 1972 the Equity Funding life insurance group sold a total of $2.5 billion of new life insurance; — bringing our total insurance in force to $6.5 billion. We estimate that Equity Funding's life insurance subsidiaries, taken as a group, would now rank in the top one percent of the industry in terms of U.S. sales of individual insurance. Among U.S. stock life companies, we believe that the Equity Funding life insurance group will have moved up to fourth or fifth place in individual sales.

INVESTMENT PROGRAMS

The EQUITY FUNDING Program, now in its twelfth year, remains one of the most innovative financial planning vehicles developed in the U.S. In 1972, 16,028 new EQUITY FUNDING programs were sold by our marketing organization.

ENTRY INTO VARIABLE LIFE INSURANCE MARKET

Equity Funding, we believe, is well positioned to participate in the marketing opportunities inherent in variable life, which could account for more than 20 percent of the total insurance market by the end of this decade. No other financial services company, we believe, can equal our experience in the marketing of equity-linked insurance products with a sales force of such proven effectiveness.

We are confident that variable life will become a basic financial planning tool for American families, and that Equity Funding will again be a leader in developing an important new product that meets current economic and social needs.

SALES ORGANIZATION

The average productivity of our sales force has increased steadily over the past several years, reflecting increasing selectivity in recruitment and new training and supervision programs. A key index of sales productivity, the average amount of life insurance sold per branch office salesman, has risen from $138,000 in 1969 to approximately $311,000 at the end of 1972.

PLANNING FOR PROFITS

One of the fundamental responsibilities of management is planning for the future, and Equity Funding's progress reflects the ongoing implementation of plans made in past years. Two major areas of corporate planning during 1972 and in the current year are related to the continuing increase in our retention of new insurance business and to the further lowering of administrative costs.

Increasing our retention of new business serves to assume greater future revenues and earnings. In the late sixties, nearly all business written by Equity Funding Life was ceded to other insurers to recapture heavy first-year costs.

As Equity Funding Life grew, and was joined by two well-established life insurers, Bankers National and Northern Life, we were able to increase the proportion of new business retained by our subsidiaries. In 1971, retention was raised to

50 percent and in 1972 to 60 percent. In the current year we expect to further increase the proportion of new business retained and to continue this trend in the future.

During the transition period to full retention, special efforts are being made to further lower costs throughout our field and home office operations by accelerating the integration of administrative functions, terminating or consolidating marginal operations and achieving maximum economies of scale.

Administrative costs dropped in 1972 to 14 percent of revenues from 15 percent in 1971 as a result of continuing management review of operations.

On February 2nd of the current year, we announced our intention to acquire First Executive Corporation, which owns two medium-sized life insurance companies, one headquartered in California and one in New York, and a newly-formed life insurance company in West Germany.

Consideration of future acquisitions focuses primarily on sound regional life insurance companies with good market penetration in areas of the country where we do not as yet have adequate representation.

Our strongest asset remains our highly effective sales organization, whose technical and sales skills, dedication and loyalty have made it possible for Equity Funding to be singled out by *Fortune Magazine* in its May 1972 "Top 500" issue as the company with the highest 10-year earnings growth rate of the top 50 diversified financial companies in the U.S.

During 1973 we expect to continue and extend our past record of achievement.